COME ON! THERE'S NO TIME TO WASTE!

ドムッ

THE OTAKU ENCYCLOPEDIA
OUCH . . . !

THE OTAKU ENCYCLOPEDIA

An insider's guide to the subculture of Cool Japan

Patrick W. Galbraith

Foreword by Frederik L. Schodt

KODANSHA INTERNATIONAL Tokyo • New York • London

HI!
MY NAME
IS MOÉ!
I'M YOUR
GUIDE.

Distributed in the United States by Kodansha America LLC, and in the United Kingdom and Continental Europe by Kodansha Europe Ltd.

Published by Kodansha International Ltd., 17-14 Otowa 1-chome, Bunkyo-ku, Tokyo 112-8652.

ISBN 978-4-7700-3101-3

First edition, 2009
18 17 16 15 14 13 12 11 10 09 12 11 10 9 8 7 6 5 4 3

Library of Congress Cataloging-in-Publication Data

Galbraith, Patrick W.
The otaku encyclopedia : an insider's guide to the subculture of cool Japan / Patrick W. Galbraith ; foreword by Frederik L. Schodt.
-- 1st ed.
p. cm.
Includes bibliographical references.
ISBN 978-4-7700-3101-3
1. Subculture--Japan. 2. Japan--Civilization--1945- 3. Youth--Japan--Interviews. I. Title.
HM646.G35 2009
306'.1095209045--dc22
2009015264

www.kodansha-intl.com

CONTENTS

FOREWORD

FOLLOWING OTHER WORDS THAT ORIGINALLY came from Japan like *geisha*, *manga*, *anime*, and even the *honcho* in "head honcho," *otaku* is gradually entering the English lexicon. I first started hearing it used in North America at the beginning of the nineties, mainly at early anime conventions. It appeared with no translation on the cover of the premiere issue of *Wired* magazine in 1993. In 1994, American fans formed an annual anime convention named "Otakon"—cleverly combining the word *otaku* and *convention*—and by 2008 it had a weekend attendance of 25,000. By now, to most young Americans *otaku* is a familiar word, usually referring to hardcore fans of anime and manga.

As is often the case when words are imported, their usage morphs to adapt to different environments. Most English-speakers are not aware of the history and complicated nuances of the term *otaku* in Japan, where in its most popular incarnation it is actually quite new, dating back only to the 1980s.

In Japan, *otaku* signifies far more than manga and anime fanboys and geeks. It is a new type of culture—one that blurs the world of children and adults, worships pop culture minutiae, fetishizes objects real and virtual, and at its worst spawns an almost autistic, inward-looking possessiveness. *Otaku* is beyond a noun, for it has even spawned an adjective (as in *otakii*). It encompasses not only manga and anime culture, but also video games, dolls, plastic model kits, music, and even an obsession with military minutiae, as in *miritarii* or *gunji otaku*.

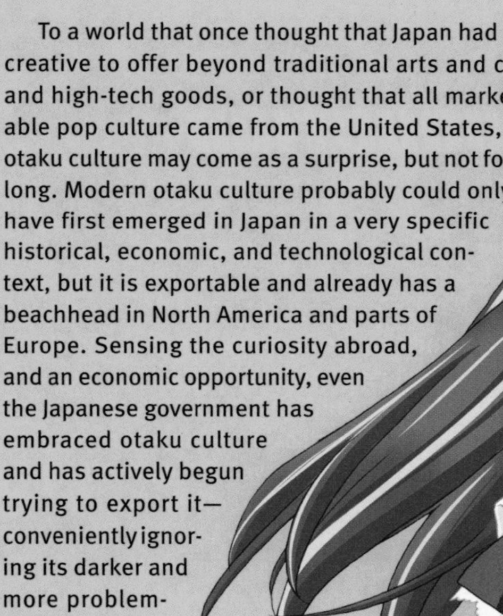

To a world that once thought that Japan had nothing creative to offer beyond traditional arts and crafts and high-tech goods, or thought that all marketable pop culture came from the United States, otaku culture may come as a surprise, but not for long. Modern otaku culture probably could only have first emerged in Japan in a very specific historical, economic, and technological context, but it is exportable and already has a beachhead in North America and parts of Europe. Sensing the curiosity abroad, and an economic opportunity, even the Japanese government has embraced otaku culture and has actively begun trying to export it—conveniently ignoring its darker and more problematic aspects.

In recent years many wonderful English-language books have been published explaining specific aspects of Japan's thriving pop culture. But there has long been a desperate need for a reference book that covers otaku culture in its broader context, for without an understanding of this culture it becomes difficult to understand modern Japan. In his tirelessly researched *The Otaku Encyclopedia*, Patrick W. Galbraith performs a vital service—exposing to the world Japan's otaku culture in its full glory, illuminating not only its breadth and depth, but its dark sides and oft-ignored edges. Prepare for a wild, educational, and entertaining ride!

Frederik L. Schodt • SAN FRANCISCO, 2009

INTRODUCTION

IT WAS FALL 2004 WHEN MY MOTHER DISOWNED ME. Well, not actually my mother, but my "host mother," a stern lady who was looking after me while I studied in Tokyo. Being from rural Alaska, I am by nature a bit antisocial and ill mannered, and found myself limited to her as a conversation partner. She'd asked about my hobbies, so I casually replied, "I'm an otaku." I remember her face turning pale as she solemnly warned me never to say that in public—and several months later she cancelled my housing contract. After that I moved in with a kimono model, but she too unceremoniously evicted me from her life, even beating me with an umbrella when she overheard me talking to her friend about *moé* anime on a crowded street.

At first I couldn't see the connection between being an otaku and my abject status. My otaku ways were nothing to hide. At university, friends and I would quip about our otaku-ness. It was a badge of honor to fail a test because you were strung out from binging on anime, or to miss a family gathering because it overlapped with a comic convention. When my academic advisor at the time asked about my future, I told him my plan to be the "Otaking," the King of Otaku. I learned Japanese watching anime and reading manga, tattooed my body with anime characters, and devoted my life to my obsessive hobbies. While others were angling for dates, I ran myself to ruin working at a mill in Montana to raise money for a signed figure of Sailor Moon. Cultish and extreme? Perhaps, but not out of line with the rising wave of otaku at the time.

But while waiting for the bruises from the umbrella to heal, it slowly dawned on me that my image of otaku was at odds with mainstream Japanese society. (It wasn't my first misperception about Japan; I had also long assumed Japanese girls were al quiet and submissive.) So, true to my otaku nature, I decided to investigate these cultural differences further. I returned to the United States in fall 2005, sold what few things I owned (keeping only my Sailor Moon figure), and arrived in Tokyo in winter 2006 to make a new life, nerves steeled and a chip on my shoulder about otaku discrimination.

But this time the word was everywhere, and it wasn't being used pejoratively. Politicians, pop idols, average men, women and children—all "otaku." Returning to my old haunts in Akihabara, I found camera crews chasing otaku in the streets for their commentary on "Cool Japan." In the span of the few months I'd been away, the otaku world had completely turned upside down. Dumbstruck, but fascinated by the polarity and schizophrenia of otaku culture all the more, I doubled my conviction to research the subject. This led me to the Ph.D. program at the University of Tokyo and the book you now hold.

During my research I found the perception of otaku was infinitely complex. Although Japan's "otaku culture" was now "cool," and had become a global phenomenon, more than a few people were uncomfortable talking to me, or being included in this book. Some were even outraged and refused outright. It was clear that there was still conflict between old, negative concepts of otaku and the newer, more international view that had been adopted by politicians and celebrities who claim to be otaku.

When I was researching Akihabara's evolution into a tourist destination for international otaku, seven people were murdered in the street by a man labeled an otaku by much of the press. Nine days later, the original "otaku murderer," Miyazaki Tsutomu, was executed amid a media brouhaha. Suddenly "good" otaku, who sought to promote the culture, were having to defend themselves against the "bad" otaku image. For all the positive change that had occurred over recent years, it seemed "otaku" was still a problematic word. This was driven home to me personally when my hero, Okada Toshio, renounced his title as the Otaking.

In his 2008 book *Otaku wa Sude ni Shindeiru* (You Are Already Dead), Okada declared otaku culture dead, and when

I spoke to him for this book I couldn't help bu squirm under his gaze when he told me he really doesn't understand "moé otaku" like myself. could feel the tattoos of moé anime characters burning under my shirt as he outlined the dif ferences between today's otaku and those of his generation. Contemporary otaku, he claimed, no longer want to be creators or to invest in learning beyond selfish interests But I was not convinced. There is great cul tural creativity seen in post-consumption media mixing, such as *doujinshi* and online activity. The abundance of otaku, and the information targeting them does not necessarily mean a fatal saturation and division, but it does mean a chaos tha can, at times, be difficult to fathom. I felt all the more that a sur vey of the culture, to promote mutual understanding between the different generations of otaku, was crucial.

After Okada I spoke to other experts such as Morikawa Kaichiro, Murakami Takashi, and Ichikawa Koichi, and heard from maids, idols, and creators about what it's like to be a the center of otaku attention. I was especially struck by anime director Yamamoto Yutaka's simultaneous criticism of and commitment to otaku. Otaku are annoying and weak he admit ted, but stressed that they will only die out if they abandon one another and become apathetic. It is my sincere hope tha this book will bridge gaps between otaku both young and old inside and outside Japan, and encourage criticism and future discussion. May otaku curiosity and community never die and may we continue to evolve for decades to come.

Patrick W. Galbraith ● TOKYO, 200

* The title of this *doujinshi*, (萌えあがれ!!ガンダムさん) *Moé Agare!! Gundam-san (Improve you moé!! Miss Gundam*), is a play on the lyrics of the *Kido Senshi Gundam* (*Mobile Suit Gundam* opening theme song. However the *kanji* used for "moé" in the original lyric, 燃えあがれガンダ (Get fired-up Gundam), has been switched to the kanji for the term "moé" (萌え) used by otaku to describe their desire for anime characters (see page 154).
Being **a)** a doujinshi, **b)** a reference the the otaku favorite *Gundam*, and **c)** created by mo otaku, it sums up beautifully the state of otaku today.

AA: ASCII Art. Images made from letters and symbols, from simple emoticons such as (^_^) to more complex drawings on online bulletin boards.

A-boy (Aボーイ): Akiba-boy. A put-down for the geeky wimps who frequent AKIHABARA, but sometimes used as a term of endearment. See also AKIBA-KEI.

Aca-fan: Academic fan. A term associated with fan studies.

ACG: Abbreviation for ANIME, comics, and games, considered by many fans (especially outside Japan) to be the core interests of otaku.

Afureko (アフレコ): Dubbing of an audio track. A transliteration of the words "after recording." This is the method of choice for TV anime in Japan. See KUCHI-PAKU.

Aho (アホ): A rough way to say "dumbass." Mainly used by people from Kansai in Western Japan. See also BAKA.

Aho-ge (アホ毛): Slang for "stupid hair." The most classic example is a single lock of hair standing up like an antenna. It often marks a DOJIKKO (lovable loser or klutz).

Akahon manga (赤本漫画): Red books. From the mid-1940s to the mid-1950s, MANGA bound in red covers started to sell in Osaka and Tokyo. TEZUKA OSAMU dominated the akahon manga market, and the quality of his stories, especially *Shin-Takarajima* in 1947, which sold 400,000 copies, inspired many to emulate him. These sparked a revolution in manga culture.

Akanbe (あっかんべー): A childish facial gesture and taunt that appears quite often in ANIME and MANGA. It's made by pulling down one lower eyelid to show the red of the eye while sticking out your tongue. It's best when accompanied by the sound "behhh-dah!"

AKB 48: A massive music IDORU group that performs daily at the AKB 48 stage in Akihabara. There are around forty-eight members broken into three teams: A, K, and B. Members range from twelve to twenty-six years of age, with the average age being sixteen. They are a goldmine for their promoters, who release material for each of the three teams, keeping the girls competing and fans coming back again and again to see them. They encourage fans to support them with purchases and OTAGEI dances. After one hundred visits fans receive the honor of seeing their name engraved on a brass plaque on the theater wall. The girls were first selected during a nationwide series of auditions in 2005, and by September 2008 AKB 48 had performed 1,100 times for 27,000 visitors.

Akiba (アキバ): Local name for AKIHABARA. During the Edo period (1600–1868) fires were a major problem for the residents of Edo (old Tokyo), and in 1869 the Meiji Emperor ordered a shrine be erected to protect the area around what is now Akihabara. Three gods were enshrined in the shrine (Chinka Jinja), and the locals mistakenly believed Akihadaigongen—the god from Akiha Jinja in Shizuoka—had been enshrined there. In the local dialect "ha" becomes "ba," and they referred to the god as "Akiba-sama." In turn they called the shrine "Akiba Jinja," and called the firebreak around the shrine "Akibahara" (Akiba's field). Japan Railways leveled the shrine in 1888 to make way for a train line from Ueno, and named the station "Akihabara." This became the official name, although locals continued to call

the area “Akibahara,” and later “Akiba.” A small memorial to Akiba Jinja remains in the maze of small electrical parts stores beneath the JR Sobu Line railway tracks by Akihabara Station.

Akiba Blog (アキバBlog): One of the first Japanese websites written by, about, and for people who love AKIHABARA. Founded in January 2004, by 2007 it had had 510 million page views, 20 million a month from regular readers. An English version was launched in 2008, and it is now widely considered the number one source for news on Akihabara. The blog is written by the enigmatic Mr. Geek, who avoids giving his real name and having his picture taken, believing it might impair his freedom to mingle in Akihabara. URL: www.akibablog.net

Akiba-kei (アキバ系): Akiba-type; geek. The kind of OTAKU who hang out in Akihabara. Akiba-kei tend to be particularly interested in the MOÉ (pronounced *moéh*) side of ANIME, MANGA, video games, and IDORU. That is, they like pure, little-girl characters and want plenty of FAN SERVICE in their dating simulators and DOUJINSHI (amateur comics). Although many Japanese consider these kind of otaku repugnant, there has been an boom in the sale of ironic Akiba-kei souvenirs—such as T-shirts and caps—since the TV series *Densha Otoko* became popular in 2005.

Akihabara (秋葉原): Tokyo’s famous electronics district and the center of the OTAKU world.

In the years following the end of World War II, the area from Akihabara to Ueno became a gathering spot for open-air black markets, with rare and high-quality radio parts being particularly common. The close proximity of a school, which would later become Tokyo Electronics University, meant the area was full of students making and selling makeshift radios for the information-hungry masses. In 1949 the Occupation Forces forced the markets to move to make way for the construction of new roads, creating a rabbit warren of stores under the raised Sobu Line rail tracks (originally erected in 1932).

AKIHABARA

The convenience of shopping for parts or ready-made radios in the dense market near Akihabara Station helped the area flourish and become the seat of the electronics and household appliance boom in the 1960s. As Japan became more affluent, people yearned for the kind of lifestyle seen in American sitcoms and movies. They dreamed of owning the so-called “three sacred items” of the day—a television, a washing machine, and a refrigerator—and buying these things became a family event. In 1958, only 8 percent of Japanese households had a TV, but by 1966 95 percent did; Akihabara at the time had 10 percent of the market, making it a family hot spot. Big events such as the Tokyo Olympics in 1964 and the lunar landing in 1969 made TV a must.

MORIKAWA KAICHIRO

MORIKAWA KAICHIRO (37) IS A DESIGN THEORIST and the author of *Learning from Akihabara: The Birth of a Personapolis*. He is an associate professor at the School of Global Japanese Studies at Meiji University and is the driving force behind the planned Tokyo International Manga Library. Morikawa was also behind "Otaku: Persona=Space=City" at the Japan Pavilion at the 9th International Architecture Exhibition at Venezia Biennale (2004)

PG: When and why did Akihabara become an otaku space?

MK: The real transformation began in 1997 when the anime *Neon Genesis Evangelion* was shown in theaters. It was able to attract an audience beyond regular anime otaku, and shops selling figures and DOUJINSHI boomed as interest in the show and its characters grew. A GARAGE KIT before *Evangelion* sold maybe 3,000 pieces per character. But when kits of *Evangelion*'s lead female character, Ayanami Rei, were released, they sold around 30,000 almost instantly.

At the time otaku were congregating in Akihabara around the specialist and hobby microcomputer market, but there were very few shops in the area that catered specifically to otaku. The Toranoana store had started selling doujinshi on a small backstreet in 1994, but there was little else. However, the *Evangelion* boom was enough to entice the figure company Kaiyodo to move its main store from Shibuya to Akihabara in 1997, and they sold merchandise like hotcakes. There was an enormous market accumulating in Akiba and there were no competitors. All the other stores saw this and followed en masse. Household electronics stores were losing sales, at the time, opening up shop space, and the otaku sanctuary really expanded at the end of the 1990s.

PG: There were figure and doujinshi stores all over Tokyo, so why move to Akihabara?

MK: Otaku often have a strong fear that they are looked down on, especially by women, and if you went to an otaku-type store in Shibuya or Ikebukuro, you had to pass through mainstream [mainly female] culture before you reached the otaku culture in the backstreets.

When stores in Akihabara began to shift away from consumer electronics to personal computers, women became largely absent from the area. So what attracted otaku here was not necessarily the presence of personal computers but the absence of mainstream culture. It didn't have to be Akihabara specifically, but the kind of women that otaku feel inferior to were absent, and that is why they came to Akiba. They could be comfortable and do as they liked without fear.

PG: What is mainstream culture?

MK: In Japan the mainstream culture is always what's been adopted from foreign cultures. Subculture is where the most Japanesque culture lies. This is historical fact. Since the Meiji period the most

K-BOOKS

influential culture has been American or European, and before that it was Chinese culture. From a foreign perspective, what's original about Japanese culture is mostly its subculture.

PG: But why do otaku shy away from mainstream culture?

MK: Otaku were the losers at school. They weren't sportsmen and didn't appeal to girls. They have this inferiority complex toward the mainstream. To them, anime and games are a kind of escape from this realm of mainstream culture. Otaku-ism is a form of escapism, and that has a very negative connotation in English. But I believe otaku culture is an escapist culture in a positive way because it fuels creation.

PG: Is otaku creativity different from technological innovation?

MK: When pressure from abroad, or *gaiatsu*, is weak, original Japanese subculture flourishes, but when gaiatsu is strong, technology tends to flourish. The cultural history of Japan is a repetition of this presence and absence of gaiatsu. For example, the 7th century was a period of strong gaiatsu, from China. Buddhism was imported and used by the government to control the people. Then around 894 there was chaos in the Chinese government, so Japan ceased to send scholars there. This allowed an original Japanese subculture to arise. It peaked in the 11th century, and is symbolized by the *Tale of Genji*, which was written by a woman, and written in Japanese *hiragana* characters—both minor presences in the society of the day. After Japan repelled the Mongol invasions in 1274 and 1281, its own original culture continued to grow and during the Muromachi period (1333–1568) the tea ceremony, Noh theater plays, and Zen gardens were developed. This was followed by the Sengoku era (Warring States period), when once again foreign technologies were adopted as guns were imported from Europe. The dominance of subculture returned in the Edo period (1600–1868) when Japan completely shut out foreign influence, and arts such as *ukiyo-e* and *kabuki* emerged. Then when the Americans forced the government to reopen the country at the start of the Meiji period (1868–1912) gaiatsu was felt again.

Historically speaking, the main exports of Japan have been design and art. At the end of the 20th century I think we entered another era of subculture. This is symbolized by Akihabara, which went from a place known for electronics to a place of otaku culture.

> **In Japan the mainstream culture is always what's been adopted from foreign cultures. Subculture is where the most Japanesque culture lies.**

PG: What is the future of Akihabara?

MK: It's impossible to predict. The media attention during the Akiba Boom had great impact on the mass-image of the place, much more than the high-rise redevelopment which simultaneously took place in Akiba. For most of the postwar period Akihabara was a place where people came to shop, but never a place for sightseeing, especially not for domestic visitors. But with the Akiba boom, people started to come to here simply to see otaku culture as if this was some sort of cultural zoo. This peaked in 2005 and I'm not sure when it will fully fade.

Over the following decades Akihabara's reputation as the place to buy cheap electrical goods continued to grow, and it was often the first stop for duty-free bargain-hunting tourists seeking the most modern "Made in Japan" gadgetry to take home. However, as the bubble economy of the 1980s deflated into the recession of the 1990s, the market for consumer electronics moved away from Akihabara to the suburbs or large chain stores—such as Yodobashi Camera, Sakuraya, and Bic Camera—situated at the commuter centers of Shinjuku, Shibuya, and Ikebukuro.

To deal with this crisis, stores in Akihabara began to shift away from consumer electronics and started to sell computers, software, and peripherals that were too specialized to be carried in large stores. Families stopped coming to the area and only specialists and hobbyists remained, most often young males who were more interested in computers, anime, and games than outdoor activities and social relationships. The face of Akihabara had changed, and by the 1990s it was populated with nerds or, as they were becoming known, OTAKU.

In 1997 the figure maker Kaiyodo moved from Shibuya to Akihabara, and scores of other otaku-oriented stores followed, moving into bankrupt or struggling electronics stores. The otaku ghetto slowly grew, and around 2003 the media came looking for the face of Japan's booming pop culture. This culminated in Akihabara's starring role in the TV drama *DENSHA OTOKO* in 2005 and the following Akiba Boom. Land prices jumped 20.4 percent between 2006 and 2007, and today, the area is being redeveloped into a tourist destination and showcase of COOL JAPAN.

Akihabara Incident (秋葉原無差別殺傷事件): On June 8, 2008, Kato Tomohiro, a twenty-five-year-old dispatch worker from Aomori in northern Japan, and stationed in Shizuoka to Tokyo's west, rented a truck and drove to AKIHABARA, where he proceeded to run down visitors walking on Chuo-dori street, which at the time was shut to traffic every Sunday for what Japanese call a "pedestrian paradise." He then jumped out of the truck and began to rampage through the streets with a survival knife, finally killing seven and injuring ten.

Kato was described as a poor, working-class man from the countryside who was estranged from his family and dissatisfied at work. Despite having had an elite high-school education, he failed the entrance exams needed to enter a good university and ended up in a dead-end job. He was apparently discouraged by a lack of friends or significant other, and upon arrest said "I'm tired of life" and "I have no place to go back to." On cell phone bulletin board system (BBS) sites prior to the attack Kato logged around 3,000 unanswered posts, and even mentioned his plans "to kill people in Akihabara." He was soon labelled an "OTAKU" and when some people online showed outpourings of empathy for Kato—calling him a "god"—the media

began to criticize otaku and Akihabara. As a result Chuo-dori was once again opened to traffic on Sundays, effectively killing public activity and preventing otaku from gathering there. Since the attack numerous people have been arrested for posting threatening notices on BBS sites, including 2CHANNEL.

Akira (アキラ): Arguably the greatest ANIME of all time, and one of the most influential science fiction films of the 1980s. *Akira* deals with the corrupting influence of social isolation and power, and was originally a 2,000-page MANGA by OTOMO KATSUHIRO written between 1982 and 1990, at the height of Japan's "bubble" economy.

SPOILER ALERT!! STOP READING NOW IF YOU DON'T WANT TO KNOW WHAT HAPPENS!

The setting is post-apocalyptic NEO TOKYO after World War III, where gangs of alienated youth ride motorbikes through the urban wasteland. The government is meddling with superhuman psychics, and one of the bikers, Tetsuo, is caught up in their experiments, which awaken powers within him to disastrous effect. His friends, led by the story's hero, Kaneda, team up with anti-government rebels and try to rescue Tetsuo, but are unprepared for how his new powers have changed him. Ultimately Kaneda must face his friend and fight it out in a battle that threatens to destroy the city.

Akira won the 1984 Kodansha Manga Award and was published as six volumes by that company before being published by Marvel in the US in 1988. It was one of the first manga to be released in English in its entirety.

Otomo was offered a deal for an animated *Akira* movie, and he agreed on the grounds that he maintain creative control. With its release in 1988, *Akira* became the single most expensive anime ever made, with a price tag of $11 million and a CEL count of 160,000. This was the last really massive anime movie made in the 1980s, and it was the first Japanese anime movie to break out of small overseas science-fiction fan clubs and reach an art house and mainstream audience.

Two live-action movies based on the manga and produced by Leonardo

KANEDA ON HIS BIKE IN AKIRA

DiCaprio are due to be released by Warner Brothers sometime before 2011. However, the decision to set the movie in a futuristic New Manhattan, rather than Neo Tokyo, has upset many fans.

Akushukai (握手会): Handshaking event, where people privileged by purchase, membership, or prior attendance get to shake hands with an IDORU, or creator. When it also involves signing autographs, they are called *sign-kai* (signing events).

Amecomi (アメコミ): American comic books, such as the works of Stan Lee, Frank Miller, and Todd McFarlane.

AMV: Abbreviation for "Anime Music Video." Any ANIME clip or montage put to music that was not in the original production or broadcast, usually done as homage by fans but also used for introductions and trailers. These are rife on Internet video-sharing sites such as YouTube and NICO NICO DOUGA.

Androgynous: See RYOUSEI.

Aniki (兄貴): Bro; a rough way to say brother. The female equivalent is *aneki*.

Animation (アニメーション): Generally, the art of making the static appear to move. Specifically in Japan, an animated movie or film that is enjoyed by adults, rather than children, and is typically expected to have smoother movement than the "limited ANIME" seen on TV. As such it is sometimes referred to as "full animation." The term *animation* was introduced to Japan in the 1960s to integrate "line-drawing films" (*senga douga*) and "movement films" (*douga eiga*); it was shortened to anime in the 1980s.

Animation sannin no kai (アニメーション三人の会): A meeting organized in 1960 by manga artist Kuri Youji, designer Yanagihara Ryouhei, and illustrator Manabe Hiroshi. They aimed to create an alternative form of expression in animation. A regular meeting was held at Sougetsu Art Center until 1967 to show short animated films. At these meetings, artists from different areas, such as TEZUKA OSAMU, Yokoo Tadanori, Wada Makoto, and Tanaami Keiichi, also exhibited their works.

Animax (アニマックス): The first and largest television network in the world devoted entirely to ANIME. Began in 1988 as a twenty-four-hour satellite channel in Tokyo. As of 2008, it reached 41 million households in forty-seven countries and fourteen languages. Shareholders include Sony Pictures Entertainment, Sunrise, TOEI ANIMATION, TMS Entertainment, and Nihon Ad Systems.

Anime (アニメ): Japanese cartoons. That is, Japanese animated TV series or animated movies. A major outlet for artistic expression and mass entertainment in Japan.

In other countries, the term usually refers to animation from Japan or in the style of Japanese animation. To most Japanese, however, anime is something shown on TV and targeting kids, and it is seen as distinct from high-quality animated feature films. Anime for adults is qualified as hobby or late night (*shinya*) anime and OVA (original video animation).

Linguistically the word is not, as some believe, derived from the French *animé* but is a shortened, Japanese pronunciation of the English noun "animation." The use of the word "anime" by itself did not really take off in Japan until the book *Terebi Meisaku Anime Gekijo* in 1975; before that it was sometimes used in combination with other words such as *anime-douga*, *anime*-manga, and *anime*-movie.

The first Japanese animated feature film was the black-and-white navy propaganda film, *Momotaro no Umiwashi* (*Momotaro's Sea Eagles*) in 1943. The first color animation was the Toei production HAKUJADEN (*The Tale of the White Serpent*, 1958), and the first TV anime was NHK's *Mitsu no Hanashi* (*Three Tales*), aired on January 15, 1960. The first breakout success came in 1963 with TEZUKA OSAMU's TETSUWAN ATOMU (*Astro Boy*).

The first wave of popular animation in Japan began at this time. Anime from this period were mostly adapted from sweeping manga series by Tezuka, ISHINOMORI SHOTARO and YOKOYAMA MITSUTERU. Much of this was slapstick comedy and action. However, these early creators pioneered narrative-style anime, with complete story arcs that adhered to cinematic logic and form. Anime became popular because it provided a more interesting alternative to the underdeveloped live-action industry of the time. Unlike America, where live-action TV shows and films had generous budgets, the live-action industry in Japan was, and still is, a small market suffering from budgeting, location, and casting restrictions. The lack of Western-looking actors, for example, made it next to impossible to shoot films set in Europe or America.

These early anime series were shown on TV, which at the time had a limited variety of programs, meaning most Japanese watched the same shows and share the same memories of them. Because of this, anime from this period are often described as "cultural," "national," or "nostalgic" anime—wholesome fare that everyone in Japan can love and be proud of.

The second stage of anime's evolution in Japan was during the 1970s, when there was a surge in the popularity of manga—especially those of Tezuka, which were often turned into anime. As a result of Tezuka's work, and that of other pioneers, anime developed certain characteristics and genres that are still fundamental elements of the art.

Around this time several important trends in TV anime emerged. Series for both boys and girls were marked by goal-oriented characters and narratives. Classics of world literature were animated, including *Heidi* by Johanna Spyri and *A Dog of Flanders* by Marie Louise de la Ramée. *Shojo* and *shonen ai* manga also

MOMOTARO NO UMIWASHI FROM 1943

adopted European settings, culminating in anime such as Ikeda Riyoko's *The Rose of Versailles* in 1979. Monkey Punch's *Lupin III* character even had French roots, and the show used mature humor and violence to lure adult viewers. NAGAI GO came onto the scene in the early 1970s, with *Cutie Honey*, *Devilman*, and *Mazinger Z*, introducing sexy transforming girls, violent themes, and macho fighting robots. And MATSUMOTO LEIJI also arrived with challenging and emotional space operas, including *Space Battleship Yamato* in 1974. These tapped a society aching for sci-fi amid the continuing space race and technological innovation. This came to a head with TOMINO YOSHIYUKI's *Mobile Suit Gundam* in 1979, a realistic MECHA series that heralded the third age of anime in Japan.

In the 1980s, the anime market was booming; studios had funding, and anime made its way from TV to theaters. Not only was Matsumoto Leiji at the height of his feature film career, but MIYAZAKI HAYAO was churning out hits with *Nausicaä of the Valley of the Wind* in 1984 and *Laputa: Castle in the Sky* in 1986. Adaptations of TAKAHASHI RUMIKO's manga *Urusei Yatsura*, *Maison Ikkoku* and, *Ranma ½* carved out the romance anime genre and mixed the slapstick comedic elements of the 1960s with the serious emotions of the 1970s. The *Urusei Yatsura* movies *Only You* (1983) and *Beautiful Dreamer* (1984) in particular were major successes.

As movie budgets started to shrink, the home video revolution arrived and companies began to distribute experimental and niche titles directly to market as OVA. VHS also made it possible for fans to record, play back, study, and share anime, marking the start of the first otaku generation.

Toward the end of the 1980s three of the biggest and most costly animated movies of all time were released: *Wings of Honneamise* by GAINAX in 1987, Miyazaki's *My Neighbor Totoro*, and OTOMO KATSUHIRO's *Akira* in 1988. The result, however, was that the anime market imploded. Japan went into recession, and studios turned to making computer games and other supplementary products targeting otaku (see ANIME BUBBLE).

WINGS OF HONNEAMISE BY GAINAX

As otaku became its main consumers, anime became a product unto itself, meaning it was sometimes not based on manga and ceased to be narrative based. Its characters were no longer goal oriented, and romance among or even *with* them took center stage. The recessionary economy could no longer support the production of massive cinema anime, animators were torturously underpaid, and TV series were so unprofitable production was farmed out overseas. The OVA market was saturated with niche series, and companies moved toward producing computer games, figures, and idoru singers instead of anime. Anime itself simply became, with few exceptions, a base on which to build profitable lines of merchandise. Late-night anime • 山本寛

YAMAMOTO YUTAKA

YAMAMOTO YUTAKA, OR "YAMAKAN," was born in 1974 in Osaka. He is among the most talented of Japan's new generation of anime directors and is known among otaku for directing the animated dance sequences in *The Melancholy of Suzumiya Haruhi*, *Lucky Star*, and *Kannagi*. After a myste-rious brouhaha concerning his direction of *Lucky Star* in 2007, he was demoted and left Kyoto Animation to found Studio Ordet.

PG: What anime do you respect?

YY: I wrote my graduation thesis at Kyoto University on Miyazaki's *Princess Mononoke* and the movie version of Anno's *Neon Genesis Evangelion*. These were epoch-making films. I don't think anyone in our generation will make an anime that moves the industry, Japan, and the world as these two did.

PG: So no anime will ever match these?

YY: I hope it will. I don't know what post-*Eva* anime is, but it's insulting to these masters if we don't try to make it. It's also irresponsible not to try and make work that resonates with our times. But no matter how you look at it, what can be done in anime has been. Genres, forms of expression, themes, characters, it's all been exhausted. So what can we do? Only copy, and add our own little bits along the way.

PG: Are you targeting otaku with your anime?

YY: I just want to make anime. I'm an otaku, so naturally similar people are attracted to my work, but I personally don't like it when otaku monopolize anime. Anime made by otaku for otaku, that sort of narrow conception isn't good. I want people who like anime, from the old to the young, to watch my work.

PG: What does "otaku" mean to you?

YY: People who are unpopular with the opposite sex and blame that on the anime and games they love. I was that way, so I can say it. Otaku are people who don't get along well with others. In truth, it isn't my favorite word.

PG: What are otaku fans like?

YY: As an otaku I can say they're generally rude and selfish. It's tiring to be with them. Miyazaki Hayao, Anno Hideaki, and Okada Toshio all gave up. They aren't trying to communicate with otaku but rather to be rid of them entirely. The worst thing about otaku is their tendency to think they're different from everyone else and cut others off to retreat into their own world. Maybe Miyazaki, Anno, and Okada just don't recognize that about themselves. . . . If we abandon otaku now, it won't result in happiness for anyone. I can just come out and say it, "Otaku are annoying," but we still have to find some way to get along.

PG: Is your anime MOÉ?

YY: I say I make moé anime because it's convenient, but I have no idea what moé is. I can't deny that some characters are moé but if we try and define those elements we end up creating separate camps o

fans that cut themselves off from one another. I'm not criticizing moé anime, and it's fine if moé elements are there, but making it on purpose and categorizing it isn't good. Anime as anime is just fine, so we should leave it that way.

I'm not criticizing moé anime, but making it on purpose and categorizing it isn't good. Anime as anime is just fine, so we should leave it that way.

PG: At a *Kannagi* event in 2008, you announced you're married. Are you still an otaku?

YY: Yes. I'm not all that sociable. For me, being an otaku is a persecution complex, like everyone despises me. I don't think Okada's generation felt that. Otaku don't have the power to change society or create culture the way Okada wanted them to. Otaku are people with a complex about being otaku. The same way I hope for another anime masterpiece to emerge, I hope that otaku will become stronger.

PG: Anime such as *Haruhi* were instrumental in the phenomenon of otaku making pilgrimages to certain locations (*seichi junrei*). Did you expect that?

YY: To some degree it was predictable because seichi junrei is a part of otaku culture. I myself did it as a student, going to Higashi-Koganei in search of Ghibli. But it wasn't my intention. If you draw settings from your imagination, you end up with Doraemon or Sazae-san, with their boring, uniform backgrounds. Anime is better if we add a sense of reality to the unreal.

PG: Is your use of IDORU similar, like giving reality to movement? For example when you used the group Berryz Kobo as a basis for the *Haruhi* dance.

YY: No, it's because I like idoru. They're like water, food, and air, something I can't live without. I always thought I wanted to make an anime idoru dance. Just doing it had meaning, and that is something I can take pride in. Forgive me for that.

PG: How do you define idoru?

YY: If you translate "idol" into Japanese it is "image." Like an image of Christ. And when you say image, it means something that's not real. It's shrouded in lies. Communal worship of the image is what creates an idoru. An idoru is about remaining as close to the image in the minds of the believers as possible. I want idoru to remain wrapped in lies, and I don't care what the real person is doing. In a way it's a sad existence, but that tragedy is also appealing. It's similar for anime characters. Anime is a lie, drawings of a human form. But when wrapped in the right lies the character can create a sense of moé in the viewer.

PG: What do you want to do from now?

YY: As a creator, I have a responsibility to change anime. We need to stop categorizing, suppress the tendency to cut ourselves off from others in the community and liberate anime and bring it to the masses. If we don't, then we will continue to retreat into smaller groups watching more specialized anime until we perish.

PG: What is coming up for you?

YY: I have a new anime in 2010. I can't say anything detailed, but it will be an original story. I want it to be a work that overthrows the "moé anime Yamamoto Yutaka" image. There will be no more dancing in my anime. I'm also working as a critic writing and lecturing.

anime began to take off in the late 1990s, as this time slot limited risk for the investors. This marked a shift from prime time to otaku anime.

During the mid-to-late 1990s anime became increasingly popular overseas, and in 2001 anime accounted for a $49 billion global market. When *Spirited Away* won the Academy Award for Best Animated Feature in 2003, even the Japanese government took notice (see COOL JAPAN).

Anime has been called the savior of the Japanese content industries, and it is so popular it accounts for over 60 percent of all children's animation shown in the world. The number of Japanese-language students has increased in recent years due largely to the appeal of anime worldwide. Anime has grown to be a truly global addiction, and people seem unable to wait for their next fix. Sean Leonard, a researcher at Massachusetts Institute of Technology (MIT), estimates that within forty-eight hours of the Japanese broadcast of an episode from a popular series such as *Naruto*, it is downloaded by approximately 18,000 fans worldwide.

Anime Ambassador: In 2008, the Japanese Ministry of Foreign Affairs named Fujiko Fujio's character Doraemon, a lovable robot cat from the future who has been an ANIME icon since 1969, the Anime Ambassador of Japan. Doraemon *taishi* (ambassador) limited his first visits to East Asia because the US Federal Communication Commission used a mascot called "Broadband" a round cat with a striking resemblance to Doraemon.

Anime Bubble (アニメバブル): Following the unbelievable success of the ANIME *NEON GENESIS EVANGELION* in 1995, production committees began to pour funds into new series looking for the next big anime hit. They were desperate to capitalize on this bright spot in the recessionary economy of the 1990s. The anime bubble was basically characterized by the pouring of funds into multiple studios and a glut of anime series. Resources began to be spread too thin, with studios working to impossible deadlines. At the peak of the bubble, sixty to seventy anime series were being aired each week, and there were simply not enough skilled animators or studios to keep up the quality. *Evangelion* famously ran out of funds toward the end of its twenty-six-episode run and ended with still shots and pencil sketches. After *Evangelion* came the legendary Yashigani Incident in 1998, so called because episode four of *Lost Universe*, called "Yashigani Hofuru," was aired with hardly any in-between frames and the characters basically just jerked around on-screen. For a time, any bad anime was called a "Yashigani." In another case, the *Gundress* film hit theaters in 1999 in a state of semicompletion. Soon after this the Japanese anime industry almost completely collapsed and studios were forced to farm anime out to foreign studios. Focus shifted to blue-chip works by proven MANGAKA and directors, and the costs of producing anime were supplemented by various cross-platform tie-ins and collectible merchandise.

DORAEMON ANIME AMBASSADOR

AnimeCon '91: The fourth full-blown, dedicated ANIME convention in the United States, held in San Jose in 1991. It was the beginning of mass OTAKU and convention culture in the US. With an attendance of 2,000, it was the first anime event to break the 1,000-person mark and receive official support from both the American and Japanese anime production studios. It was the predecessor to ANIME EXPO, the largest convention in the US. The event was dominated by *Nadia: Secret of Blue Water* and the *MINNA AGECHAU* ♥ CONTROVERSY—heralded by the American media as the coming of Japanese pornography rather than anime.

ANIME EXPO:
FROM LEFT TO RIGHT: TAKADA AKEMI, KATO HIROMI, HIDAKA MASAMITSU, ANDO MASAHIRO, NAKAGAWA SHOKO, AND THE DUO JYUKAI

AnimEigo: One of the earliest US licensors and localizers to adopt subtitles. It is most famous for importing *Bubblegum Crisis* and *Urusei Yatsura*, two landmark series of the Third Wave of international fans. Interestingly, it doesn't carry HENTAI titles, which almost all other distributors do.

Anime Expo: Also known as AX, this is North America's largest ANIME event, with an attendance of over 35,000 in 2007. Founded in 1992, it takes place on the Fourth of July weekend in Los Angeles, California, under the auspices of the non-profit Society for the Promotion of Japanese Animation (SPJA). AX has frequently collaborated with the anime industry, and as the convention has grown, so has the visibility of AX's industry sponsors with their towering presence in the exhibition halls. Many new products are unveiled at AX, and Japanese guests, usually singers, often perform (see SHOKO-TAN). Fan events and competitions of anime music video (AMV) and COSPLAY also play a major role in the convention's appeal.

Anime fandom (international): Anime fandom outside Japan can roughly be broken down into five waves. The First Wave of international fans began in the 1960s and early 1970s with the syndication of TV shows such as *TETSUWAN ATOMU* (*Astro Boy*), *JYANGURU TAITEI* (*Kimba the White Lion* or *Jungle Emperor*), *Eitoman* (*Tobor, the Eight Man*), *Kaitei Shonen Marine* (*Marine Boy*), *Tetsujin 28-go* (*Gigantor*), and *Mach Go Go Go* (*Speed Racer*). These were a huge impact on the media landscape of the time, leading some to describe this as the height of Japanese anime's influence on the international market. Decades later *Jungle Emperor* inspired *Lion King*. It must be noted, however, that at the time most fans probably didn't realize that these cartoons were from Japan.

The Second Wave of fans were those who cut their teeth on anime in the 1970s on MATSUMOTO LEIJI's *Uchu Senkan Yamato* (*Space Battleship Yamato*) and YOSHIDA TATSUO's *Kagaku Ninjatai Gatchaman* (*Battle of the Planets*). Epic stories, deep characters, and science-fiction themes and settings characterize this era of animation. It was at this time that anime truly began to be taken seriously among fans as an art form to be enjoyed by adults. Anime fans started appearing at SF conventions, forming clubs, and networking. This wave also marks the beginning of a crucial division in localizing techniques, with the relatively light edits of *Yamato* standing in sharp contrast to the complete "Americanized" rewrites of *Gatchaman*.

The Third Wave came onto the scene in the 1980s when Matsumoto Leiji's space operas were dwindling in influence and anime on VHS was on the rise. Fans clustered around TAKAHASHI RUMIKO's *Urusei Yatsura* beginning in 1981; the *Transformers* anime between 1982 and 1987; and Studio Nue's *Super Dimension Fortress Macross*—better known as Harmony Gold's *Robotech*—in 1985. *Robotech* was the first major hybrid anime, combining *Super Dimension Fortress Macross* with the unrelated *Super Dimension Cavalry Southern Cross* and *Genesis Climber Mospeada* to meet the American broadcast minimum of sixty-five episodes. The English dub of MIYAZAKI HAYAO's *Nausicaä of the Valley of the Wind*, a hack job called *Warriors of the Wind*, also hit the shelves in 1985, convincing fans to stick with the Japanese material. OVA (original video animation) releases such as *Bubblegum Crisis* in 1987 also made an impact, and *Akira* in 1988 started the mainstreaming of gritty, adult sci-fi anime.

The Fourth Wave of fans became acquainted with anime in the 1990s through specialty comic shops and pirated copies. They experienced a wide variety of anime and usually saw it in the original form without heavy edits. At this time the devaluation of the US dollar doubled anime and merchandise prices. Nonetheless, dedicated fans meant Manga Entertainment's release of *Ghost in the Shell* debuted on the Billboard Top 10 for video sales in August 1996. The release schedule for official titles was slow, and a lack of reliable information made fan-subs, tape dealers, and information sharing at conventions the norm. This generation of fans tends to prefer subtitles because they grew accustomed to the manuscripts they printed off the Internet or bought at conventions.

The Fifth Wave starts with fans who became acquainted with the medium through *Sailor Moon* and *Dragon Ball Z* on Cartoon Network's TOONAMI programming block in 1998, sporadic Sci-Fi Channel late-night specials, and Fox Kids and Kids WB offerings. They could buy videos or DVDs from mainstream shops such as Suncoast. They witnessed the *Pokémon* phenomenon in 1998, thought "Gundam" meant 2000's bishonen spectacular *Gundam Wing*, and saw *Spirited Away* take the Academy Award for Best Animated Feature in 2003. This wave went online and established communities in contact with one another and monitored otaku activity in Japan. With the mainstream market in the US saturated by anime and manga, and the raw supply of licensable stock in Japan shrinking in quantity, the cost of localizing a series has inflated to the seven-figure range.

GATCHAMAN
KNOW OVERSEAS AS "BATTLE OF THE PLANETS"

With the flow of new material slowing, fans—who could be called post-fifth wave—now tend to download or watch series on the Internet for free.

Anime Festival Asia 2008 (AFA'08): An event in Southeast Asia celebrating Japanese pop culture. Held in November 2008 in Singapore as a large-scale extravaganza sponsored by Dentsu, BANDAI, and ANIMAX. It was also partly sponsored by the Embassy of Japan and the Japan Foundation, clearly marking it as part of the COOL JAPAN goodwill campaign. AFA'08 was a warm-up for the Japan Creative Centre, which opened in 2009 to showcase Japanese culture and content in Singapore. Many performers and artists came from Japan, and over 45,000 locals attended the two-day event. Organizers compared the event to the TOKYO INTERNATIONAL ANIME FAIR and ANIME EXPO, indicating it might become a regular regional fixture.

"THE KING OF ANISONGS" MIZUKI ICHIROU (IN JACKET) WITH COSPLAYERS AT ANIME FESTIVAL ASIA 2008

Anime Kentei (アニメ検定): The National Comprehensive Animation Cultural Knowledge Certificate Examination, also known as the Anime Kentei, was established in 2007 to promote interest in and understanding of the industry and culture of Japanese animation, although knowledge of titles from around the world is also necessary. It's a written exam in five grades, Grade One being the hardest as examinees need to be intimately familiar with secret stories and insider knowledge. The exam is run out of the Tokyo Anime Center in AKIHABARA. Preregistration is compulsory, and each attempt costs about $50, not including official textbooks.

Anime musicals (アニメミュージカル): Beginning with BANDAI's 1993 stage version of *Sailor Moon* at Sunshine Theater in Ikebukuro, Tokyo, many ANIME have been made into stage musicals. Examples include *Sakura Taisen*, *Prince of Tennis*, and *Dear Boys*, with other bizarre examples including *Bleach* and *Naruto*. These live theatre productions typically follow the original anime plotlines but also add a lot of new material. They generate numerous IDORU, photo albums, and CDs. The *Sailor Moon* musical (or *SeraMyu*), for example, played over 800 performances and released twenty CDs. The combination of the intricate costumes, emotional songs, and beautiful boys makes these musicals particularly popular among FUJOSHI.

Anime News Network: Or ANN. One of the largest and most dependable online sources for information on OTAKU activity in Japan and North America. It also runs the magazine *Protoculture Addicts*. ANN is mostly dedicated to the anime industry, although MANGA, J-POP, and assorted other happenings also make headlines. Content is made up of reviews, editorials, forums (including the Edit List, where differences between original and localized anime are documented), and listings of anime and manga titles and production staff. Founded in 1998 by Justin Sevakis.

Anime Shinseiki Sengen (アニメ新世紀宣言): New Age of Anime Declaration. An event held in Shinjuku on February 22, 1981, to commemorate the release of the first of three *Mobile Suit Gundam* ANIME films. Over 15,000 young Japanese gathered to hear director TOMINO YOSHIYUKI's speech questioning the idea that anime was somehow low quality or vulgar.

Aniparo (アニパロ): ANIME parody. A DOUJINSHI or YAOI work that features characters from popular ANIME series in alternative worlds or relationships; parody here does not imply ridicule, it is an homage and is often very sexual.

Anisong (アニソン): ANIME song. A colloquial term used to describe songs that are associated with anime, but it can also include *TOKUSATSU* songs. It usually refers to the addictive opening and ending theme tunes. There are basically two types, the old-school 1970s retro type; and J-POP sung by leading performers. The retro sound is inherited from the early days of ANIME when these songs defined the style of music associated with anime, while the more modern J-Pop songs were pioneered by the record labels King Records and Star Child in the 1990s. Many respected artists and composers, such as TM Revolution and KANNO YOKO, have crossed into anisong production to improve the quality of music, but the classic anisong sound stubbornly remains. In 2005 Mizuki Nana's "Eternal Blaze" made it to number two on the Oricon sales charts, the highest ever for an anime-related song, and set the scene for SEIYUU (voice actors) to dominate the charts. While sales of CDs are falling globally due to the popularity of download sites, anisong CDs continue to sell well to otaku who covet the extras that come with the CDs. Their demand for nostalgia and simplicity in music shapes the market. There are groups who meet online, sing anisong at KARAOKE (see PASERA), and make anisong remixes. There is a massive annual event for anisongs, called "Animelo Summer Live" where famous singers, old and new, perform their hits live.

Anmoku no ryokai (暗黙の了解): Unspoken agreement. The principle rule governing DOUJINSHI production in Japan and FANSUBS and FAN-DUBS in the US. The publishers, licensors, and distributors agree to look the other way as long as fans don't go too far in their productions, don't make too much money, and don't stop being good consumers of the licensed, official, and commercial products. In a November 2007 article in *Wired* magazine Daniel Pink—speech writer to former US President Bill Clinton and a doujinshi fan—suggests that anmoku no ryokai is the heart of a new business model because allowing consumers to produce keeps fans interested in the work, cultivates new talent in amateur artists, and provides free market research on what is popular and what people want. Fans aren't infringing on rights to copy for profit but are creatively rewriting it for entertainment. The balance, however, seems to work a lot better in Japan than it does in the United States. In fact, in 2008 Kadokawa made a landmark deal to allow amateur MAD MOVIES of their popular *Suzumiya Haruhi* anime franchise as long as creators mark videos with the Kadokawa logo when they post them online.

Anna Miller's (アンミラ): First opened in 1973 in Hawaii, this was one of the first themed, costume chain restaurants in Japan. It's famous for the uniforms its waitresses wear, which consist of a white blouse, an orange or pink jumper-style miniskirt—with the waistline cut underneath the breasts—a matching apron, and a heart-shaped nametag. They have been an important influence on the current MAID CAFÉ boom. Passionate fans call this place "Anmira" and are attracted by the large-breasted, pie-slinging gals—not unlike the Hooter's girls in the United States.

MYSTERIOUS ANNA MILLER'S COSPLAYERS

Anno Hideaki (庵野秀明): Born in 1960 in Ube, Yamaguchi Prefecture. One of Japan's most influential anime luminaries, Anno was the main director for, and a founding member of, GAINAX. He's known for his philosophical touch and psychological deconstruction of characters. He began as a film student at Osaka College of Arts with friends and roommates Akai Takami and Yamaga Hiroyuki. In 1981, they explored their passion for ANIME and film and created the opening animation for DAICON III, one of the sci-fi conventions at the center of the early OTAKU movement. Anno worked on the anime *Macross* from 1982 to 1983, but he was still largely unknown. In his spare time, he directed parody works of SENTAI (masked superhero) shows, including *Patriotic Squadron Dai-Nippon* (1982), about the Russo-Japanese war, and *Return of Ultraman* (1983), a special-effects bonaza that replaces New Ultraman with a giant Anno in Ultraman cosplay. It went on to become a promo for Daicon IV in 1983. Anno and Daicon Film also created the classic opening animation for the event. Anno then responded to an advertisment posted in *Animage* magazine by MIYAZAKI HAYAO, who was making *NAUSICAÄ OF THE VALLEY OF THE WIND* and was short of animators. Anno met with Miyazaki, who was impressed enough by his work to give him the task of drawing the detailed sequences of the God Soldiers at the end of the film. When the work came out in 1984, along with Anno's GENGA (key frames) work on *Macross: Do you remember love?*, he became a sensation and co-founded Gainax. His directoral debut was the *Gunbuster* OVA in 1988. Anno's greatest influence can be seen in Gainax's TV anime such as *Nadia: Secret of Blue Water* (1990–91), a series originally proposed by Miyazaki as a counterpart to *Laputa: Castle in the Sky* (1986). Anno was given very little creative control and fell into a four-year depression after the work. He came back with *NEON GENESIS EVANGELION* (1995–96), which revolutionized the field with innovative techniques, grand narratives, and philosophical

CUTIE HONEY MOVIE DIRECTED BY ANNO HIDEAKI

themes. Not everyone was happy with Anno's style, however, and disappointed fans insisted he redo the controversial ending of *Evangelion*, even threatening his life. In response he gave them a twisted and brutal ending in the film version. He resigned from directing at Gainax after disputes over his treatment of *His and Her Circumstances*, a school romance drama and Gainax's first attempt to adapt an existing (manga) story into anime. He left the show in the hands of his protégé, Tsurumaki Kazuya. He has since directed or been involved with the non-animated films *Love & Pop*, *Cutie Honey*, and *Strings*. He also directed short films for the Ghibli Museum, and in 2000 he directed the live-action *Ritual* for Studio Kajino, Ghibli's film arm. In 2006, he started a new studio called Khara to "rebuild" *Neon Genesis Evangelion* into four new films. The works are in conjuction with Gainax. Tsurumaki is directing, and original character and MECHA designers Sadamoto Yoshiyuki and Yamashita Ikuto are back. The first of the films, *Evangelion: 1.0 You Are (Not) Alone,* was released in 2007, *Evangelion: 2.0 You Can (Not) Advance* in 2009, while *Evangelion 3.0* and *Final* have yet to be announced.

Anorak: A British-English term similar to OTAKU, complete with the negative connotations of poor social skills and an obsessive interest in a topic that seems strange or boring to others.

Arashi (荒し): Vandalize; to lay waste to. When a blog or site gets so many hits or comments (often meaningless ones) that it can no longer be, or no longer is, managed and goes out of control on a spiral of destruction.

Arts Vision (アーツビジョン): A Japanese talent agency founded in 1984 and known for its voice actors (SEIYUU). Some famous examples include HAYASHIBARA MEGUMI, Mitsuishi Kotono, Hoshi Soichiro, Horie Yuri, Takagi Wataru, and Miyamura Yuko.

Asahara Shoko (麻原彰晃): See AUM SHINRIKYO.

Asimov, Isaac: Born in 1920 in Petrovichi, Russia. Died in 1992. After moving to the United States, this biochemist and author became known for his realistic approach to science fiction. A humanist and a rationalist, he is one of the Big Three SF writers (along with Robert A. Heinlein and Arthur C. Clarke). He wrote and edited more than 500 books and an estimated 9,000 letters and postcards. The Science Fiction Writers of America in 1964 voted "Nightfall" the best short science fiction story of all time. His most famous works are the *Foundation* series, the *Galactic Empire* series, and the *Robot* series, where he proposed his famous LAWS OF ROBOTICS to avoid the SF trope of killer robots and probe their socio-cultural significance. He was also behind the *Lucky Starr* series of juvenile SF novels and numerous works on popular science.

Asobi (遊び): Play. The indulgence of emotional and physical pleasure. Also, someone getting carried away and going beyond normal limits, even getting a little crazy.

Aso Taro (麻生太郎): Born in 1940 in Iizuka, Fukuoka. This businessman-turned-politician became leader of the ruling Liberal Democratic Party and the prime minister of Japan on September 24, 2008. While he was Minister of Foreign Affairs, he actively promoted Japan as "the nation of pop culture" and was the chief proponent of COOL JAPAN. Aso's tough talk and crooked smile may make him look like a gangster, but he relates to AKIBA-KEI OTAKU and claims to read thirty MANGA a week. He idolizes *Golgo 13* (about an assassin) and has praised the goth-styled doll ANIME *Rozen Maiden*. Because of this he's sometimes called "Rozen Aso" or "His Excellency Rozen." In a 2006 campaign speech in Akihabara, Aso famously described his love of manga and his foreign policy goals for Japanese pop culture. Stock prices for anime-related companies jumped by 18 percent, and young people were so enthralled with his antics that manga-like images of him and his catch phrases soon adorned "Taro-chan" souvenir products.

In 2008, after the prime minister misread *kanji* (the Chinese alphabet, which stupid characters in anime often can't read), it was widely speculated that his habit of reading too much manga had kept him from his studies. The word otaku was again evoked to describe him, but this time in a derogatory manner. His ratings in both public and political polls dropped drastically thereafter.

Atari: The first company in the world founded solely to make video games. The name comes from the word said when placing a chip in the Japanese board game *Go*. In 1972, it was a North American company owned by Nolan Bushnell and Ted Dabney, but it is currently a subsidiary of French publisher Infogames Entertainment SA. Atari pioneered arcade games, home consoles, and computer technology with games such as *PONG* and the Atari 2600 system. But later consoles such as the Jaguar, Atari's answer to NINTENDO's Famicom, sold terribly. Today, the company develops and distributes games for all major consoles and for the PC.

AU: Abbreviation of "alternative universe," a catchall

phrase used to refer to a side story or spinoff series based on an existing work. The spinoff doesn't take into account the events, character interactions, or realities of the original, and so takes on a new, alternative flavor.

Aum Shinrikyo (オウム真理教): The Aum Supreme Truth sect, a 20th-century religious movement in Japan notorious for its 1995 gassing of the Tokyo subway. Also known for its links to OTAKU culture. Asahara Shoko (born Matsumoto Chizuo), the cult's blind guru, styled himself as the captain of the "Space Battleship Mahayana" and described the production of sarin gas as "Cosmo Cleaner," both references to MATSUMOTO LEIJI's *Space Battleship Yamato*. Aum operated a store in AKIHABARA called "Mahaposha," and later "The Graceful," to recruit youth who were unhappy that the world promised in ANIME never arrived. *Genma Wars* is an early example of an apocalyptic anime that inspired the group, and *Neon Genesis Evangelion* is eerily similar to their world view of invading spirits and apocalyptic cleansing. Asahara succeeded in gathering some 10,000 followers. After disastrous attempts at political campaigning in Shibuya, and under police investigation for alleged abuse of cult members, Asahara ordered sarin gas to be released on the Tokyo subway, killing twelve and injuring thousands. He was sentenced to death in 2007 and is awaiting execution. During his trial, Asahara was repeatedly referred to as "anime like" or "otaku like" in his behavior, driving home negative stereotypes of otaku and fear of their behavior.

AV: Either "audio-visual equipment" or "adult video," usually the former among older generations and the latter among younger ones. Specifically AV means live-action porn flicks. It's a massive industry and many beautiful "AV girls" become internationally famous among guys who watch this stuff. Even a cursory Internet search for "Japanese AV" shows that it's hugely popular outside Japan.

Avatar: A representation or projection of the self in a virtual space. From the Sanskrit word for incarnation of a holy being in worldly form. These days it mostly refers to the customizable 3D models and 2D icons, users, viewers, or game players use to identify themselves online. The author Neal Stephenson popularized the word in his CYBERPUNK novel *Snow Crash* in 1992. As the Internet expanded, hackers and users on BBS forums started employing avatars of about 100 square pixels. The AOL Instant Messenger was the first major software to use avatars. Online virtual worlds such as *Second Life* feature the most sophisticated avatars.

Awase (合わせ): Getting together with like-minded people to form a group. Especially used for COSPLAYers wearing costumes from the same series and posing together.

Azuma Hideo (吾妻ひでお): Born in 1950 in Tokachi, Hokkaido. He debuted as a MANGAKA in 1969 and pioneered *FUJORI* GAGS and LOLICON MANGA. He was influenced by greats such as TEZUKA OSAMU and ISHINOMORI SHOTARO, but his works are dominated by surreal science fiction and BISHOJO (beautiful girls). He started in the SHONEN MANGA (boys' comics) genre before moving on to SHOJO (young girl) MANGA and SEINEN (youth) MANGA. His manga from the 1980s are considered crucial in defining the OTAKU movement. The fact that he was working on shojo manga and brought those influences, for example androgyny and romance, into male fantasy is also important. Works include *Fujori nikki* (1978), *Shisso nikki* (2005), and *Cybele* (1979), the first LOLICON DOUJINSHI in Japan.

B

Back lighting: See TOUKOU.

Baka (バカ): Stupid. Often the first Japanese word that foreign ANIME fans learn. It can mean idiot or fool, depending on the listener, atmosphere, and region. "Baka" is rude but generally more acceptable in Tokyo than it is in Western Japan, where it is a serious insult. See also AHO.

Bakunyuu (爆乳): See KYONYUU.

Bandai: A Japanese toy maker famous for plastic models (PURAMO) and Gashapon vending machine toys (see GACHAPON). Bandai is one of the world's largest toy producers. Some Bandai group companies and partners produce ANIME and TOKUSATSU (special effects) programs, which become the basis for Bandai toys. The company is most well known for its giant robot anime series and merchandise tie-ins, which began in the 1980s with the epic space opera *Mobile Suit Gundam*. After an equal power-share merger with game developer and amusement facility operator Namco, the company is now officially known as Bandai Namco Holdings in Japanese, and Namco Bandai Holdings, Incorporated, in English.

Bangyaru (バンギャル): A girl into VISUAL-KEI bands. A groupie. They tend to dress in GOTH-LOLI fashion.

Bara (バラ): An old term for homosexual men. See YURI.

Bareru (ばれ): To come out; to be exposed. Especially used for coming out of the closet, in this case admitting to being an otaku.

Barnett, Josh: Born in 1977 in Seattle, Washington. A mixed martial arts heavyweight pro fighter popularly known as the "strongest OTAKU in the world." This is because, in addition to being incredibly macho, he famously makes trips to AKIHABARA and NAKANO BROADWAY to buy FIGURES, games, and ANIME when in Japan. He's said he loves anime because of the lessons it teaches about the intensity of relationships between people. He idolizes the character Kenshiro from *Fist of the North Star* and uses its theme tune, "*Ai wo Torimodose*," when he enters the ring. He once called out former Pride Heavyweight Champion, Fedor Emelianenko, with Kenshiro's famous line "*Omae wa mou shindeiru*" ("You're already dead"). As a result, Japanese fans

TOKYO BIG SIGHT

have taken to calling him the "blue-eyed Kenshiro."

Since Barnett, a host of otaku fighters have appeared, including Nagashima Jienotsu Yuichiro, who wears COSPLAY to the ring, uses ANISONGS as ring music, and speaks 2CHANNEL jargon.

Bedroom café: See JOSHIRYO.

Beta (ベタ): Areas of the MANGA page that are black; colored areas are called "tone."

Beta (ベタ): Typical, predictable. A beta story is a cookie-cutter one that anyone can understand.

Betamax (ベータマックス): Also called βマックス (βmax) in Japan, with the Greek *beta*. A half-inch-thick videotape recording format introduced by Sony in 1975. It was a vast improvement on the chunky, professional one-inch U-matic cassettes and could be used at home. Sony fought fiercely with JVC's video home recording system VHS (introduced in 1976) but lost the fight because Beta's recording time was too short and VHS was adopted by the porn industry. Even so, OTAKU who adopted Beta early and claimed it was a superior system continued to support it for many years.

JOSH BARNETT "STRONGEST OTAKU IN THE WORLD"

Big Sight (ビッグサイト): Or Tokyo Big Sight, is the popular nickname of the massive Tokyo International Exhibition Center, which opened in 1996 in the Odaiba bay area of Tokyo. It has an iconic silhouette thanks to the upside-down pyramid shapes of the Conference Tower. The "King of Sentai Songs" Kushida Akira sang an ANISONG in 2002 called "*Shouri da! Big Sightron*," which parodied the towers' likeness to the giant robot Macross City and the close proximity of a massive saw-like sculpture that appears to be its weapon. Big Sight hosts COMIKET, WONDER FESTIVAL, TOKYO INTERNATIONAL ANIME FAIR, and countless other OTAKU events.

Bimbo yusuri (貧乏揺すり): Poor man's fidget. To fidget or shake, as in bouncing the knee or twitching nervously. It's rude.
Binyuu (微乳): See MUNYUU.
Biseinen (美青年): Beautiful adolescent; but basically means "beautiful man." It is typically used to describe characters of any age older than BISHONEN (beautiful boy). However, bishonen don't necessarily grow into biseinen, as the aesthetic pleasures in both are somewhat distinct.
Bishojo (美少女): Pretty or cute girl, although the literal translation is "beautiful girl." These comprise an entire genre of characters in ANIME, MANGA, HENTAI, and GYARUGE. The Japanese obsession with bishojo is obvious in the many weekly magazines cataloging these girls, the myriad of online sites worshipping them, cute girl characters in DOUJINSHI, and so on. Bishojo characters tend to stretch the limits of femininity with stereotyped and cliché personality types, and they often have a distorted, hypersexualized anatomy, such as unnaturally long legs and absolutely massive breasts.
Bishojo games (美少女ゲーム): A general term for dating simulator games on personal computers. See GYARUGE and EROGE.
Bishonen (美少年): Beautiful boy. Bishonen characters in MANGA are drawn to be beautiful—in a rather feminine way—because that makes them nice for women to look at and fantasize about. The strong homoerotic undertones in the deep relationships between male characters provide fertile ground for FUJOSHI and DOUJINSHI artists.
Biyojo (美幼女): Beautiful infant girls. Distinct from the concept of BISHOJO or BISHONEN. These are not merely KAWAII, but rather are MOÉ characters that appeal to those OTAKU whose preferences steer toward LOLICON. Biyojo are immature, innocent, and non-threatening.
BL: See BOYS' LOVE MANGA.
Black-ink drawing: See KUROBETA.
Blank space: See YOHAKU.
Boke (ぼけ): The idiot, crazy, or loose character in traditional Japanese standup comedy duos (see MANZAI). This is also used in daily conversation to describe a foolish person. It can be used as a verb to mean "space out."
Bome (ボーメ): Pronounced "bow may." The most famous FIGURE sculptor in Japan, well known for his meticulous, OTAKU depictions of BISHOJO. Bome appeared in the early 1980s as one of the first amateur producers of GARAGE KITS, or resin pieces of a figure roughly molded and left for the buyer to put together, finish, and paint. The high quality standards and creativity of these kits, mostly inspired by the "hobby" anime that dominated the OVA era, formed the basis of the commercial figure market. Bome initially worked part-time for KAIYODO, but

he eventually became an employee and debuted with them professionally in 1986.

Collectors praise Bome for his accurate paintwork, fine detail and ability to capture and represent characters in natural poses. But what elevated Bome to godlike status was his skill at overcoming the "three-dimensional contradiction," that girls who exist on the pages of manga could not possibly exist in the real world. Bome somehow managed to take the ridiculous proportions of two-dimensional women and transform them into glorious, eye-popping 3D. Because of this, fans enjoy photographing his works, in turn prompting Kaiyodo to release the first ever photo collection for a single figure sculptor, *BOME • EX* (1995).

Bome has long been an inspiration to MURAKAMI TAKASHI and collaborated with him on the life-size bishojo figure "Miss ko2 (Project ko2)" in 1995. The humble model maker was then recognized as an artist and given his first exhibition at Feature Ink in New York in 1998. This set the stage for Murakami's "Ero Pop Tokyo" in Los Angeles that same year and the "SuperFlat" installations in Tokyo and Los Angeles in 2000 and 2001—all three featured Bome. Bome then stood alongside Murakami at "Un Art Populaire" (Popular Art) held by the Cartier Contemporary Art Foundation in Paris in 2001, where the curator deemed Bome the "king of otaku." Bome has his own collection of bishojo figures, the Monsieur Bome Collection for Kaiyodo. His works are now on permanent display at the Figure Museum in Shiga. See INTERVIEW ON PAGE 74.

Book (ブック): A technique in animation where a background is traced onto an animation CEL, which is placed on top of the character cel for a layered effect. The character cel is between the background and the special traced cel in front of it like it is sandwiched in the pages of a "book."

Boryokudan (暴力団): "Violent group," or gang. When used in Japan, this refers to organized crime. The members of these groups are individually called YAKUZA, but this word is often mistakenly used by those outside of Japan to describe the syndicates themselves. Groups of yakuza consider the term "boryokudan" an insult, preferring to be called *ninkyo dantai*, "chivalrous organizations." Boryokudan specialize in crime such as prostitution, clubs, gambling, and loan sharking.

Bosozoku (暴走族): Motorbike gangs known for their extreme devotion to each other, violent temperament, internal discipline, and loud revving of their engines. Many members are YANKIIS. While once a common sight in Japan—when gangs of well over a hundred bikers would cause havoc, riding through towns, bashing cars with baseball bats, and wielding samurai swords—the ranks of bosozoku have dwindled in recent years.

FIGURE OF TAMAKI FROM *TO HEART 2* BY *BOME*

These days it's mainly in rural areas that you might see, or more likely hear, the odd small gang of youngsters trying to recapture the bosozoku glory days.

Botsu (ボツ): To sink; or making a failed attempt or unpopular decision. This is used by OTAKU to denote a poor story development, character, or idea in a creative work.

Boy's Love manga: Mainstream commercial manga of the YAOI genre. It's often abbreviated to "BL" MANGA. These erotic manga are not always pornographic, and they focus on romances between male characters. Due to their mainstream nature they feature original stories and characters, unlike other forms of yaoi, such as DOUJINSHI. Readers are often somewhere between SHOJO MANGA fans and hardcore FUJOSHI. Fans overseas typically choose another term such as yaoi or *shonen-ai* because "boy's love" sounds too much like "boy-love," a type of pornography for male pedophiles.

Boy phobia: See DANSEIKYOUFUSHO.

Bromides (ブロマイド): Or promide. An old kind of IDORU trading card named after a chemical used in the photographic process. Asakusa's Marubell Do, established in 1921, is one of the oldest idoru stores in Japan and specializes in these rare cards. Many current idoru, especially STREET IDORU and MAIDS in AKIHABARA, have reclaimed this practice, as well.

Burachira (ブラチラ): Bra shot. Catching a glimpse of a girl's bra or the gratuitous use of such an image; very much like a PANCHIRA flash of panties. If the cleavage or whole breast is exposed, it is called *munechira*.

Burikko (ぶりっこ): A put-down describing someone who is too cute. A reaction to the overly cultivated, forced cuteness in characters or idoru like MATSUDA SEIKO, the first and archetypal burikko IDORU of the 1980s.

BURUSERA
ARE PRETTY
CUTE HUH?

Burusera (ブルセラ): A combination of *buru*, meaning "bloomers," and *sera*, meaning "sailor." Specifically refers to the bloomer-like sportswear and sailor-style school uniforms of the kind traditionally worn by schoolgirls in Japan. Both items are a serious fetish for many men in Japan. Burusera are often bought and sold in backroom establishments also aptly named "Burusera." In the past, there was a lucrative industry for high-school girls who were willing to sell their used panties and clothes. They could fetch even higher prices if their underwear was *nama* (fresh, as in taken off in the store) and included a picture of the seller. Legendary tales of vending machines selling used underwear emerged in the 1990s; but these days it is technically illegal to sell second-hand underwear, as they fall under the auspices of the revised antique sales law. Men entranced by undies now feed their need at peeping cafés (see NOZOKI) or even by stealing them (see SHITAGI DOROBO). See also SUKUMIZU

Butler Café: See SHITSUJI CAFÉ.

Cameko (カメコ): See KAMERAKOZO.

Candies (キャンディーズ): One of the first IDORU bands in Japan and partially responsible for popularizing the idoru boom in the early 1970s. Candies was comprised of three girls who came together in 1973 and stayed at the top of the charts until 1978, when they announced they wanted to "return to being normal girls." They paved the way for Pink Lady later in the decade (best remembered for NBC TV's abysmal *Pink Lady and Jeff* circa 1980) and the Onyanko Club in the mid-1980s. Onyanko Club (which means "Kitty Kitty Club"), had over fifty members and was the paradigm for mass idoru groups such as Morning Musume in the 1990s and AKB 48 in the 2000s.

Candy Girl doll: A brand of sex doll created by the Tokyo-based company Orient Industry. The company was founded in 1977 to develop the perfect sex doll partner. Candy Girls, feature supple silicon flesh over an aluminum, stainless steel, and industrial plastic skeleton. In sharp contrast to anatomically correct Real Dolls from the United States, the most popular Candy Girls are anime or childlike characters that do not approximate realistic sex partners. As creepy as that may seem, Orient sells fifty dolls priced between $1,300 and $6,900 each month. There are also doll "rental spaces" in Tokyo. Candy Girls are of such interest in Japan that Vanilla art gallery in Tokyo's posh Ginza area hosted Orient's 30th anniversary exhibition in June 2007.

CANDY GIRL DOLLS

Canning: See KAN-ZUME.

***Captain Harlock* debacle:** MATSUMOTO LEIJI's epic space pirate manga *Uchuu Kaizoku Captain Harlock* became a televised anime in 1978 directed by TEZUKA OSAMU's student Rintaro. With split screens and flashbacks, it is a classic in the anime cannon. But when Ziv International edited a handful of episodes into *Captain Harlock* in 1981, the result was one of the worst anime edits of all time. When it was made, conventional wisdom was that anything created for the Japanese market was too weird to be anything but comedy. In Ziv's episodes two and three, the dialogue was only sometimes correct, Daiba Tadashi was renamed "Tommy Hairball," and there was suddenly and inexplicably a gay robot. The wide distribution of the Ziv edition by Family Home Entertainment in the United States sullied the import ANIME record for some time. The original 1978 series was released again in 1985, this time by Harmony Gold. Using the same method it did for *Robotech* to reach the minimum sixty-five episodes for broadcast anime, Harmony Gold spliced *Harlock* with another series, *Queen Millennia*, to form *Captain Harlock and the Queen of a Thousand Years*. This was a controversial choice, as these series are unrelated, but Harmony Gold decided it was too expensive to buy the rights to the next *Harlock* series, *Endless Orbit SSX*. Scenes were fragmented and developed in a nonsensical way inconsistent between episodes. Entire plot points were confused or dropped; the *Queen Millennia* story arc wasn't even carried through to the original conclusion. Despite the title, Harlock and Millennia never appear on screen together.

***Captain Tsubasa* (キャプテン翼):** A mega-popular SHONEN (boys') MANGA series about a soccer team written by Takahashi

THE MANGA VERSION OF *CAPTAIN TSUBASA*

Yoichi in 1981. It has also been made into ANIME and video games. It was promoted by the Japan Football Association to assist in establishing the sport in Japan. Various famous international soccer players, including Nakata Hidetoshi, Zinedine Zidane, Francesco Totti, Fernando Torres, Matias Fernandez, Alexis Sanchez, and Alessandro Del Piero, were apparently all inspired by *Tsubasa* to play professionally.

When Japan sent Self-Defense Force personnel to Iraq in 2004, *Captain Tsubasa* decorated the water trucks; they went unattacked for two and a half years. In 2006, the government subsidized a dubbed *Captain Tsubasa*, or *Captain Majed*, to air on Iraqi network TV. The program is said to have been an inspiration to the Iraqi soccer team.

Perhaps even more interesting, however, was the show's impact on female manga fans in Japan. In 1985, this series sparked an enormous outpouring of YAOI DOUJINSHI featuring the characters in various relationships and sexual couplings. The *Tsubasa* harem was so rich that it dominated the female doujinshi side of things for years. Clamp, the famous SHOJO

MANGAKA group, also got its start writing *Captain Tsubasa* doujinshi.

Caricature: See HITOKOMAMANGA.

Cartoon/Fantasy Organization (C/FO): One of the first ANIME clubs in the United States. It was founded in Southern California in 1977 to view and discuss Japanese animation, and it has been meeting monthly since. After opening a branch in New York, the club reorganized to have groups in multiple cities with a central information-sharing magazine for networking and tape trades. The original C/FO was renamed the Los Angeles Chapter. In the early 1980s, there were 500 members and three dozen chapters in North America, and even one in Japan on the US Air Force base at Misawa.

After infighting among the leadership, the C/FO disbanded as an international organization in 1989. The club system itself gave way to more democratic and flexible online groups in the 1990s. The Los Angeles club, still operating, is now the only C/FO. See also PATTEN, FREDERICK WALTER.

Catch copy (キャッチコピー): Slogan. Phrase used to brand a product, usually said along with the name of that product.

CCC: Also known as 3C, or the Three Cs that define otakudom: Collection (*shuushuu*), Creativity (*souzou*) and Community (*komyuniti*). These were isolated in the 2004 NOMURA INSTITUTE REPORT on otaku.

Cel or Cel-ga (セル画): The transparent sheets drawn on by animators. Because different objects are drawn on different sheets, only moving objects have to be redrawn, which saves time and money in the production. Tracing on the sheets also improves continuity. "Cel" can also describe analog, hand-drawn cel animation in contrast to digital techniques. The name comes from the tradition of using celluloid for animating from the 1910s to 1950s. Cel animation was invented by John Bray, and Earl Hurd in 1914. In 1927, Oofuji Noburo used cel animation for part of his *KAGE* ANIMATION "Kujira." The technique continued to be very limited due to cost until the 1930s. Some artists washed cels and reused the scarred and wrinkled material three times before moving on. Even *Tetsujin 28-go* suffered from this practice. With the anime boom in the late 1970s and 1980s, cels became highly valued among collectors and fans, and Toei Douga started selling them in its Animepolis Pero store. Today, cels by famous Japanese creators are bought, sold, and auctioned all over the world. Mandarake, for example, carries an extensive collection of cels for sale. In the late 1990s and 2000s, Japanese studios started moving to digital animation. The family series *Sazae-san* was the last to hold out, but it eventually went digital, causing some to say that full cel animation is a thing of the past. Most anime today use a combination of background and mechanical digital animation and cels for characters.

Chakuero (着エロ): Non-nude erotica. Defined as finding partially or fully clothed women more appealing than those who are naked. For example, when seeing a woman in a tight dress, fishnet stockings, and high-heels—or girl in a BURUSERA and LOOSE SOCKS—the clothes themselves become highly eroticized, fetishized targets of desire. This is quite common in ANIME and IDORU videos. See CHIRARI-IZUMU

Chakugoe (着声): Ring tone; a derivation of *chakumero*. Sound bites of popular phrases or music. There was a particularly embarrassing period from 2006 to 2007 when many cell phones in Tokyo had chakugoe ring tones from the anime *Suzumiya Haruhi* or more general MAID lines such as "*Okaerinasaimase gosshujin sama!*" ("Welcome home, Master"). There was scarcely a passenger train in the city where such sounds couldn't be heard.

Cheki (チェキ): An instant-photo camera from Fujifilm. "Cheki" also refers to the actual photos taken with such a camera. Until the advent of mobile phones with built-in cameras, cheki were a popular accessory for young girls in Japan (see ONNA NO KO SHASHIN). These days they have been adopted by MAID CAFÉS, where personal messages are often written on the souvenir snapshots. These photos are highly collectible, and some regular customers have hundreds of them. See also PURIKURA.

Chibikyara (チビキャラ): Short or small character. Usually very cute and young in appearance, for example Chibiusa from *Sailor Moon*. They often function as mascots or comic relief. The term is sometimes confused with SD (super deformed) versions of normal characters, but *chibi* is a character type and SD is a style.

Chidol: A child idol. See JUNIOR IDORU.

Chikan (痴漢): Groper; especially of women on trains. Groping is somewhat of an epidemic in Japan, where long commutes on crowded trains is the norm. Also, the cultural aversion to causing a scene, breaking the peaceful atmosphere, and drawing attention to a potentially embarrassing situation means most victims and bystanders stand quiet. There has recently been a crackdown on chikan by the police, with posters warning against trying it, and the introduction of "Women Only" carriages on trains at peak hours. Because of this, chikan have had to look elsewhere, and a new industry in AV, HENTAI, and MIZUSHOBAI clubs replicating train rape fantasies is on the rise.

Chinpira (チンピラ): A punk, or low-level YAKUZA. These entry-level thugs are quite dangerous, and tend to have cheap suits and bad hair.

Chirarizumu (チラリズム): Or *chirari shuugi*. The idea that it's better not to see everything, because catching even the slightest glimpse of something you shouldn't be seeing is way more of a turn on.

Chiyogami animation (千代紙アニメーション): Patterned-paper animation. The paper—which features traditional Japanese designs (sometimes called *yuzen*)—is folded and cut into shapes, then used to animate scenes. Part of the early development of ANIME.

Chogokin (超合金): Super alloy. The fictitious material that *Mazinger Z* is supposedly made of, later appropriated as a brand name for diecast metal robots toys sold by Popy, a subsidiary of BANDAI. The Chogokin Mazinger Z toy, released in 1974, kicked off a craze for robot toys in Japan that lasted for more than a decade, both in Japan and abroad—where they were marketed variously under the brand names "Shogun Warriors" and "Godaikin." It was quickly followed by Chogokin portrayals of many other ANIME robots and TOKUSATSU characters, making the brand name synonymous with any diecast metal toy. In response to the popularity, numerous other companies scrambled to make diecast toys, including Takatoku, Takemi, Bullmark and Nakajima, all now defunct. In spite of their metal content Chogokin were quite fragile, meaning that few pristine examples survive today. In the 1980s, stores feeding the emerging otaku subculture, in particular MANDARAKE, began touting "dead stock" (mint condition) Chogokin as "rare" or "vintage" antiques, making them hot collectibles. With the rise of complex transforming robot toys in the early Eighties, diecast figures fell out of favor. The current incarnation of the toys, Bandai's "Soul of Chogokin," targets nostalgic adult collectors rather than children.

Chojugiga (鳥獣戯画): Humorous scrolls drawn by Bishop Toba (1053–1140) in the 12th century. The name literally means "humorous pictures of birds and animals," and they depict caricatures of people as animals (for example, a frog dressed as a priest). Thought by some to be the root of MANGA in Japan, these scrolls display various conventions still used today, from speed lines and thought balloons to animal characters and bawdy humor. TEZUKA OSAMU was apparently a big fan of these, but only saw them later in his career. Some argue this historic element is a domestic counterweight to the later influence of foreign artists like Walt DISNEY and Max FLEISCHER. But others suggest that theories linking manga to older, more traditional Japanese art are deeply tied to nationalistic ideas of Japaneseness.

Choo, Danny: Born in 1972 in London. He moved to Tokyo in 1999 and his website (www.dannychoo.com) has become one of the most trusted English-language sources for up-to-date information on Japanese pop culture. He's a graduate of London University's School of Oriental and African Studies, and in his free time he likes to dance around the streets of Tokyo wearing a *Star Wars* "storm-trooper" costume.

C

Circle (サークル): In general this means a group of people, with a common interest and goal, cooperating to achieve something beyond the individual. The smallest unit in the production of DOUJINSHI is not an individual, but a "circle" that supports and makes the creation possible. There are said to be no "customers" in this cyclical arrangement, as everyone participates. Before the 1980s the high cost of printing and labor-intensive production methods meant membership-style, hierarchal doujinshi circles were common in Japan. But from about 1981 onward the move was to smaller groups, and these days some individuals—who create, publish, and distribute their work alone—even call themselves a "circle." At COMIKET, 71 percent of doujinshi circles are female, and the average age is twenty-eight.

CM: TV commercial.

Coin (コイン): Online slang for "to score" or "to gain points." It refers to NINTENDO's hit video-game franchise *Super Mario Brothers*, where characters would score points by grabbing coins.

Combini (コンビニ): Convenience store. An essential part of daily life in Japan. The combini has developed tremendously since arriving in Japan in the 1970s and lives up to the term "convenience" infinitely better than stores in other countries. Aside from food, alcohol, and cigarettes, they also offer postal and courier services, cell phone and electronic money charging, photocopying, fax, ATMs, credit card and finance services, and bill and tax payment services. And they sell tickets for concerts, attractions, and travel. For entertainment, people hang out by the magazine racks and read MANGA for free (see TACHIYOMI). You can literally live out of combini, as was shown in Koreeda Hirokazu's 2004 film *Daremo Shirani* (*Nobody Knows*). There are approximately 44,000 combini in Japan, dominated by 7-11, Lawson, and FamilyMart.

Comic (コミック): The general English term for a panel comic strip or comic book. For many, a distinction is made where "comic" refers to American or European cartoon styles and MANGA refers to Japanese work.

Comic city (コミックシティ): A series of DOUJINSHI sales events held throughout Japan almost every month. Established in 1988, the major events happen about fifteen times a year in Osaka and Tokyo in venues ranging from 3,000 to 22,000 square meters. Many of the smaller events in rural areas, or with niche topics, attract many women, particularly FUJOSHI, who generally call these events "city."

Comic market (コミックマーケット): General term for a convention to buy and sell comics; typically events where amateurs can

A DOUJINSHI CIRCLE MEMBER AT COMIKET

YAOI DAY AT COMIKET

display their work. Outside Japan these are often tied to various trade or industry events, but in Japan they are almost always independent public events.

Comics Journal, The: One of the few academic journals focusing exclusively on comics and MANGA as an art form.

Comiket (コミケ): Pronounced as *comike*. An abbreviation of "comic market." The biggest amateur MANGA (DOUJINSHI) sales event in Japan. It was first held in 1975 with 700 people attending and has since grown to be massively popular. In 2008 as many as 550,000 people and 35,000 DOUJINSHI CIRCLES attended. This makes Comiket the largest indoor, non-government, non-profit public gathering in Japan. The event has been held in various places over the years, including MAKUHARI MESSE, which denied the event venue space in 1991 after the MIYAZAKI TSUTOMU INCIDENT, when the "OTAKU murderer" revealed he'd attended Comiket, and it was thought the event must be for wackos.

Comiket is now firmly entrenched in the massive Tokyo BIG SIGHT complex in Odaiba, which it occupies for three days, twice a year. Comiket attracts many YAOI fans, and women have historically dominated the number of registered booths. The second day is yaoi only. Comiket says 57 percent of attendees are female, while 71 percent of the CIRCLES that attend are made up of women. The average age of circle members is twenty-eight, and buyers are on average twenty-five years old. Due to space constraints, a lottery has comiket · 市川孝一

ICHIKAWA KOICHI

TO HIS COLLEAGUES, ICHIKAWA KOICHI (41) is just another full-time enginee from Tokyo. But in his free time, Ichikawa moonlights as one of three power sharing Partner Representatives at the top of the Comic Market Prepara tions Committee—the organizers of Comiket. He's been a regular a Comiket for over twenty-five years and prefers to keep his identity hidden

PG: What got you into DOUJINSHI?

IK: When I was young, I watched *Kikaider* and *Cyborg 009*; I was a normal Japanese boy. But then I saw TAKAHASHI RUMIKO'S *Urusei Yatsura*. It had the first harem, and the character Lum-chan. She was a super sex-symbol in Japan, what movie stars are to France and America, and was my first love. Lum-chan is the source of MOÉ, the queen. She's the first TSUNDERE character. The show had everything, and I was really interested in comparing the MANGA and the ANIME, the anime and the movies, and eventually in getting my hands on things that weren't in stores.

PG: What was the reason behind starting Comiket?

IK: When I was still a kid, the *manga taikai* (manga convention) was formed to explore and market the medium. At the time, professionals and amateurs were working together in the same space. But this didn't last, because there was serious criticism, and restriction of styles and forms of expression. Comiket was founded as an alternative meeting for people that broke from the manga taikai. They wanted to have the freedom of expression, to be able parody, criticize, and rewrite established works. Comiket was founded as a space of free expression, and I hope this doesn't change for another hundred years.

PG: Why do you think OTAKU emerged in Japan?

IK: In general I think Japanese have very otaku-like traits. We like to collect things study, and create. So, manga, anime, FIGURES, otaku things, arrived in an environment particularly suited for otaku activity.

After the war kids applied this natura otaku spirit to popular culture, but they had to grow out of it and redirect thei energies as adults. Those who didn't were kind of isolated and hidden. However, so many boom series, of manga and anime began to appear that everyone was captivated and entered into the otaku mindset

Over the past five years, some celebrities have come out as otaku, otaku musi is topping the Oricon charts, commercia products target otaku, and the media is fixated on otaku. These days no one gets too upset if you're an otaku, you don' have to hide it, and you can make friends being yourself. This is an environmen ripe for developing otaku, so maybe we can call it the otaku generation. If the culture is accepting, then it expands. Now think it's become a culture of its own. The world seems to be getting more into otaku culture, too, with the spread of anime and other media. But Japan is still the core because of the prevalence of otaku products. Japan is also traditionally a

COMIC MARKET 74
2008 SUMMER
企業ブースパンフレット
西地区4階にて無料配布中。
ICHIKAWA-SAN IS SUCH A MAN OF MYSTERY!

publishing culture with cheap and abundant printed material. You can't go anywhere in Japan without finding manga of some kind. Otaku goods are still very cheap, too, which seems different from overseas where only a bourgeois otaku elite can afford things. Being an otaku in Japan is starting to get expensive, though, which is maybe another reason affordable DOUJINSHI are popular.

PG: What makes good a doujinshi?

IK: Doujinshi are best when the original work is not too perfect and there are still things to say and explore. I can't imagine making a doujinshi of the film *Roman Holiday,* which is testament to its near perfection. If a work isn't perfect, but you really like it, then good doujinshi can be made. If some aspects are not explained, or some stories or ideas are not developed, the characters can be used in new and creative ways to explore and expand on the original story that inspired the doujinshi.

PG: What about the issue of copyright at Comiket?

IK: Well, we can't say this too loudly, but the copyright laws are generally looser in Japan. Historically and culturally, there's been some allowance for copying in appreciation and study. People who participate in Comiket are manga readers and buyers and are the driving force of the industry. The communication among CIRCLES creates even more interest in popular manga series. Besides, I think Comiket is so large, prosperous, and well known now that they can't shut it down. They could maybe bust us if we were a smaller operation. Of course, it is not OK to copy exactly, and we enforce that rule. But if you're making something new using the characters and story, it's OK. We police ourselves and keep what's really shady out. Nothing is pure white, mind you, but we are operating in the gray area. Dark gray.

PG: How does Comiket resolve problems?

IK: We try to learn from any problems and mistakes made before, and improve each time. But it's the participants who are most responsible for the market's smooth operation. Everyone is a participant and part of the community, so everyone shares the responsibility for the upkeep of the space and the success of the event. They are well mannered and mindful of our position. It's common sense not to disturb the well-being of the community. We welcome anyone who shares these values to join us. I personally want to see more influence from outside Japan; it's a good chance to learn from others and examine their form of expression.

Doujinshi are best when the original work is not too perfect and there are still things to say and explore.

PG: What lies ahead for Comiket?

IK: More participants are coming from overseas, so we need to think how to accommodate them. There are many communication problems right now. I really can't say if Comiket will become any bigger—maybe if we had a giant convention space somewhere like Frankfurt—but we are doing our best to make things more comfortable. I mean, we want people to be able to get what they want when they want it, and say what they want to. It's very sad for us when we have to censor doujinshi or tell circles that they have to limit their expression. I want to contribute to a world where there is no need for that.

been in place since 1979 to determine which circles can attend; only 80 percent who want to come make it. A registered circle at Comiket pays $85 for half a table and two chairs. Admission is free, but purchasing the $20 catalog is encouraged. Otaku watcher Patrick MACIAS estimates Comiket generates around ¥1 billion at each event. Comiket Inc., a legal public entity, was formed in 1985 to make it possible to do business with commercial and legal entities participating in Comiket. There are 2,400 volunteers in the Preparations Committee Organization. Comiket maintains a socialist structure, claiming everyone is an equal participant and "there are no customers or authority figures" (see DOUJINSHI and CIRCLE). There is, however, now an industry section at Comiket with 150 booths doing PR and giveaways.

Comiket Firebomb Incident: Amid intense hatred for OTAKU, a bombing incident occurred at Comiket 54 in 1998. Security has been tightened since then, but threatening letters are still not uncommon. There was another bomb threat at the summer Comiket in 2008, though the culprit was kind enough to post on 2CHANNEL precisely what he planned to do and when; he was arrested upon entry.

Comitia (コミティア): Founded in 1984, this has become Japan's largest event for the direct buying and selling of original MANGA published outside official channels. The DOUJINSHI bought and sold here are not parodies of other works. It has gone from 103 participating CIRCLES to 2,036. It does not call itself a doujinshi event but rather an "exhibition and sales event for independent manga productions." Unlike COMIKET, it does not make distinctions between amateurs and professionals and encourages everyone to display high-quality, original works—anything from manga and games, to critical essays and goods. Copyright tends to be respected, so fan works featuring established characters are limited. The event is held four times a year (February, May, August, and November), with 10,000 people gathering at Tokyo BIG SIGHT.

Con: Slang for a convention, or massive gathering of fans, called *event* (イベント) in Japanese.

MANGA ON DISPLAY AT AN EXHIBITION OF COOL JAPAN

Cool Japan (クールジャパン): A concept, movement, or government policy that proposes Japan as a world trendsetter for entertainment, technology, art, fashion, music, and contemporary culture. In 2002 journalist Douglas McGray wrote a ground-breaking article called "Japan's Gross National Cool" for *Foreign Policy* magazine that suggested the country's real power came through the global appeal of its pop-cultural output such as MANGA, ANIME, and games. Ironically, it was this article, written by a foreigner for a foreign audience, that first inspired many Japanese to take their own pop culture seriously. The article was translated into Japanese the following year, and Cool Japan became a hot topic among politicians like ASO TARO. Indeed, JETRO (Japan External Trade Organization) reported that between 1992 and 2004, the average rate of Japan's export growth was 20 percent, but that exports in anime, manga, music, fashion, and films grew by 300 percent.

In 2003 *Spirited Away* took the Academy Award for Best Animated Feature, and promoting OTAKU culture soon became government policy. The Ministry of Foreign Affairs' 2004 Diplomatic "Blue Book" said, "Contemporary Japanese culture has attracted attention around the world as 'Cool Japan'" and suggested that a way to revitalize "Japan's economy, society, and culture" was to "proactively spread Japan's charm abroad as a brand name . . . in particular, Japan's so-called subculture, such as animation, movies, comics (*manga*), and Japanese cuisine."

Also in 2004, The Contents Industry Act was ratified and anime- and manga-related projects flourished; The Tokyo International Anime Fair and World Cosplay Summit were two examples. Also, who became prime minister of Japan in September 2008, has openly stated that he intends to use Cool Japan "soft power" to improve economic and international relations. In discussing the potential of all this, the media focused on Akihabara, the Electric Town and the supposed heart of the content industry, which has led to reinvestment in and sanitization of the area. However, criticism of this national mobilization has not been slight. American academic Laura Miller has accused Japan of "pimping popular culture," and Japanese philosopher Azuma Hiroki has pointed out that McGray is an expert on neither Japan nor the content industry and the government has no business seriously taking his advice. Maybe in response to this, in 2008 the government announced plans to conduct its own

COSPLAYERS AT THE 2008 WORLD COSPLAY SUMMIT IN NAGOYA. A SHOWCASE OF COOL JAPAN

market research on Cool Japan—the first serious assessment of the policy.

Core (コア): Akin to the English term "hardcore." In Japan this identifies knowledge, behaviors, or people that have a singular focus and intensity that put them at the center of the topic in question. For example, core-anime is anime targeted at an audience who really know their stuff.

Cospa (コスパ): "Costume Paradise." Japan's first professional, mass-market COSPLAY tailor and retailer. Founded in 1995 by former staff of the OTAKU goods merchandiser Broccoli, Cospa operates out of Tokyo's fashion center, SHIBUYA. Its Cospatio brand of ANIME and video game character costumes start at around $500, while bespoke costumes can cost several thousand dollars. In partnership with Broccoli, Cospa temporarily opened the first MAID CAFÉ, the Welcome to Pia Carrot Café (August 1998), followed by Gamer's Café (February 2000). Cospa founded the first permanent maid café, Cure Maid Café in March 2001. It is now targeting casual Japanese fans and tourists and has aspirations to spread its annual $18 million empire across the globe.

Cosplay (コスプレ): "Costume" plus "roleplay." The act of dressing up as a favorite character from ANIME, MANGA, or video games. It most likely has its roots in the *Star Trek* conventions of the 1960s in the US. In 1978 the science-fiction critic Kotani Mari attended the Japan Sci-fi Convention wearing a costume from TEZUKA OSAMU's *Umi no Triton* (*Triton of the Sea*) and is often mistaken as the first cosplayer in Japan. But according to Kotani people were already cosplaying at COMIKET the year before.

Fans in the US claim the term "cosplay" first appeared in 1984 when Japanese journalist Takahashi Nobuyuki visited World-Con, a sci-fi convention in Southern California, and returned to Japan with stories of crazy American "masquerades," a word he changed to the more easily pronouncable "cosplay." Takashi himself says he first coined the term in a June 1983 issue of the Japanese magazine *My Anime*.

COSPLAY AT
COMIKET

With intense fandom and massive conventions, cosplay in Japan quickly developed, and a cosplay industry started to emerge in 1994 selling professional-grade outfits. In the late 1990s, with the burgeoning interest in Japanese animation, cosplay was exported back overseas, but with one amusing difference. Due to the habit of FLOPPING in the early days of translated manga, many non-Japanese cosplayers would design their costumes in the mirror image of the original. It was not uncommon to see uniforms buttoned up the wrong way or kimonos folded in reverse, much to the amusement of Japanese obsevers.

COSPLAYER AT THE 2008 WORLD COSPLAY SUMMIT

In 2007, Cure, Japan's largest cosplay social networking site, estimated there were approximately 200,000 dedicated cosplayers (REIYAA) in Japan; about 90 percent are women in their teens or twenties. Cure's data comes from its 270,000 registered users, growing by about 200 new members a day. Interestingly, an opinion poll on the site revealed that cosplayers from Osaka are the most respected in Japan, apparently because Osaka girls wear such brash and bold fashion. In 2007, Net research firm iSHARE released survey results showing 46.8 percent of women between the ages of twenty and forty said they want to try cosplay, and 18.9 percent said they had already done it.

Most cosplayers belong to CIRCLES, making it easier to create their own costumes, and they organize events to take pictures of one another. Photographers who take pictures of cosplayers are known as KAMERAKOZO and are essential to the see-and-be-seen ritual of cosplay. Many of these photographers have websites or create photo albums of the best cosplayers.

The cosplay industry is big business in Japan, worth $350 million annually, according to ITmedia, an information service site for IT and technology firms. There is a national cosplay association called Cos-Most; summer COMIKET in 2008 drew 14,000 cosplayers, who each paid $8 to participate; and in 2007 Vantan—Japan's largest and most respected fashion school—started offering cosplay courses, costing $5,000 for three months or $8,000 for six months. There are also major companies dedicated to cosplay, the most successful of which is cosplay retailer COSPA.

Cosplay outside Japan has also come a long way from those early costume mix-ups, and today cosplay.com, the world's largest English-language cosplay site, has over 100,000 members. This kind of interest has even inspired the WORLD COSPLAY SUMMIT in Nagoya each year. According to a survey in 2007 on NHK's "Cool Japan" program, about 87.5 percent of foreigners think Japanese cosplay is cool.

Cosplay café (コスプレカフェ): A general term for a café where the staff dress up in costume and play out a fantasy role assigned to them. This can also mean a café that lends customers costumes so that they can experience COSPLAY and join in the fun.

Cos-plays: A rather interesting take on COSPLAY, this refers to stage plays where scenes from an ANIME or video game—original ones or DOUJINSHI—are acted out before a live audience. These were invented by fans outside Japan as events on the convention circuit; they are not as prevalent in domestic Japanese fandom.

Coupling (カップリング): A fantasy relationship between two characters. Usually used to describe DOUJINSHI or fan fiction, particularly YAOI, that feature characters—from the same or different stories—in a romantic encounter. In this usage, it is sometimes abbreviated to "CP." Unlike "slash fiction," which indicates the dominant partner in front of the submissive separated by a "/," yaoi couplings have a variety of possibilities that are described by simple but slightly mathematical formulas.

The type of coupling is often clearly written in online posts—and to a lesser extent in text heavy doujinshi—making working out the kind of coupling a snap once the formula is mastered. The most standard is "x," which indicates a romantic relationship: for example, "A x B." The name before the "x" is the *seme* (dominant) and after is the *uke* (submissive). An arrow, on the other hand, marks a simple attraction: "A→B" means A likes B; or "A←B" means B likes A. Other forms include "A x B→C" as in B is drawn to C while involved with A. "A x B←C" indicates C is drawn to B. More complicated settings can be A→←B, meaning a love that is unspoken. "A + B" is simple friendship. And "ABA" means flexible gender roles, so everybody is happy. See also UKE, SEME, and OUDOU.

Creative Commons: Stanford Law School professor Lawrence Lessig's concept of limited licenses that avoid copyright infringement by allowing the use of mainstream, commercial media by amateurs in their creative production of new or alternative art. See also ANMOKU NO RYOKAI.

Cross-genre, cross-platform: See MEDIA MIX.

Crossplay (クロスプレイ): Cross-dressing COSPLAY. When a person dresses up as a character of the opposite sex.

C3xHOBBY: Also known as "Chara Hobby," this is the largest toy and figure event in Japan. It's run by a coalition made up of Hobby Japan, Media Works, and the production company Sotsu Co., Ltd. Until 2003, Hobby Japan was running cosplay • 綾川ゆんまお

AYAKAWA YUNMAO

YUNMAO, A NATIVE OF GUNMA PREFECTURE, started cosplaying in 1997, when she was thirteen, went pro in 2003, and became the director of the Japanese National Maid Cooperative in 2008. She has published a book on cooking for OTAKU, works as a journalist for both Japanese and American publications, and has been seen globally in TV appearances.

PG: What are your hobbies, and do you consider yourself an otaku?

AY: I like drawing, reading MANGA, watching ANIME, and of course COSPLAY! To me, "otaku" means someone who is sincere with his or her hobby. It's about having passionate emotions. I've searched my soul and I know I'm an otaku to the core. If I'm reincarnated, I'm going to be an otaku again. It's a good life writing DOUJINSHI and cosplaying. I've been an otaku as long as I can remember.

PG: How did you get started?

AY: I've been reading manga since I was a child. From early on I was, and still am, writing doujinshi, and I started cosplaying with friends as an extension of that. I liked SHONEN stories, and we all were into *Slam Dunk, Ruronin Kenshin,* and *Yuyu Hakusho*. My friends wanted to form a cosplay group (AWASE), so I volunteered to be the male character Kurama from *Yuyu Hakusho*. There weren't wigs on the market at the time, but I was one of the few first-year junior high-school students who could do his hairstyle, and the costume was easy to make. We just thought it would be fun. But I really got hooked and started cosplaying seriously. First only at small events in Gunma, then at larger events in Tokyo. I've gone to every COMIKET with my doujinshi and cosplay CIRCLE since high school. I just couldn't get enough of it! It was at one of those larger events that I was scouted by a game company and started working as an illustrator and talent (TARENTO). Over time, my options as a professional cosplayer expanded and my work as a designer in the company slowed down. So I quit to focus on my career as a talent.

PG: Why are you so serious about cosplay?

AY: Because I can become the characters I love. When you cosplay, there's a sense that you're taking the character into you. It's like being at one with the character. That's fun, and I made more friends when I began cosplaying. I was happy. I also enjoy wearing clothes I can't in daily life. After all, anime costumes are so cute and cool! I like the designs, but couldn't wear them normally. I still make my own costumes when time allows.

PG: When did you go pro?

AY: I always have difficulty with this question, because there isn't one appearance that I can point to as a debut. It was more like somewhere along the way I noticed that I had become professional. I appeared on cell phone sites first, then as a cosplayer in specialty magazines, and finally on TV. At some point I was getting offers as a talent, and that's when it occurred to me that I was pro.

PG: What were you doing at the time?

AY: I was a regular on a variety program on TV Tokyo. We dressed as maids and did a bunch of challenges such as cooking, photo shoots, and physical competitions. It was a pretty dangerous gig, even in the variety world. Like, we once had to change clothes on a frozen skating rink!

PG: You've come pretty far in a short time. What are you up to now?

AY: I'm trying to focus my energy on being a representative of Japanese cosplay abroad. I'm a missionary for Japanese otaku culture! I've also started an online store to sell products, and I'm appearing as a guest at conventions in the United States and writing a regular column in *Otaku USA* magazine. In Japan, I'm still writing for *COSMODE* magazine, going to events when I can, and working as an instructor in the MAID KYOUKAI, but I am cosplaying abroad more now.

> **When you cosplay, there's a sense that you're taking the character into you. It's like being at one with the character.**

PG: Is the Maid Kyoukai part of that?

AY: Yes, educating maids is starting to happen overseas. We're thinking of offering courses at conventions and administering the test for maid certification.

PG: Anything else we should know about?

AY: Oh, I'm also a RACE QUEEN on weekends.

PG: A race queen? Is that a sort of cosplay?

AY: No! It's completely different. You become a campaign girl for a team or a company. You're a contracted model doing a professional job, so it's more like being a tarento than a cosplayer. You're still wearing a costume, but there's a purpose other than just becoming a certain character.

PG: Why did you want to be a race queen?

AY: I've always liked cars and bikes and wanted to see the race world from the inside. I thought the only way for a woman to do that was to be a race queen. But race queens are meant to be at least 170 centimeters tall and I'm really small. I was lucky though, and they took me on because they thought I was funny. I may well be the world's smallest race queen!

PG: How are your fans? In Japan and abroad.

AY: People overseas are friendlier. They come up and greet one another. Maybe Japanese are a little shy.

PG: Why do you think cosplay is popular the world over?

AY: Because anime and manga are interesting, and people just love the characters so much that they can't hold it in. You feel something for a character and get something from him or her by cosplaying. I think cosplay will continue to become an even more common and open hobby. Now it's kind of something that only otaku do for fun, but we're are entering a time when normal people can get into it too. You can buy good, cheap prepackaged costumes and wear them to cosplay parties. This is the same in Japan and abroad, although costume parties have existed overseas for a lot longer.

PG: What is your dream?

AY: I would like to tie cosplay to charity and host a cosplay event with activist themes that encourage meaningful volunteer work. It isn't about enjoying cosplay alone, but coming together to do something good. Cosplay will save the world!

I'VE ENTERED THE MOE MATRIX!

its own event, Hobby Expo, at Tokyo BIG SIGHT, boasting 21,000 visitors in one day. At the time, Media Works was running C3 (the Cultural Convention of Characters) at Makuhari Messe, getting 37,800 over two days. They joined forces in 2004 for the inaugural C3xHOBBY at MAKUHARI MESSE, with Sotsu as a sponsor. The mascot Hobby-chan was designed in 2006 by Yoshizaki Mine of *Keroro Gunsou* fame.

Cyberpunk: A genre of science fiction set in a dystopian future where society and technology have run amok. Hard-boiled and gritty, the genre is often described as "lowlife meets high-tech." It first emerged in the early 1980s with the release of the film *Blade Runner* in 1982—directed by Ridley Scott and based on Philip K. Dick's novel *Do Androids Dream of Electric Sheep?*—and the novel *Neuromancer* by William GIBSON in 1984. Cyberpunk stories are usually set in or around cyberspace and often feature hackers, rogue computers, androids, advanced weaponry, MECHA, and complex futuristic concepts. The stories are often visionary. For example, Gibson predicted advances in the Internet, reality TV, and virtual communities. Much of Japanese cyberpunk is influenced by Scott's vision of "the city" in *Blade Runner*, a look that was in turn partially influenced by Tokyo's futuristic neon urban landscape. Indeed, Gibson, too, was influenced by Japanese cities in his vision of *Neuromancer*. The themes, elements, and designs from *Blade Runner* return again and again in ANIME and MANGA such as *Bubblegum Crisis*, *AKIRA*, *GHOST IN THE SHELL*, and many others. The look and eel of NEO TOKYO is now intimately tied with visions of the future or sci-fi technological drama. This Japanese version of cyberpunk has returned the favor of influence to films overseas such as the *Matrix* trilogy. See also SHIROW MASAMUNE.

A CYBERPUNK CLASSIC

D&D: Abbreviation of *Dungeons & Dragons*, a fantasy tabletop role-playing game (RPG) originally designed by E. Gary Gygax and Dave Arneson and first published in 1974 by Tactical Studies Rules, Inc. (TSR). D&D is the archetypal RPG in which players invent AVATARS that adventure through stimulating fantasy realms. About five people sit around a table and elaborate a story together, guided by the "dungeon master," who moves the narrative forward with key events, battles, and meetings. Dice are rolled to decide battles, but other than this the players have nothing but a piece of paper to note down their characters' development and items. D&D fueled the now classic image of passionate, creative, and withdrawn geeks in a basement communicating through their characters.

DAICON (ダイコン): The nickname of a series of conventions held in Osaka that jumpstarted the ANIME OTAKU movement. The title can be read as "big convention" because "dai" is an alternate reading of the first kanji character in Osaka (大阪) and means "big." In 1981 the 20th Japan SF Convention was held in Osaka for the third time, thus the name DAICON III. The high point of the event was an 8mm anime film about an ass-kicking little girl who is attacked by giant robots (including *GUNDAM*), *GODZILLA*, and spaceships (from *SPACE BATTLESHIP YAMATO*, *Star Wars*, and *Star Trek*) while trying to deliver water entrusted to her by aliens. With the water she grows a spaceship that looks like a giant white Japanese radish (also called *daikon*). The creators—who went

DAICON IV ARTWORK

on to form the company GAINAX—were a bunch of college students lead by a young ANNO HIDEAKI. They came back in 1983 and rocked DAICON IV with a sequel anime on 16mm film.

This second film centered on a flying bunny girl (perhaps an older version of the DAICON III girl) with magical powers and features an eclectic cast of characters from global popculture, pet sidekicks, lots of missiles, and another daicon spaceship. Set to the song "Twilight" by Electric Light Orchestra, the world ends and begins anew, as bunny girl kicks the snot out of Darth Vader, Spiderman, SENTAI (masked superhero teams), KAIJU (monsters), a dragon, an alien, a Macross VF-1 Valkyrie, a Klingon battle cruiser, and more. The camera pans across hundreds of characters as bunny girl surfs the sky on "Stormbringer," the sword of chaos. The animation—which is now easily found on the Internet—is a cult classic symbolically connected to the emergence of hobby anime and otaku culture. The opening titles to *DENSHA OTOKO* (2005), for example, reference the DAICON IV anime and use the same theme song.

Dakimakura (抱き枕): Hug pillow. Oversized pillows designed to be extremely huggable. These are security objects and usually never leave the grasp of sleeping Japanese children. So addictive is the comfort provided that many older men and women still use them. There has also been a boom among OTAKU buying slightly risqué pillows. These body-size dakimakura are adorned with life-sized images of IDORU and sexy ANIME girls. They can cost over $100, but they're probably still cheaper than a girlfriend. See also HIZAMAKURA and MONOKATARI NO HITOBITO.

Damé (ダメ): Useless; no good or hopeless.

Damé-elite (ダメエリート): A lovable but no good loser who somehow makes it to the top of a given strata. For example, Himura Kenshin from the manga *Ruroni Kenshin* is the world's deadliest samurai assassin, but he is also a cute HETARE (loser).

Damé ningen (駄目人間): A useless human. A self put-down in OTAKU discussions. Often accompanied by the ASCII ART (AA) _|￣|O, which depicts a defeated man on his hands and knees.

Damé shikou (ダメ指向): Vector toward DAMÉ. Architect-turned-OTAKU commentator MORIKAWA KAICHIRO believes that OTAKU are on a path toward bad and no good things. For example, the first generation of otaku liked sci-fi, the next turned to sci-fi ANIME and robots, and those after preferred BISHOJO anime. The focus shifted from a sense of wonder for the future to nostalgia, and this was encapsulated by dating simulator games (GYARUGE) that emerged as an alternative to anime. "An otaku is someone attracted to things that are

DAKIMAKURA COVERS FEATURING POPULAR ANIME CHARACTERS

considered indecent by the general public," Morikawa has said, "there is no such thing as a MIYAZAKI HAYAO otaku."

Danseikyoufusho (男性恐怖症): Boy phobia. A female fear of boys. It's said to be rather common in girls who spend their formative years in cloistered schools devoid of male influences. The other way round, many OTAKU seem rather intimidated by women.

Danso (男装): A girl dressed up as a BISHONEN (beautiful boy).

DANSO BAND FUDANJUKU

Danso café (男装カフェ): Cafés where waitresses dress up like beautiful boys to serve their mainly female customers. First appeared in Tokyo's Ikebukuro OTOME ROAD distinct in the mid 2000s. Somewhat akin to the popular host clubs in Japan in which handsome men entertain women. Danso cafés serve coffee and cakes that are incredibly sweet, mixing girly femininity with the desires and fantasies associated with YAOI manga. Recently these cafés, and the girls dressed as beautiful boys, have become popular with men too, and many danso cafés have also appeared in AKIBA. Most MAID CAFÉS also now have danso staff to bring in the ladies and pleasantly mix up (or confuse) the desires of men.

Darudere (ダルデレ): A character that is usually very relaxed, lethargic, and apathetic, but then suddenly snaps at others with biting comments. The word combines *darui* (lazy), and *dere dere* (lovey dovey). An alternative rendering, *tsundaru*, swaps *dere* for *tsun*, which means "to scorn." Tsundaru is actually closer to the meaning, but darudere is favored for the way it sounds. The term gained popularity after the anime *The Melancholy of Suzumiya Haruhi* aired in 2007, as a way to describe the character Kyon, who was considered a special kind of TSUNDERE. See also YANDERE.

Date Kyoko: See VIRTUAL IDORU.

Datsu-ota (脱オタ): Breaking free of OTAKU-ness. It can mean either an otaku who improves his or her communication and social skills or one that gives up his or her hobbies (see also SOTSUGYOUSHITAHITO). In 1998, several sites online started announcing fashion tips to help otaku avoid social prejudice. These came to be known as datsu-ota fashion sites, and they provided the groundwork for how-to guides today (see also *DENSHA OTOKO*).

DD: An acronym meaning *daredemo daisuki*, or "love anyone." It's used to describe people who don't commit to one person, object, or hobby and instead wander from one pleasure to the next. Many young OTAKU are DD, loving whatever ANIME, FIGURE, or IDORU strikes their fancy at a given time. It can also be used as a compliment for those who find good in all things.

DESIGN BY NIWANO NORIKO

DECO DEN (DECORA DENWA)

Decora (デコラ): A kind of GYARU (gal) fashion characterized by its over-the-top decoration. Examples include dresses with dangling jewelry; fingernails decorated with glittering rhinestones; and cell phones, studded with plastic gems, that have so many accessories attached to them they must be carried in separate bags. The trend echoes both the drawing style of SHOJO MANGA—with their carefully designed flower and jewel motif backgrounds—and the fashion of the female characters. See also OTOME-CHIC.

Dengon dial (伝言ダイヤル): Telephone clubs for voice-mail personal ads. Known to be used by sex clubs to organize prostitution. These were very popular in the 1990s when it was reported that some teenage schoolgirls (KOGALS) used the service to arrange meetings with older men for ENJOKOSAI (compensated dating).

Denpa (電波): Electomagnetic wave. Also used as an adjective to describe saccharine-sweet, supercharged IDORU, characters, and products. OTAKU researcher Shingo, author of a report on *MOÉ* on the Heisei Democracy website, says this is one of the four major types of moé.

Denshamania (電車マニア): See TETSUDO OTAKU.

***Densha Otoko* (電車男):** *The Train Man.* A popular TV drama and film, based on a 2004 novel of the same name. It began as an allegedly true story that unfolded on a 2CHANNEL bulletin board for single men to bemoan their woes. The tale tells how a twenty-four-year old OTAKU saves female passengers from being molested by a drunk on a train. He receives Hermes brand flatware as thanks from one of the women, asks his online friends how to respond, and successfully dates her.

The book, which is simply a collection of the posts that appeared on 2CHANNEL, was published under the pseudonymn Nakano Hitori, a name that can be read as *naka no hitori*, meaning "one of those people." The producers, however, insist the story is true and say they were in contact with the original densha otoko, whose true identity—if he exists—was never revealed. To end the myriad of lawsuits, Hiroyuki, the man behind 2CHANNEL, claimed the rights for the story.

The TV series aired on Fuji Television in 2005, and the tale struck gold with its message that otaku are not cultists or psychopaths, but actually misunderstood, sensitive, and passionate guys. The last episode was watched by 25.5 percent of the national viewing audience. The movie starred teen heartthrob Yamada Takayuki and award-winning actress Nakatani Miki. The story was then made into four MANGA.

DENSHA OTOKO

I LOVE DISNEY!!

Digital Hollywood University (デジタルハリウッド大学)**:** Also known as *dejihari* or DH. Founded in 1994 and located in Akihabara, this is Japan's first school specializing in digital content. It also launched the first international graduate program in ANIME in Japan. Major sponsors include companies such as Hitachi, Ltd., Uchida Yoko Co., Taito Corp., Kansai Telecasting Corp., and Namco Ltd.

Disney: The Walt Disney Company. An animation studio founded in California in 1923 by the brothers Walt and Roy Disney. It has become one of the largest media and entertainment corporations in the world, valued at $3.8 billion and boasting 137,000 employees in 2007. It has a Hollywood studio, eleven theme parks, and several television networks.

The studio began by making short gag cartoons based on *Alice in Wonderland*. This was followed by a stint producing work for Universal Studios, including the creation of the character Oswald the Lucky Rabbit (which would prove popular in Japan many years later). In 1928 Disney lost control of Oswald and created a new character, Mickey Mouse, to star in the short films *Plane Crazy* and *Steamboat Willie*, both of which were widely praised for their innovative use of motion, sound, and music.

DIGITAL HOLLYWOOD UNIVERSITY IN AKIHABARA

Other iconic characters such as Minnie Mouse, Pluto, Donald Duck, and Goofy followed.In 1937, Walt Disney made the world's first animated full-length feature film, *Snow White and the Seven Dwarfs*, which received a Hollywood premiere. Disney's works would become a huge influence on emerging postwar Japanese anime creators such as TEZUKA OSAMU.

Walt Disney died in 1966 after pioneering many animation techniques, establishing Disney as a TV and film franchise, and founding Disneyland. There was a long period of decline after his death, but things started to turn around when *Dumbo* was released on VHS in 1981. A renaissance began with *The Little Mermaid* in 1989, which had superb animation and music. *The Rescuers Down Under* in 1990 was the first film to make wide use of CG animation techniques. In 1991, *Beauty and the Beast* became the only animated film nominated for the Academy Award for Best Picture. 1993 saw the release of Tim Burton's *Nightmare Before Christmas*, a massive hit with the GOTH-LOLI crowd in Japan.

From then on the interplay with Japanese anime, for better or worse, becomes impossible to ignore. In 1994, *The Lion King* became the highest grossing animated film in history. It was the first Disney film not based on an already exisiting work, but it was widely speculated that Disney had borrowed from Tezuka Osamu's JYANGURU TAITEI (*Jungle Emperor*). The official response from Disney lawyers was that their animators were not influenced by Tezuka's anime and all similarities were coincidental.

Disney is obviously dearly loved in Japan. In 1983 Tokyo Disneyland opened, followed in 2001 by Tokyo Disney Sea. Both are part of the Tokyo Disney Resort, which—despite being the only Disney park not owned by the Walt Disney Company—is the most profitable Disney park in the world. This is largely due to huge merchandise sales and the Japanese custom of buying souvenirs for friends and family—most young women own at least one Disney product.

This symbiotic relationship between Disney and Japan has also helped the spread of Japanese pop culture worldwide. In 1995, Disney purchased DiC Entertainment, which dubbed and released the first two seasons of the mega-hit *Sailor Moon*, and in 2002 Walt Disney Studios acquired Saban Entertainment of *Power Rangers* fame. In the same year Disney's subsidiary Miramax acquired the US rights to the fourth *Pokémon* movie. In 2003, Ghibli's *Spirited Away* became the first anime film to win an Oscar for Best Animated Feature, and Disney distributed it, along with other Ghibli films.

Dojikko (ドジっ娘): A loser or screw-up girl; a girl who is always making mistakes. An ANIME and MANGA character type that appeals to the NON-ABILITY crowd. Failure only makes the character cuter as she keeps on trying to overcome weaknesses and throws herself upon the mercy of the audience.

Doll (ドール): A figure representing a human. Japan has a long and deep history with dolls, or *ningyo* as they are more correctly called in Japanese. A potent mixture of Shinto animism and Zen Buddhist object worship is reflected in Japanese doll culture, and it is believed dolls have a spirit. From as early as the Heian period (794–1185), dolls have helped people explore and mediate important life-stage transitions. Examples include the presentation of dolls during various festivals intended to give young girls and boys role models, the gift of bride dolls at marriage, and dolls for safe childbirth.

Because of a popular belief that dolls should be treated with proper respect, when they are discarded they are burned in a special ceremony called *ningyo kuyo* (last rites for dolls). Dolls are also sometimes married to the dead to sooth their spirits, and during WWII kamikaze pilots were given female "mascot" dolls to keep them company.

A CUSTOMIZED VOLKS DOLL

Starting in the 1960s, the doll-making boom hit Japan, spearheaded by Yotsuya Simon, who was influenced by German-born French surrealist Hans Bellmer's work from 1935. Doll fandom spread with the advent of art and photography books. Many artists started to make life-sized, ball-joint dolls.

Some life-sized dolls were, of course, made for purposes other than art, and in 1977 Orient Industry was founded in Tokyo to develop the perfect sex doll. Their most famous dolls are the CANDY GIRL series.

Dolls have long been working their way into popular media. A string of movies and manga in the 1960s and 1970s—including MATSUMOTO LEIJI's *Sexaroid* (1968), TEZUKA OSAMU's *Yakeppachi no Maria* (1970), and ISHINOMORI SHOTARO's *Sexadoll* (1971)—established their place in pop culture. Cyborgs, too, were prominent in sci-fi anime during the 1980s, culminating in OSHII MAMORU's *Ghost in the Shell* in 1995.

The real doll renaissance, however, came with *Neon Genesis Evangelion* and the doll-like character Ayanami Rei. Such was her popularity that she spawned a PVC figure boom and contributed to a wave of doll-like characters in anime. In 1996, Paper Moon, a doll manufacturer founded in 1987 in Gifu Prefecture, made thirty life-sized ball-joint Ayanami dolls, which sold out despite a $4,500 price tag. Other companies followed suit and started to make dolls.

In 1999, VOLKS, a Kyoto company founded in 1972 to make resin garage kits, used the same materials to create its Super Dollfie series. As the popularity of smaller ball-joint dolls increased, manga about dolls also started to appear, the most influential being Peach-Pit's manga *Rozen Maiden* (2002–2007) about a young man who becomes a slave to his doll. In 2004 Oshii Mamoru delved even deeper into the theme of dolls with *Innocence: Ghost in the Shell 2* which featured android robot sex dolls that resembled Hans Bellmer's ball-joint dolls.

DOLL FAN AT A DOLPA

Doller (ドーラー): A slightly derogatory term for a doll user, or a person who loves dolls. It's especially used to refer to those who use sex-dolls. In early 2008, one major retailer of such dolls, Orient Industry, estimated there were 20,000 such people in Japan. Users are divided into *wet* users (emotionally invested), and *dry* users (interested in collecting). Dollers consider a purchase to be an "adoption" or a marriage.

Dollfie: See VOLKS.

Dolpa (ドルパ): An abbreviation of "Dolls Party." Large markets where fans of VOLKS dolls can buy, sell, trade, and share dolls, many of which are customized by fans. Fifteen thousand people attended Dolls Party 19 on April 27, 2008, to celebrate the 10th anniversary of the Super Dollfie series of Volks' dolls. These events started in 1999 and are usually held at Tokyo BIG SIGHT during the long holidays in May and December, and in March in Kyoto, the hometown of Volks.

Douga (動画): Moving pictures, or an animated film. The homonym *douga* (童画) means art drawn for children.

Doujin no sakuhin (同人の作品): A general term for the wide spectrum of homage works created by fans of an existing artistic property. The most famous example is DOUJINSHI (amateur comic books), but also included are *doujin soft* (games), *doujin* goods, and *doujin anime* (often erotic). If it can be made, it has, and someone is doing it by him- or herself in a CIRCLE to make it better or to better suit their tastes.

Doujinshi (同人誌): An amateur or professional magazine, most often MANGA, published independently by a group of fans (CIRCLE). They are roughly equivalent to fanzines or fan fiction but differ greatly in the scale and intensity of production and consumption. There are massive events devoted to buying and selling doujinshi (see COMIKET), and stores deal in such products year round (see TORANOANA). Comiket data shows there were 2,496 new doujinshi titles published in 2003, each with an average circulation of 13,546.

In the broadest sense, the prototypes of doujinshi are the magazines distributed in private literary circles and academic gatherings, but what is known as doujinshi in Japan today tends to be fan-produced manga. Initially this kind of work consisted of original stories and characters, but it shifted to "parody" by taking characters from established series and placing them in new stories, alternative COUPLINGS, or parallel worlds. The plots are often created by diehard fans who want a story to continue after it officially ends. Others are more interested in seeing their favorite characters in sexual encounters that were never intended by the original creators.

Although doujinshi often infringe on copyright, most professional manga artists respect this activity as the creative right of fans and, in return for looking the other way, tap them for new ideas (see ANMOKU NO RYOKAI). Professional mangaka such as Togashi (*YYH*) and Kuwabara Mizuna (*Mirage of Blaze*) also write doujinshi. Hagiwara Kazushi himself created *Bastard - Expansion*, a pornographic doujinshi with characters from his work *Bastard!!* The other way round, some doujinshi authors become professionals,

DOLPA EVENT IN TOKYO

for example four women who drew *Captain Tsubasa* doujinshi in the 1980s later became the manga artist collective CLAMP. Doujinshi researcher Gunnar Hempel estimates there are 8,000 "professional" doujinshi artists in Japan scraping by on an average of $1,200 a month. However, they gross on average $3,200 from large sales events.

Doujinshi Datsuzei (同人誌脱税): Doujinshi tax evasion. An incident in which Shinagawa Kaoruko (real name Shimosato Mizue), a doujinshi author famous for her *Prince of Tennis* doujinshi, was sued in 2006 by the Nagano Prefecture government for unpaid back taxes. The audit came amid accusations of plagiarism and flagrant copyright infringment. Shinagawa reported her annual income from doujinshi sales as 20 million yen over three years, when it was actually estimated to have been closer to 200 million yen ($1.9 million). In 2007, she was ordered to pay 93 million yen in back taxes and fines. This is one of many cases of stricter control being asserted in the world of doujinshi, but it was arguably one of the most legendary due to Shinagawa's fame and final estimated income from doujinshi.

Dousen (動線): Speed lines. Lines drawn to suggest motion in a still image. Traditional Japanese art also displays these, but they are put to ingenious use in MANGA and ANIME.

Doutei (童貞): A male virgin. Some people identify themselves this way online. The female version is *shojo* (処女), though people seldom call themselves that.

DQN (ドキュン): Pronounced *dokyun*. Slang for someone who lacks common sense. It's also an onomatopoeia meaning "shot through the heart," and comes from TV Asahi's show *Mokugeki Dokyun* (1994–2002), which was something akin to Jerry Springer's tabloid talk show in the United States. The guests were working class and tended not to be the smartest of folks. In 1998 on the online site Ayashii World, user Mummy Ishida started to use the term to insult people he, or she, felt lacked an education. It caught on and spread to mean a painfully stupid person. 2CHANNEL users soon picked it up, although Ayashii World responded that 2channel was itself a DQN hangout.

Dress-up dolls: See KISEKAE NINGYO.

Dutch wife (ダッチワイフ): Refers to full-sized, lifelike sex dolls—from a rather discriminatory historic term referring to Dutch merchants and their practices. See also CANDY GIRL DOLL.

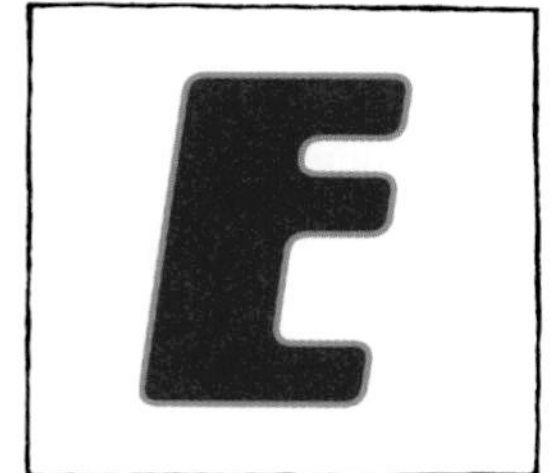

Ecchi (エッチ): See H.
Educational manga: See GAKUSHU MANGA.
Egakimoji (描き文字): Hand-lettering.
Ekonte (絵コンテ): Storyboard. In planning animation, the basic idea of the work is done in brief sketches to show ideas, positions, transitions, and flow.
Emonogatari (絵物語): Picture story.
Enjo (炎上): Blazing up. Slang for to "flame" someone by putting a bunch of meaningless filler comments on an online discussion to silence someone.
Enjokosai (援助交際): Compensated dating. Sometimes abbreviated to *enko*. A euphemism in Japan for "dates" where older men pay middle- or high-school girls for their company. Often, but not always, this is blatant prostitution. Enjokosai hit the headlines in the mid-1990s and caused much public outrage, when it was suggested that KOGALS in Shibuya were turning tricks to buy designer-brand goods. Author Murakami Ryu wrote a novel about enko called *Topaz II*, which ANNO HIDEAKI made into the film *Love & Pop* (1998). Enko continues to make news and there are regularly stories in the media about men—from politicians to school teachers—paying teenage girls for sex.
Eroge (エロゲー): Erotic video and PC games. Eroge are explicitly sexual, and the player's avatar has sex with, or molests, numerous girls in a fantasy harem.The most representative example is the game *To Heart* by game company Leaf. See also the parallel genre of GYARUGE.

Ero gekiga (エロ劇画): Realistic, pornographic comics from the 1960s and 1970s.

Ero-guro (エログロ): Erotic plus grotesque. "Tentacle sex" is the most obvious example (see SHOKUSHU KEI), although *guroloil* (grotesque Lolita) fashion and *kimo-kawaii* (gross but cute) characters are right up there. This is nothing new, actually. The famous description of vibrant and chaotic youth culture from the 1920s to the 1940s was *ero-guro-nonsense*. This was often simply a way to dismiss the shifting morals and practices of youth and popular culture, which was struggling to deal with modernization, Westernization, and militarization. On the manga side of things, Suehiro Maruo (*Shojo Tsubaki*) is probably the best-known ero-guro manga artist.

ENGLISH VERSION OF SUEHIRO MARUO'S *ERO-GURO* MANGA *SHOJO TSUBAKI*

Erokawaii (エロ可愛い): Erotic and cute. Often shortened to *erokawa*. A term first used to describe the J-POP idoru Koda Kumi, although the basic look has long been popular in the OTAKU world. It is considered the most sexualized of the four types of MOÉ.

Ero-puri (エロプリ): Erotic *purikura* (sticker photos). A subgenre of sticker photos in which people, especially young women, try to look as sexy as they can, often posing semi-naked. See also YABA-PURI and ONNA NO KO SHASHIN.

Essay manga (エッセイマンガ): A manga genre made popular by ultra-conservative thinker Kobayashi Yoshinori in the early 2000s. The essays are often propagandist entertainment using manga to push a single idea. The author appears in drawn avatar or textual comments to openly state his or her opinion.

Etsuransha (閲覧者): A reader/viewer, or more specifically a lurker on a popular site such as 2CHANNEL keeping track of developments without participating.

Event (イベント): In Japan this means convention. There are numerous subcategories to denote what kind of an event it is; these include DOUJINSHI, figures and toy, and industry showcases. Many fans treat these events as a chance to meet members of the opposite sex, hoping to find partners with similar hobbies.

Expo '70: Held in Osaka in 1970, this was Asia's first World's Fair. The theme was "progress and harmony for mankind," and many bright, utopian visions of space-age futures were presented. However, economic, social, and ecological disasters cast a long shadow over that realistic possibility. OKADA TOSHIO, MORIKAWA KAICHIRO, and MURAKAMI TAKASHI all believe it was soon after this event that Japanese youth began seeking alternative futures in ANIME, MANGA, and video games.

Eye catch (アイキャッチ): Segments of anime or still shots—usually timed to music and lasting only seconds—appearing after a commercial break in the middle of a televised anime. The purpose is to draw viewers back to the show.

I THOUGHT I'D GIVE YOU SOME *FAN SERVICE!*
F

Fanboy or fangirl: An English equivalent for a geeky OTAKU enthusiast, but without the Japanese connotation of being a creepy loner.

Fan-dub: Fan-produced vocals dubbed over a film's original dialogue. Similar to FAN-SUB.

Fan-fiction, fan-art: The Western equivalent of what Japanese call DOUJINSHI, but usually based online.

Fan service: Showing a series' characters in risqué or compromising positions to give the fans a thrill. This can be as simple as a gust of wind blowing up a girl's skirt, or as titillating as a naked girl stepping out of a shower, hidden only by steam. Showing down a girl's top as she bends forward is also a classic.

Gentle teasing such as PANCHIRA (panty shots) has existed as long as the anime medium itself. In the 1970s, NAGAI GO's transforming-girl show, *Cutie Honey,* took fan service to new heights, as would the magical-girl genre that followed. By the 1980s, full frontal nudity and the shower scene became stock elements of all anime. In the mid-1990s, director ANNO HIDEAKI made a scathing critique of fan service in his anime series *NEON GENESIS EVANGELION.*

Anno had promised every episode would have something for the fans to drool over, but he ended up giving viewers less as the series became increasingly traumatic. Then, when he did put in fan service, he would question the viewer's desire by juxtaposing a characters' pain with their sexuality. Famously, he showed his male protagonist, Shinji, beside a hospital bed, masturbating over the comatose body of the female character, Asuka, as he mutters "I'm so fucked up."

Since this self-referential watershed, fan service rarely includes full nudity.

Fan-sub: A fan-produced, subtitled version of work not available in a given country. Using a Macintosh II and the ColorSpace II video board, Robert Woodhead and Roe Adams made the world's first fan-sub with the *Vampire Princess Miyu* OVA in 1988. They went on to form AnimEigo, the first anime-centric licensing firm in the United States. The first online fan-subber was Sue Shambaugh, a translator who posted translations of anime series that could be printed off by those who owned the Japanese tapes and could not speak Japanese. She sent neat manuscripts by mail for a modest $3 charge.

Fazacon (ファザコン): Father complex. An intense longing for the father figure, which often manifests in preferred character type or even sexual preference. For example, the older gents in YAOI couplings tap into this desire for daddy dearest.

Fechi (フェチ): Fetish. When attached directly to a word in Japanese, this means "obsessive about." For example muscle-*fechi*.

TELETHA TESTAROSSA FROM FULL METAL JACKET FIGURE BY BOME FOR KAIYODO

Fighting girls: See SENTO BISHOJO.

Figure (フィギュア): Figurine. A collectible character or mecha toy, usually from ANIME, MANGA, LIGHT NOVELS, or video games. The size can vary from a few centimeters tall to life-sized *toshindai* models. Collectible anime figures really took off in the 1990s, but companies such as the Aoshima toy company were making model airplanes as early as 1929. Toys of early anime were also around in the 1960s and 1970s, and KAIYODO, best known for its anime-related figures, began in 1964 making *SHOKUGAN*, food or candy with toy prizes. BANDAI imported capsule toy machines from the United States in 1977 and went on to produce mecha figures with plastic models (*PURAMO*) of *Gundam* in 1980. That same year, *Hobby Japan* magazine ran advertisements for a resin kit of Robby the Robot from the film

SHOKUGAN TOYS FROM KAIYODO

Forbidden Planet (1956), which jump-started the amateur resin kit boom in the 1980s. General Products, the predecessor of GAINAX, and BOME, all got started in figures during this time. In 1982, Kaiyodo began launching original figures, many from live-action and anime franchises. General Products started WONDER FESTIVAL in 1984 to buy and sell GARAGE KITS, giving fans the outlet they needed. The boom in OVA and theatrical anime gave these craftsmen plenty of niche characters to use as subjects. Companies dealing in these products began to emerge, and mass production was made possible by factories in China. Famous figure companies Wave, Kotobukiya, Yellow Submarine, and VOLKS all took off at this time. Kichijoji, a suburb in western Tokyo became a hotspot of resin kit figure activity, with the Wave showroom located there.

Meanwhile, Takatoku and Takara started making mecha figures of the *Macross* and *Transformers* franchises, as well as SENTAI action figures. Figure craftsman Araki Gentaro started experimenting with advanced and detailed models in the magazine *SMH* in 1995. That same year, the TV anime *NEON GENESIS EVANGELION* and GYARUGE *Tokimeki Memorial* became smash hits that fueled a figure renaissance. Kaiyodo and Tsukuda Hobby especially concentrated on producing *Evangelion* figures, the latter developing highly detailed, prepainted, hollow PVC (plastic) figures. They were affordable and very popular but had a tendency

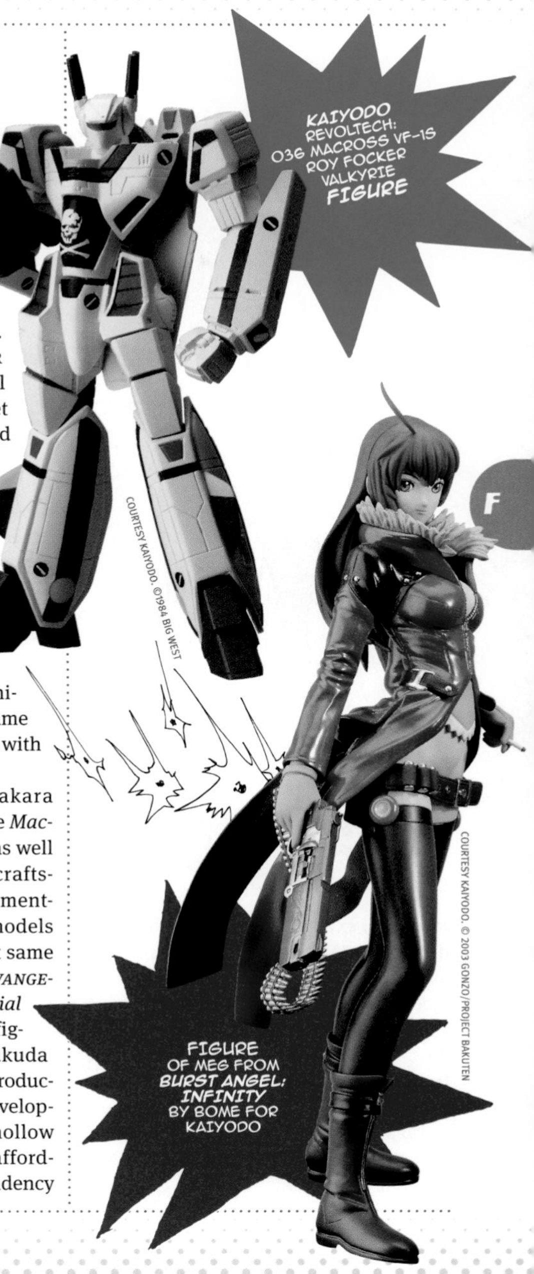

KAIYODO REVOLTECH: 036 MACROSS VF-1S ROY FOCKER VALKYRIE FIGURE

FIGURE OF MEG FROM *BURST ANGEL: INFINITY* BY BOME FOR KAIYODO

to bend if exposed to heat and fade if in direct sunlight. To solve this problem, vinyl and soft vinyl began to be used. The model maker Akiyamakobo appeared in 1996 and would pioneer human-size figures. When Kaiyodo moved its Tokyo store from Shibuya to Akihabara in 1997, the time of figures had come. Since 2001, GOOD SMILE COMPANY has innovated the industry with its high-quality figma and Nendoroid figures.

COURTESY KAIYODO. © KOBAYASHI MASATOMO
HOMARE CHARACTER FIGURE BY BOME FOR KAIYODO

According to the Japan Toy Cooperative, toys in Japan were a $7 billion industry in 2007. The otaku stuff, including puramo and figures, constituted $1.3 billion of that total. That does not include garage kits, which is a wild free-for-all and anyone's guess.

Figuremation (フィギュメーション)**:** Stop-motion animation using figures and toys. Went through a spurt of popularity in 2007 with *Akiba-chan*, a cute and bubbly show brought about in part by Tsuburaya Entertainment, the firm behind the long-running *Ultraman* franchise.

***Final Fantasy VII*:** Or *FF7*. An RPG video game released by Square (now Square Enix) in 1997. Taking three years, 120 artists and programmers, and $30 million to develop, it was the first in the series to use 3D computer graphics for fully rendered characters and prerendered backgrounds. This was made possible because FF7 was the first in the series not made for Nintendo, whose N64 cartridges did not have the graphic capabilities needed. Instead Square went over to the Sony PlayStation, which had enough graphics power for the 3D game-play and enabled the game to have forty minutes of cinematic in-game movies.

Long-time *Final Fantasy* character designer Amano Yoshitaka was replaced by Nomura Tetsuya, whose manga style was easier to adapt into 3D. Composer Uematsu Nobuo created an orchestral score that became a classic, including the first *Final Fantasy* song with digitized vocals, "One-Winged Angel."

SPOILER ALERT!! STOP READING NOW IF YOU DON'T WANT TO KNOW WHAT HAPPENS!

The story is set in a technologically advanced, dystopian world where a ruthless mega-corporation called "Shinra" is draining the life of the planet to use as an energy source. The game-play follows the main character, an antisocial mercenary named Cloud Strife, who fights Shinra to overcome his past. Along with eight other characters, he faces the most badass villain in video game history—Sephiroth, an elite, genetically engineered soldier. In what is often described as gaming's most shocking moment, Sephiroth stabs the heroine Aeris Gainsborough in the back, killing her.

FF7 is without question one of the most popular games ever made; it sold 2.3 million copies within three days of its 1997 release in Japan, and helped Japanese RPG games find favor worldwide. Its North American release in the same year was prefaced by TV commercials on major networks, a promotion with Pepsi, and advertisements in *Rolling Stone*, *Details*, *Spin*, *Playboy*, and Marvel and DC comic books. In one weekend it sold 330,000 copies, and sales crested to 1 million copies by the end of the 1997. In all, FF7 has sold over 9.8 million copies worldwide, making it the second biggest PlayStation title after *Gran Turismo*. The game has been voted the best of all time by many publications and regularly tops popularity rankings.

Such was the force behind this beast of a game that Square couldn't resist cashing in with cross-platform and multimedia tie-ins. These include prequels, sequels, and alternate universes such as the mobile-phone game *Before Crisis: Final Fantasy VII*; the CGI film *Final Fantasy VII Advent Children*; the anime *Last Order: Final Fantasy VII*; the third-person shooter *Dirge of Cerberus: Final Fantasy VII*; the PSP game *Crisis Core: Final Fantasy VII*; the novellas *Maiden Who Travels the Planet* and *On the Way to a Smile*; and cameos by the game's characters in the *Final Fantasy*–Disney crossover series *Kingdom Hearts*.

Flag: The prompt box that appears in dating simulators, or GYARUGE, informing the player to get into the action, or make a decision. It also means a story development is foreshadowed. The word "flag" has worked its way into OTAKU conversation to mean "say something!" For example:

> Cute maid: "You look handsome today master. Is that a new tie?"
> Speechless male otaku: "..........."
> Otaku's friend: "Hey ... flag!"

Flaming: See ENJO.

Fleischer, Max: Born in 1883 in Krakow, Poland. Died in 1972. After moving to the United States, he became an important pioneer in the development of animation. He brought such characters as *Betty Boop*, *Koko the Clown*, *Popeye*, and *Superman* to the screen and was responsible for a number of technological innovations such as the rotoscope, which simplified animation by allowing movement to be created by tracing frames of live-action film, and the Stereoptical camera, which allowed a horizontal camera on a tabletop to film three-dimensional miniature sets so that animation CELS could pass in front or behind. After his death, *Time* magazine named Fleischer the "dean of movie cartoonists."

I WONDER IF BETTY BOOP WAS THE FIRST MOÉ CHARACTER?

BOME

BORN IN 1961 IN OSAKA, Bome is the best-known bishojo model figure sculptor in Japan. Even after collaborating with Murakami Takashi and being touted as a pop artist the world over, Bome remains humble. He goes to work from 9 a.m. to 11 p.m., sometimes even on weekends, and produces ten to twenty models a year. As a salaried employee, he sees no bonus for all the hype surrounding him.

PG: When did you start making figures?

B: When I was twenty, I went to Tokyo to be an animator, but it didn't work out. I was hanging around Tokyo when Kaiyodo opened a branch there, and I started working there part-time. They eventually took me on full-time and sent me back to Osaka. When I was twenty-five, I was told to try my hand at sculpting models.

What's interesting about Kaiyodo is that we have regular work from 9 a.m. to 6 p.m., but after 6, we can use our desk to make anything we like. If what we make is good enough to be a product, they merchandise it.

PG: So you started out producing garage kits?

B: Yes. I've been at Kaiyodo doing this kind of stuff for about twenty-five years now. When I was a kid in Osaka, Kaiyodo's store was in a shopping arcade near my house. I went there often and used to make things, calling the guy who is now senior director "big brother." The model makers there called me "Bome" because I wore a hat (*boushi*) and glasses (*megane*).

PG: What was the first thing you made for Kaiyodo?

B: It was a clay Cyclops, a monster from Ray Harryhausen's *The 7th Voyage of Sinbad* (1958). But after that, well . . . there are others who can make better monsters and robots than I can. Kaiyodo has some great masters working on animal figures. Bishojo was the last genre left for me. I'd always liked anime, and I was sort of making those things but didn't think it would last as long as it has. You know, creating figures of monsters and heroes, like Kamen Rider, is all about making it realistic. However, bishojo figures are based on two-dimensional pictures. Bringing them to life is based on aesthetic sense, and if the customer likes my interpretation then they buy it. I think that's where bishojo figures give greater opportunity to the creator. There is no one answer. I think that makes them more interesting. That's why I create them. Bishojo figures are based on 2D pictures, and the genre constantly evolves and changes as new people come into the field. I find it interesting to watch the trends. Like, characters from ten years ago are not popular anymore. Godzilla doesn't change in ten years, but for bishojo ten years is a long time. The genre has an accelerated consumption cycle. Following that is fun as well.

PG: Who was your first bishojo love?

B: Um . . . I think Lum-chan from *Urusei Yatsura*. At that time, the TV series was on and many people were making Lum-chan

figures, including me. We all were kind of like, "My Lum-chan is better than yours!" There was a time when Lum-chan overwhelmed Comiket. People said when you put her on the cover, that book would sell. I believe she was a revolutionary character. Before that, there were no shonen manga or anime that had a female character as the lead. Do you know Lum-chan?

PG: Yes, I love her, too.

B: I see. American fans are kind of persistent, but in good way. Once they've found a character they like, they stick to it for a long time.

PG: What is your major focus when making a character?

B: There's many, but the pose, I guess. I take great care in whether the pose looks cute or cool. I like challenging myself to really express what is drawn in the picture. It's funny, people used to say I'm not good at making figures that look like the original picture. They say my figures have "Bome face."

PG: What's most difficult about making figures?

B: Well . . . I guess everything is difficult. It's hard to know whether your feeling for the character comes across and is understood by others. Wonder Festival is the best place to gauge the reaction of customers. If it doesn't sell well, that means it wasn't good, and if it sells well, that means my feeling was understood by the customers. Wonder Festival is my best and only battlefield, or stage.

PG: What would you like to do in the future?

B: I'm going to continue creating figures. There is a warmth in creating 3D things by hand. Computer graphics are great, but you can't touch them. When I'm making figures I can really feel them, and I can also hand them to other people and they can touch, feel, and keep them with love. That gives me pleasure. It's an analog rather than virtual experience. It's like some people say the first *Star Wars* is better than the digitally edited version. think so too.

PG: Where do you find your inspiration?

B: I am constantly reading manga, magazines, and books and watching anime. On days off I go to otaku shops in Osaka's Nipponbashi and buy tons of books to bring back. I go there to find the seeds o ideas to create figures.

> **There is a warmth in creating 3D things by hand. Computer graphics are great, but you can't touch them.**

PG: Have you thought about a career as an artist?

B: No, I'm not that kind of person. I me Murakami Takashi and things developed so we could show figures in New York. I was meant to be my "debut as an artist." But I really didn't think of it that way, so didn't go. Murakami got really angry. He said there are many people who want to study art in New York and have the chance to exhibit in those galleries. So the nex time, when Fondation Cartier in Paris invited me, I went to France. Anyway, still think I'm not an artist, just a modeler The exhibition at Parco in Shibuya in 2008 was promoted as the 10th anniversary of my debut as an artist, but i doesn't make sense to me at all.

PG: What is the difference between an artist and a modeler?

B: I don't understand the difference. Ever

though I create figures, I don't understand art. I like Michelangelo, but I see it only as a reference. I don't understand the heart of art at all, and the border dividing what's art and what's not is unclear to me. When I collaborate with Murakami, there's a gap between us. He says, "Fix this, and then it will be art," but I don't understand what he means at all.

PG: The *Miss ko2 (Project ko2)* you made was art, though.

B: I made the basic model, and then it went to the manufacturers. After that it kept developing. I just did it like any other job. Murakami was not famous at the time, and it was my mission to help him. Kaiyodo likes people with the kind of interesting story Murakami had. So I made Koko-chan. I didn't expect that this figure would sell for half a million dollars five years later. Nevertheless, at that time, Murakami was saying, "Please think five years into the future." It's certainly amazing that what he said came true.

PG: Do you have a hobby?

B: I like creating things like puramo and figures, but that's my job! So I'm looking for a hobby now. I like reading books, watching videos, and playing games. I made my main hobby into my job, so there's no end to it.

PG: Of all the figures that you've made, what's your favorite?

B: There are many, but my favorite is "Oni-musume" (Japanese Ogre Girl). That's my most representative work. It's been seen everywhere, and we went to Paris together. Her look goes right back to Lum-chan. The basics, like her tiger bikini, horns, and a club, are the same. I like those motifs, so I keep trying different things with them.

ONI MUSUME [SHE=DEVIL] FIGURE BY BOME

Flopping: The process of flipping pages of Japanese MANGA so they can be read from left to right. The US-based manga publisher VIZ Media, under the leadership of Horibuchi Seiji, was responsible for establishing this practice in 1987, but many artists resented these mirror-imaged manga, including Toriyama Akira of *Dragon Ball* fame. In 2002 TOKYOPOP, under the leadership of Stuart Levy, published manga in their original form in its wildly successful "100% Authentic Manga" series. Until Tokyopop, unflopped manga were translated by fans in what are known as SCANLATIONS available online. For many fans, reading it in the original form was a badge of honor.

4channel: Or 4chan. An English-language, online bulletin board founded in 2003 as a copy of Japan's 2CHANNEL. Because of this, many of the various boards and threads are devoted to Japanese pop culture and related topics. As with 2channel, anyone can anonymously post comments, so things have a tendency to get lively and irreverent. Even the originator of the site is only known by the handle "Moot." Although images can be posted, some parts of the site still display ASCII Art (AA) in homage to 2channel. 4chan now has 3 million monthly users.

FPS: First-person shooter. A type of video game where players take a first-person perspective and blow their enemies away.

Freeter (フリーター): A person who makes a living by stringing together part-time work. An amalgamation of the English word "free" and the German "arbeiter" (worker).

Fujori gag (不条理ギャグ): Absurdity, irrationality, or inconsistency in a gag. It's surprisingly common in ANIME and MANGA of the 2000s, reflecting the surreal state of things. First seen in the pages of *Garo* magazine in the 1970s and refined by AZUMA HIDEO in the 1980s.

Fujiko Fujio (藤子不二雄): Pen name of the MANGAKA duo Fujimoto Hiroshi, 1933–96, and Abiko Motoo, 1934–, both from Toyama Prefecture. Together they were best-selling sci-fi MANGA and ANIME authors and an inspiration to many young Japanese OTAKU. Their cynical short works are especially respected. In 1953, they published *Utopia: The Last*

I'M SO GLAD THEY DON'T FLOP MANGA ANYMORE!
!

World War and moved to Tokyo in 1954 to go professional. They lived in Tokiwa-so, where many mangaka gathered. They left in 1959, and in 1963 received the Shogakukan Manga Award for their manga *Susume Robot and Tebukuro Tecchan*. They then established animation Studio Zero with ISHINOMORI SHOTARO and others. The duo had many hits, including *Obake no Q-taro*, *Kaibutsu-kun*, and *Paaman*. Fujimoto became a favorite of kids with *Doraemon* (from 1970), while Abiko continued targeting young adults with *Warau Salesman*, *Mataro ga kuru*, and *Black*

Shokai Henkiro. *Doraemon* has received the Nihon Mangaka Association prize for excellence (1973), the Shogakukan Manga Award (1982), and the first TEZUKA OSAMU Cultural Prize Grand Prize (1997). The anime version became a massive cultural hit in and is their most beloved work. The *Doraemon* anime has yet to be dubbed into English. The duo broke up in 1988.

Fujoshi (腐女子): Rotten girl. An ironic pun on the homonym "*fujoshi*" (婦女子), meaning "woman" or "lady." Girls who read YAOI or BL MANGA. These days *fujoshi* is the common term for a "female OTAKU," but this fails to acknowledge their unique interests. They are quite different from JOSEI NO OTAKU (female otaku), who have similar interests as men. Recently genres such as yaoi and fujoshi hangouts like Ikebukuro's OTOME ROAD have grown in popularity and men have also begun to join their ranks. Men who read yaoi are called *fudanshi* (rotten boys).

Fukidashi (吹き出し): Speech or thought balloon. Traditional convention in comics around the world, but thought to have existed in Japan since very ancient times. Examples include the 12th-century humorous animal scrolls, CHOJUGIGA, and 19th-century HOKUSAI MANGA.

Fukyo-katsudo (布教活動): Proselytizing. An otaku trying to assert his or her hobbies and convert others like a missionary trying to spread religion.

Full animation (フル・アニメーション): Anime created for OVA or theater release. Unlike TV or limited anime, full animation production typically has a large staff and boasts massive cel and frame-per-second counts. The result is fluid, rich movement.

Furry or furries: Animal characters or people dressed as them. This term comes from the United States, but is applicable to KIGURUMI and NEKOMIMI.

Furuya Toru (古谷徹): Born in 1953 in Yokohama, Kanagawa Prefecture. He is a veteran SEIYUU most famous for playing Amuro Ray in the seminal *Gundam* series. He also played Hoshi Hyouma (*Kyojin no Hoshi*), Pegasus Seiya (*Saint Seiya*), Yamcha (*Dragon Ball*), Kasuga Kyosuke (*Kimagure Orange Road*), and Chiba Mamoru/Tuxedo Mask (*Sailor Moon*). He often appears on TV and has been attending conventions around the world to drum up international interest in ANIME, seiyuu, and Japan, and he has been a commentator for the annual WORLD COSPLAY SUMMIT in Nagoya, Aichi Prefecture. He is considered a cultural ambassador and was praised at the Seiyuu Awards in 2008.

Fuseji (伏せ字): Hidden letters; an asterix used in place of a f**king rude word.

Fushi manga (風刺漫画): A caricature-like, satirical cartoon.

Futanari (ふたなり): A hermaphrodite.

Gachapon (ガチャポン): Capsule toy. Collectible toys usually associated with anime and purchased from vending machines in Japan. Also known as "*gacha gacha*," which is the sound made when the toys in plastic balls, the size of tangerines, rattle in the case and come out with a "*pon*" sound. BANDAI first imported capsule-toy machines from the US in 1977 and copyrighted the name Gashapon, although the unofficial name gachapon is more generally used by fans, retailers, and rival makers. The industry pulls in around $310 million a year. The toys are usually released in sets of around five pieces, one of which is bound to be near impossible to get, meaning that if you want the lot, you have to spend a fortune trying. Complete sets sell for a premium in RENTAL SHOWCASES. See SOUNDROP.

Gag manga (ギャグマンガ): Dirty, bawdy, and physical comedy MANGA, usually targeted at naughty boys.

Gaiatsu (外圧): External pressure. The influence on Japan by other countries.

GACHAPON MACHINES

THE ICONIC AYANAMI REI IN *NEON GENESIS EVANGELION* BY GAINAX

G

Gainax (ガイナックス)**:** Also known as Studio Gainax, the quintessential otaku studio founded by a bunch of fanboys with nothing but innovation, garage kits, and cameras. They came up through the ranks of the blossoming otaku generation and are a true success story. At the 20th Annual Japan SF Convention, or DAICON III in 1981, a group of film students from the Osaka area created an amateur animation under the name "Daicon Film." In 1982 they opened a specialty SF shop, and in 1983 they returned to the 22nd Annual Japan SF Convention, or DAICON IV, with a sequel animation for the event's opening. The film was a defining moment for anime otaku and has become a cult classic. Their talent was obvious, and a core group of convention organizers joined forces with Daicon Film to create General Products. Among the group were a young ANNO HIDEAKI, OKADA TOSHIO, Sadamoto Yoshiyuki, Akai Takami, and Yamaga Hiroyuki. In 1984 General Products started WONDER FESTIVAL to sell garage kits of MECHA and BISHOJO from popular anime. That same year the group officially incorporated under the name Gainax. The name combines *Gaina*, which is Tottori and Shimane Prefecture slang for "great" or "amazing," and an "x" to indicate the unknown. Under this new name the group tied up with BANDAI and tackled its first major project, the film *Royal Space Force: Wings of Honneamise*. Production started in their Tokyo studio near Takadanobaba in 1985 but later moved to a studio in Kichijoji. The film cost an astounding $8 million to make and promote, but it had a tepid reception on its release in 1987. Nonetheless, it was a technical and cinematic achievement that set director Yamaga and the Gainax crew apart. Okada's OVA *Gunbuster*, directed by

Anno, followed in 1988 and was a much bigger success. Akai then turned out the company's first computer game, *Denno Gakuen*, in 1988. On firmer ground, Gainax began producing anime for TV. It wowed TV audiences in 1990 with Anno's *Nadia: Secret of Blue Water*, a thirty-nine-episode series that was inspired by the 1870 Jules Verne classic *20,000 Leagues Under the Sea*, and originally proposed by MIYAZAKI HAYAO as a complement to his *Laputa: Castle in the Sky*.

Always taking care to keep in touch with the otaku masses, Gainax then turned out the classic dating simulator *Princess Maker* (circa 1991), in which the goal was to raise the perfect daughter or lover. Okada was accused by his colleagues of negligence as company president and was forced to resign in 1992. With the monstrous success of *Nadia* under its belt, in 1995 Gainax and Anno produced *Neon Genesis Evangelion*, a powerful twenty-six-episode series that left pretty much anyone who watched it in a changed emotional state. *Evangelion* would go on to be licensed by A.D. Vision for a price of over $1 million and become the most popular anime series in America. Gainax, however, was threatened by fans for not giving them the ending they wanted.

Things got rough for Gainax for a while. In 1998, Anno quit directing halfway through *His and Her Circumstances*, which was the company's first attempt to adapt an existing story into anime. Then a year later Gainax was accused of tax evasion and its president, Sawamura Takeshi, was charged with accounting fraud.

Gainax continues to be successful, however, and has produced a series of otaku classics, including the raunchy *Oruchuban Ebichu* (1999); the maid robot extravaganza *Mahoromatic* (2001); the depression-driven *The Melody of Oblivion* and *This Ugly Yet Beautiful World* (both 2004); the nonsense OVA series *FLCL* (2000), and *Gurren Lagann* (2007), which revived the machismo of 1970s-style super-robot anime.

Gakushu manga (学習漫画): Educational manga. Almost every school textbook in Japan contains some kind of educational manga. These cover a wide range of topics, from flossing your teeth to driving, but they have also been used to teach Japan's often controversial history syllabus and other subjects.

I KNOW YOU LIKE TO *GEEK OUT* SOMETIMES

Gal game: See GYARUGE.

Gamer (ゲーマー): Someone who enjoys playing games, usually video games, with enough regularity and skill to qualify them as a separate and distinct subcultural group.

Gangu gashi (玩具菓子): An old way to say SHOKUGAN, or candy with a toy prize.

Ganguro (ガングロ): Black face. A type of GYARU prevalent during the mid-1990s. They had very dark fake tans and wore heavy white makeup around the eyes, making them look like raccoons. The protagonist of the manga *Peach Girl* (1997–2004) is often mistaken as a ganguro, and

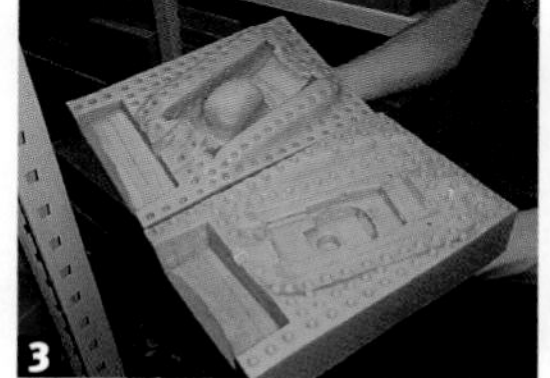

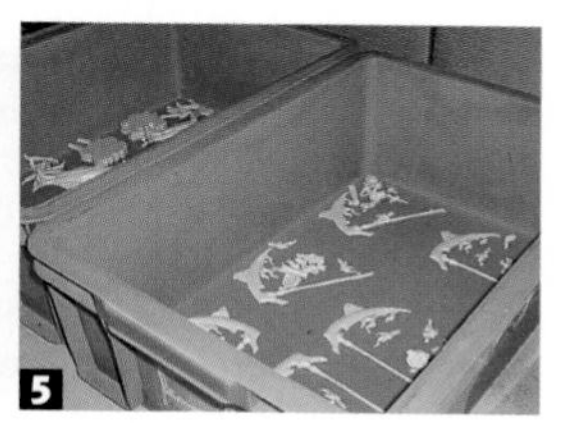

1 Artist crafts the original
2 A mold is cast
3 Silicon molds are made
4 The pouring machine
5 Sorting
6 Final sorting
7 Master painting

the Ganguro Trio in *Super Gals!* (2001–2002) are obvious examples.

Garage kit (ガレージキット): Amateur-produced model kits that are basically rough resin pieces completed by fans with extra sculpting, fastening, and painting. The term originated with dedicated hobbyists producing kits of their own in the garage because they were frustrated by being unable to find quality FIGURES of the subjects they wanted. In August 1979, the magazine *Hobby Japan* ran an advertisment for a 1/35 scale resin Robby the Robot from *Forbidden Planet* (1956), and the boom began. General Products, the predecessor of GAINAX, appeared on the scene in 1982 producing such kits. Originally kits were sold and traded between hobbyists at conventions such as WONDER FESTIVAL, but they've since gained popularity and now a number of companies, including Volks, WAVE/BJ, Kotobukiya, and B-Club, create and sell these rough kits.

Garage kits are quite hard to make, and only the most dedicated do it, claiming it gives them a way to express their feelings for the character. A popular maker can easily sell 1,000 pieces. BOME, the KAIYODO modeler, got started making garage kits in the 1980s.

Garçon (ギャルソン): The Japanese rendering of the French word for "boy," but confusingly, is often used to refer to girls cross-dressing as beautiful boys in butler cafés targeting YAOI fans in Ikebukuro, Tokyo.

G

Garo **(月刊漫画ガロ):** *Gekkanmanga Garo*. The premiere magazine for avant-garde MANGA, such as FUJORI and GEKIGA. Founded in 1964, the magazine was an outlet for social concern and criticism. Before *Garo*, college students were discouraged from reading manga, which were by and large seen as kids' stuff. The work of manga artists such as Shirato Sanpei, with his heavy anti-establishment themes, appeared in *Garo* at the height of antiwar and anti-capitalist protests and demonstrations by college students. At the peak of its popularity in 1971, *Garo* had a circulation of over 80,000. After the failed Anpo protests and the advent of more sophisticated anime such as *Space Battleship Yamato*, *Garo* lost its ability to inspire the people. By the mid-'80s its circulation was barely over 5,000, and the magazine finally closed in 2002.

Gattai **(合体):** Unite; combine into one. Also a union between robots. Generally characters in different robots join together to create a bigger, stronger robot that kicks ass. The first ANIME series to involve combining robots was *Getter Robo* created by NAGAI GO and Ishikawa Ken in 1974. The best known series overseas is *Go Lion* (*Voltron*). *Ga* can mean "combine" and *tai* means "body." You can imagine what FUJOSHI do with this in YAOI: really, really close male friends in giant robots. *Genesis of Aquarion* by KAWAMORI SHOJI is a great recent example of *gattai* anime.

GDH: The parent company of Gonzo Digimation, a studio famous for mixing 2D and 3D animation. While delving into big-budget films (*Brave Story* in 2006 with Warner Entertainment Japan and Fuji TV), GDH's real bread and butter is the otaku hobby market.

GDH was among the first studios to make anime for an international audience. President Ishikawa Shinichiro studied business in the United States and worked at the Boston Consulting Group (1991–99), giving him international connections that would benefit the company. Perhaps its best-known project is *Afro Samurai* (2007), based on a doujinshi by Takashi Okazaki. This was the first anime based on a Japanese manga to be released in English rather than Japanese and was co-produced by the actor Samuel L. Jackson, who also voiced the main characters. It also had a kick-ass soundtrack by RZA. There are plans to make a live-action Hollywood version.

Geek out: To release all inhibitions and get all geeky. Such as speaking like a really passionate fan about a particular

AFRO SAMURAI FROM GDH

object of fascination. See also the related concept of OTAKU TALK.

Gekiga (劇画): Dramatic pictures. An adult alternative to the children's manga of the 1950s. Gekiga became extremely popular in the 1960s and '70s for its messages of social strife and human struggle. These resonated with the antiestablishment ideals of youth at the time. Classic manga and anime *Ashita no Joe*, for example, defined the underdog spirit of a poor nobody taking on the big rich guy. Gekiga are known for their dark lines and gritty style, showing sweat, blood, urine, semen, and dirty streets with an unblinking eye. For that reason, they lend themselves well to erotica and sports dramas, their most enduring subgenres.

Gender bending: A theme that is deeply tied to the fantasy and play of Japanese anime. It is related to RYOUSEI and FUTANARI androgyny, gender transformation, and semi-gay themes. This plastic or flexible treatment of gender in anime has been around since at least TEZUKA OSAMU's cross-dressing *Princess Knight* (1958) and in US imports since Berg Katse (Zoltar) from Toriumi Hisayuki's *Science Ninja Team Gatchaman* (1972). Famous examples of gender bending, and blending, include *Ranma 1/2* (1989), *Maze* (1996), and *Revolutionary Girl Utena* (1997).

General Products: See GAINAX.

Genga (原画): Key frame. The limited number of images drawn by a master animator to establish the overall style and feel of an animation. The genga guides the DOUGA, or in-between frames. Can also mean "concept art."

Gensaku (原作): Original story; source material. For example, a LIGHT NOVEL that serves as the basis of an ANIME. This is also a common way to refer to the distinction between characters, as in one that is "gensaku" and another that is "original," ironically meaning *not* in the original gensaku.

Gésen (ゲーセン): Abbreviation of "game center," the Japanese term for game arcade.

Ghost in the Shell: See KOUKAKU KIDOUTAI.

Gibson, William: Born in 1948 in South Carolina, USA. An American-Canadian science fiction author who has been called the "noir prophet." He coined the term "cyberspace" in his debut novel *Neuromancer* in 1984, before the arrival of the Internet, and predicted the rise of reality TV and virtual enviroments. He is widely considered the father of cyberpunk, and in his 1996 work *Idoru*, he introduced the English-speaking world to the term "otaku," which he defined as a "pathological-techno-fetishist-with-social-deficit." Notably, Gibson did not see otaku as necessarily unique to Japan, saying in an April 2001 interview with the *Observer* newspaper that otaku are at the heart of the "culture of the web."

Glomp: The action of one person lovingly and dramatically attacking another with a hug. A glomp is often predatory and lies somewhere in the gray area between a caring embrace and a flying leap to tackle someone. The term is used extensively in convention culture. Many COSPLAY fans get glomped at events in the United States, but this is not customary in Japan.

Godzilla (ゴジラ): The original KAIJU monster from the Japanese film series of the same name. The giant beast resembles a bulky, wingless dragon, and its name is a combination of gorilla (*gorira*) and whale (*kujira*). Since debuting in 1954, *Godzilla* has been seen in twenty-eight films from Toho. It is now one of the most iconic characters in all film history. It has a star on Hollywood's Walk of Fame and was given a lifetime achievement award

gamer • 杏野はるな

ANNO HARUNA

ANNO HARUNA (21) WAS BORN IN OSAKA and raised in rural Kumamoto Pre-fecture. She now lives in Tokyo and is known as the "Queen of Retro Games." She plays games about eight hours a day but has been known to binge for thirty-six hours straight. She's undefeated in *Street Fighter II*, became a game character in *Street Fighter Online*, and a GRAVIA photo of her marks a trap in *Metal Gear Solid 4*. She can play and win *Super Mario Bros*. blindfolded, and her room holds one of the largest retro game soft-ware repositories in Japan, some 1,000 artifacts valued at over $100,000

PG: When did you start playing games?

AH: I've been playing since I was fifteen, when I left Kumamoto and came to Tokyo to become an idoru. We didn't have game centers or movie theaters back home, and I fell in love with games as soon as I touched them.

PG: You're known as a retro gamer. When did that start?

AH: Soon after I came to Tokyo I discov-ered Nintendo's Famicon and Game Watch, but I just thought they were fun. I was pretty busy putting out gravia and DVDs as an idoru and didn't have time to learn much about games. When I was sev-enteen, I started playing games at least ten hours a day, so I went deeper. I would draw myself maps, or sculpt the mon-sters out of clay. . . . I am from the N64 generation, and I didn't know anything else. When I started playing those older games and learning about them, I came to understand the way the industry had evolved and why. I didn't really appreci-ate games until I started thinking about their roots and development.

PG: You've been into retro gaming for years. What's the appeal?

AH: Playing games is a kind of communi-cation, and because I play retro games my fans are guys in their thirties from the Famicon generation. When I'm with them, they tell me how hard it was when games cost hundreds of dollars, and how they would share games with friends and find secrets. I also like the pixels in retro games. Not everything is rendered per-fectly, so you can use your imagination to bring the characters to life.

PG: What's your favorite system?

AH: Game Watch! It's so simple, just two buttons! But that's why it's deep, anyone can enjoy it.

PG: Are you an otaku?

AH: Um, I think I might be. I didn't really think about it until people started to say that about me. I guess compared to the norm I look like an otaku, because an otaku is someone who concentrates on one thing and becomes totally absorbed in it for a long time. Like, if it's a game then they don't just play it, they trans-form themselves and do things in the real world, or make things, or whatever.

PG: Do you see a difference between game otaku and gamers?

PRESS

AH: Yes, a gamer can see his or her self objectively. Like, when faced with a person who knows nothing about games, a gamer can explain the hobby in an understandable way. But a game otaku knows way too much about the topic, so they can't talk about it anymore. Their explanations to outsiders are crap. It's like otaku have forgotten about the time when they started from zero.

PG: Do you think outsiders recognize this difference between otaku and gamers?

AH: No, I think they're lumped together in Japan, and the mass media promotes this misunderstanding. Like, when there's a violent crime, they say it has something to do with the person being an otaku, or a gamer. The image is of gloomy and unenergetic people who don't like to communicate with others, or can't communicate at all. I guess there isn't anything to be done about that due to the nature of the hobby, but it still irks me. For me, games are "pop" and cool. I want to show people that gaming isn't something only lonely people do in dark, dirty rooms. I want to show that anyone, even a young girl like me, can play games. Japan invented many of the games loved around the world, but now we have these negative stereotypes and are losing out to passionate and professional gamers in Korea and Europe.

PG: But don't you think the image of gamers is changing, and that people who play multi-player RPGs are seen as happy and social?

AH: But those are online, right? There are a lot of games these days where you can play with others without ever seeing them. What I mean is there are a lot of people, in Japan anyway, who don't think of other players in these games as humans. When I play online games, people are always saying horrible things you shouldn't say to other people. Just because games are online and cooperative doesn't mean that people are really communicating with each other. Talking to people offline is completely different.

> **one of the best things about the retro game era was that normal people made games.**

PG: What do you think of the boom in light gamers?

AH: Light users, including women and older people, have been increasing rapidly with the Nintendo DS Lite and so on. Also, there's a lot of educational stuff for students, so parents kind of have to let their kids play games. We live in an age and a country, where everyone plays games and not playing means not being part of the group, so parents have to allow their kids their games. But what's important is not just playing games, but getting something out of them. Like using them to build connections with people, or getting new ideas and starting to make your own games.

PG: Do you think Japanese games need to change?

AH: Lately people focus too much on game graphics. When a game is released, people talk about how good it looks or how many cut scenes it has. It's like watching a movie. You don't even really play, it's just a waste of time. The skill element is gone. It isn't that way with retro games. In the allotted time, you can sharpen your skills and progress. The games, the way we play, and the players have all changed.

PG: Do you think it's because games have gone mainstream?

AH: I don't know. Back when games first ppeared, people played them because hey were new but didn't know what they vere. Now, even young kids know a lot bout games. That makes a big difference n the way players approach games. I think hat's an important change. The feeling of ewness at the beginning of gaming hisory has been displaced by rapid growth nd overdevelopment. People expect igh quality, so companies can't develop nything new. They are stuck making socalled good games with good graphics nd no bugs. That's why I think things ave gone a bit too far. I don't think this vill change for a while. The users are satsfied as is, and companies don't want to ake risks.

PG: So has creativity in games been slipping?

AH: Yeah, I think so. Game companie have become too large, and everythin has to be done on a huge scale. One o the best things about the retro game er was that normal people made games. I wasn't done by people at some compan meeting, but by people playing in thei free time, thinking, "Wouldn't it be fun i this was in a game?" Now it's more like "We need to make a game. What shoul we do?" That approach is holding creativ ity back. Also, there are too many peopl involved, opinions differ and the game i compromised. Some things are taken ou due to sponsors and others are forced in so the things creators want to show an convey get lost.

PG: What's in the future for you?

AH: Up till now I've been on the player o promotion side of things, but I want to b more active in creating. I'm working o the story for an adventure game, but i won't get moving until 2010 at the earliest. I'm also working on a book where I as questions like what would happen if yo had grade schoolers play older game today. Would they think it is fun or boring? Also, now that retro games are kin of disappearing, I want to travel aroun Japan and find where they remain. I'm even thinking of starting a game museum It wouldn't be run by one company, bu rather be a history of all games. Nintendo, Capcom, Konami, all those companies would be there, and there woul be a stage in the middle for events. Thes days the tendency is for one company t promote its newest games, and I thin players miss out on the connections t the past and comparisons. That's wh people think what comes out now is th best. It would be good for people to com and rediscover old games. That might b the start of someone coming up with a idea or making the next great game!

by MTV in 1996. *Godzilla* is deeply tied to Japanese postwar concerns of invasion, nuclear destruction, and natural disaster. In the original film, US nuclear tests in 1945 on the Marshall Islands awaken and mutate the beast, which then destroys Tokyo. In subsequent films it battled many monsters, starting with Anguirus. In *Ghidorah, the Three-Headed Monster*, Godzilla became a hero and the savior of Japan. A less campy Godzilla emerged in *Godzilla (1984)*, when it was depicted as a violent, insatiable force of nature and the personification of the atomic bomb. It died in *Godzilla vs. Destroyer*, but Godzilla Junior mutated to full size to carry on the legacy. *Godzilla, King of the Monsters!* was reworked with new characters and released in English in 1956. In 1961, England made its own *Godzilla*-style film, *Gorgo*, and Godzilla mania spread across Europe. Comics appeared in the US from Marvel Comics in the mid-1970s and from Dark Horse Comics in the 1980s and 1990s. Godzilla made its American TV debut in the 1978 Hanna-Barbera Saturday morning show *The Godzilla Power Hour*, in which it gained a sidekick, Godzooky, described as its nephew. A second cartoon series aired on Fox Kids featuring a juvenile Godzilla traveling around the world with a group of humans it believed to be its parents. See also KAIJU and TOKUSATSU.

Gokko asobi (ごっこ遊び): Make-believe play, especially pretending to be someone else or from another time. The new identity often gets called "X-gokko." As one might expect, this resonates with identity-seeking otaku who cosplay as their favorite characters, emulate heroes, and voyeuristically project themselves into ANIME, MANGA, and games.

Goods (グッズ): Any kind of character related merchandise, for example the "goods" sold at conventions.

Good Smile Company (グッドスマイルカンパニー): A Japanese FIGURE, SHOKUGAN, model, and accessory maker involved in planning, production, and sales. Often referred to as GSC or Gussma. Founded in 2001 well after the figure boom in the 1990s, Good Smile makes the kind of high-quality figures that were only a dream for fans a few decades ago. Aside from

GOOD SMILE COMPANY SUZUMIYA HARUHI FIGURE

G

GOOD SMILE COMPANY NENDROID FIGURES

their own activities, they also sell Max Factory, Alter, FREEing, and Kaiyodo's Revoltech products. They are especially close to the garage kit maker Max Factory and share a booth with it at WONDER FESTIVAL and other major events. Both Good Smile Company and Max Factory are located in the same building in Chiba Prefecture, and the latter also runs an Indian restaurant in the building. Aside from its spicy keema curry, Max Factory has always been known for its BISHOJO and MECHA works, which are now industry standards. Together, the two companies have sent waves through the figure world with series such as Nendroid and figma.

Gothic, Goth (ゴシック・ゴス)**:** Dark, doll-like designs and fashion, often evoking Victorian vogue. It features lots of buckles, straps, black-on-black, and embroidery. There is a conscious attempt to look nonhuman, be it as a doll or a vampire. Eye patches are sometimes worn and fake blood splattered to make the subject look scary or undead (see ERO-GURO). The Tokyo goth scene, highly visible at JR Harajuku Station, mixes in pink and red and frilly doll-like clothes influenced by VISUAL-KEI music, ANIME, and MANGA.

Goth-loli (ゴスロリ)**:** An abbreviation of "Gothic" and "Lolita." A Japanese fashion influenced by Victorian-era children's clothes, aristocrats, or porcelain dolls. It began in the 1970s with brands such as Milk and Pink House and was popularized by VISUAL-KEI idoru Mana in 1999. It's often associated with visual-kei fans, Harajuku, and Dollfie dolls. However, the single largest store devoted to this style is Marui Young (0101 Young) in Shinjuku, with four floors devoted entirely to goth-loli, and the largest event is Tokyo Dark Castle, also primarily in Shinjuku. Gothic is the heavy, dark aesthetic, while Lolita is the softer, pastel side. In combination, there is a wide variety of styles running the spectrum from mature Classic Lolita to childish Sweet Lolita, from grotesque Gurololi to Elegant Gothic Lolita. Some common traits are black and white, frilly ruffles, lace and ribbons, long skirts, bulky shoes, petticoats and bonnets, parasols, and a travel suitcase with

THE GOTHIC & LOLITA BIBLE MAGAZINE

accessories and makeup. Some adherents take cues from the Rococo and Victorian periods of European history, striving to be respectful, demure, and cultured in the ways of sewing, classical music, and the traditional observance of high tea. For the most part, however, most live similar to any average person. The style has spread overseas and is seen in fashion magazines such as the *Gothic Lolita Bible* and *FRUiTS*, and in anime like *Rozen Maiden, D. Gray Man*, and *xxxHolic*. Goth-loli can be seen at anime conventions around the world and at retailers targeting international Japanophiles. International fans tend to see it as a form of cosplay, but Japanese wearers themselves are quick to point out that they are not cosplayers or otaku, despite having an interest in anime and manga. They say fashion is a way of life, not the temporary emulation of a fantasy character.

Graduate: See SOTSUGYOUSHITAHITO.

Gravia (グラビア): Gravure, short for Rotogravure. A type of printing process used in glossy photos in magazines. A gravia IDORU is accordingly equivalent to a pinup girl. These idoru are so prevalent in Japan that saying "gravia" without further qualification refers to such idoru.

Guang Hua Digital Plaza, Taipei (光華數位新天地): Often called the Akihabara of Taipei, this is a six-story plus basement, indoor technological and electronics market known for its high density of computer, anime and games shops. Figures can also be found in the underground shopping area of Taipei Station, PURAMO in Wanhua, and so on. Taiwanese otaku refer to themselves and their particular passion with the suffix "*~mii*," meaning to be driven crazy by something. For example *anime-mii*. Near Guang Hua was Coffee Animaid, one of the first maid cafés outside Japan, which opened in 2004 but has since closed. There is another active otaku area in Taipei around Ximen Station.

Gundam: See *KIDO SENSHI GUNDAM*.

Gunji otaku (軍事オタク): Military otaku. Guys into wearing camouflage, speaking to one other in military lingo, and playing paintball every weekend. Defense Minister ISHIBA SHIGERU is a gunji otaku. In fact, there are so many like him that there is a running tour of the Defense Ministry in Ichigaya. The two-hour private tour costs nothing but must be booked about two months in advance. Similar tours are available for the Police Museum in Kyobashi and the sporadic fire station and maritime coast guard events and demonstrations. In general, however, most would rather go into the woods for paint- or air-gun combat than actually enlist in these organizations. There is also an indoor shooting range on the top floor of Asobit City-Hobby in Akihabara to satiate their thirst for combat.

Gyaku harem (逆ハーレム): Reverse harem. A female protagonist surrounded by many men, usually in a romantic adventure

GRAVIA IDORU TSUGIHARA KANA ON THE COVER OF YOUNG MAGAZINE

story. This also can refer to works with many boys for girls to ogle at, and there may not be a main female character. These often feed the production of YAOI DOUJINSHI couplings between males. See also HAREM.

Gyaru (ギャル): Gals. Young Japanese women known for outrageous fashions and hanging out in Tokyo's club districts. They have fake tans, wear short skirts, and favor accessories big on bling. They abandon traditional Japanese feminine modesty and are tough, rude, crude, and ultra-sexy. Gyaru are champions of consumption and keep in touch via communication networks on their cell phones (see TEREKURA and DENGON DIAL). Most of them hang out around Center-gai street and the 109 BUILDING in Shibuya. Gyaru characters tend to pop up in anime, like Kotobuki Ran from the anime *Super Gals!* (2001–2002) and Keiko, the little-sister character from *Genshiken* (2004).

Gyaruge or galge (ギャルゲー): Gal games. A type of dating simulator game. The player tries to navigate a relationship with one or more beautiful anime girls in a nostalgic or exotic setting. Answering prompts correctly determines the outcome of courting. Gyaruge are a huge industry in Japan. These games have been responsible for many of the terms used in the otaku world, including TSUNDERE. The first was *Night Life* from Koei for the Fujitsu FM7 in 1983. The most representative gyaruge is *Tokimeki Memorial* from 1994. These games are by and large not very sexual, instead teasing with FAN SERVICE images of the girls in various states of undress. NOVEL GAMES are the tamest, and EROGE are the most sexual.

Gyaru moji (ギャル文字): Girls' (gals') letters. A nonstandard, crass form of written Japanese used by young Japanese girls. Luckily for those of us who aren't young Japanese girls, dictionaries of gyaru moji are available.

Gyaru-o (ギャル男): Short for "gal *otoko*," or gal-guy. These are the male equivalent of GYARU. These highly decorated, fashionable, club-going young men tag along with the girls, tending to play a secondary support role.

H

H: Pronounced "*ecchi*," a euphemism for sex. It's the first letter of HENTAI (pervert), but it isn't as strong an indictment and is similar to shortening "erotic" to "ero." It was slang among female high-school students in the 1950s as a way to describe naughty boys who thought too much about sex, and it appeared in the novel *Shiroi Magyo* run in *Asahi Shimbun* newspaper in 1955–56. It became a popular in the 1960s as a way to refer to erotic materials. In the 1980s, TV talent Akashiya was looking for a word to descibe sex without saying sex, and settled on "ecchi." It soon became common use. For example, Ataru from *Urusei Yatsura* is desribed as ecchi. More recently, Haruhi-ism, the fandom surrounding bishojo anime *Melancholy of Suzumiya Haruhi*, is indicated by a giant H.

Hadashi no Gen **(はだしのゲン):** Better known as *Barefoot Gen*, this is a semi-autobiographical manga series by Nakazawa Keiji about the trials of orphans in post–atomic bomb Hiroshima, widely considered the essential antiwar Japanese work. It's read as GAKUSHU MANGA in many schools in Japan and is housed in libraries across the country. Due to its importance, a volunteer group translated it into English in 1976, making it one of the first manga available overseas. It's now required reading in many college courses on Japan. Director Yamada Tengo made three live-action films out of it, Madhouse animated two of its own and Fuji TV did a live-action TV show in 2007. Despite this, *Gen* began humbly as a serial in *Shonen Jump* in 1973, but it was canceled and finished its run in three other minor magazines in 1975.

Haijin (廃人)**:** Human garbage. Some people actually use this to identify themselves online.

Hair nude (ヘアヌード)**:** Starting in 1991, Japan's obscenity law, which basically forbade any public display of genitals or pubic hair, was loosened, allowing certain books to show the forbidden area if they were deemed "artistic." The controversy that led to the law being changed mainly surrounded the release of *Santa Fe*—a book of nude photos of idoru Miyazawa Rie—by the famous Japanese photographer Kishin Shinoyama. Miyazawa was only eighteen at the time and had made her debut in 1989 trading on her childlike innocence. This led to the new category of "hair nude" and increasingly open sexual imagery.

Hakuchi-moé (白痴萌え)**:** Literally "retard-moé," a rather vulgar term. In postwar Japan, *hakuchi* was used to insult those who are mentally challenged, and the antics of such people have come to be seen as "cute" by some otaku. Hakuchi-moé characters are extreme versions of DOJIKKO or HETARE. Those who create these characters truly go to extremes, crafting brainless, spineless, immobile creatures that take NON-ABILITY to unexplored heights. Because it's pretty sick language, it's not a term that should be used in polite company.

Hakujaden (白蛇伝)**:** *The Tale of the White Serpent*. Japan's first animated feature film in color, released by Toei Douga in 1958. Some consider it the first "anime" film, though the musical numbers and animal friends are closer to Disney-style animation. The film is an adaptation of a Chinese folktale and maintains Chinese design styles and names. Among the 13,590 staff on the two-year production was a seventeen-year-old Rintaro, the disciple of TEZUKA OSAMU who would go on to direct classic anime films such as *Adieu Galaxy Express 999*. *Hakujaden* was released in the US in 1961 by Global Pictures as *Panda and the Magic Serpent*, the first anime to make it to America. However, it had a lackluster reception.

Hamaru (はまる)**:** To go crazy for something; to be totally into something. This tendency is key to the otaku spirit and roughly synonymous with saying "my boom" (a personal interest, passion or hobby that one is just coming into).

Hanaji (鼻血)**:** Nosebleed. In Japan this signifies someone who is too excited or is thinking sexy thoughts. In anime and manga, if a character gets a nosebleed it's a sure sign they're a horny pervert.

Hand-lettering: See EGAKIMOJI.

Hanna-Barbera: American animation studio formed in 1944 by MGM animation directors William Hanna and Joseph Barbera. They were largely responsible for the establishment of the Saturday morning cartoon system that reigned from the 1960s to '80s, when weekday syndication eclipsed weekend runs and Turner bought up Hanna-Barbera. It was later absorbed

H

into Time Warner, specifically Warner Bros., Animation. It was the basis of the Cartoon Network until Japanese anime pushed classic cartoons out of prime time. Their shows include *The Huckleberry Hound Show*, *The Flintstones* (the first prime time animation), *Top Cat*, *Tom and Jerry*, *The Yogi Bear Show*, *The Jetsons*, *Jonny Quest*, *Scooby-Doo*, and *The Smurfs*.

Hanryuu or Kanryuu (韓流): The Korean Wave. A boom in South Korean TV, film, music, and idoru that came after the hit drama *Fuyu no Sonata* (*Winter Sonata*) was aired on NHK in 2003. The show was so popular it had 20.4 percent of households in Tokyo watching its 11 p.m. run. This is not unlike the Latin Lover craze that swept the United States around 2000. Until 2008, when they were overtaken by Chinese, Koreans were the largest minority in Japan, and they are still the most deeply embedded in Japanese society. The hanryuu idoru were widely promoted by ethnic Koreans living in Japan.

South Korean TV dramas usually depict beautiful people in beautiful settings living beautiful lives, and they were a throwback to the style of trendy Japanese dramas of the 1980s. The fans were mostly middle-aged Japanese housewives who say Korean men are appealing because they're studly, assertive, and buff—a pleasant side effect of their compulsory military service. They're also seen as being more kind and respectful of women and elders than Japanese men, which comes from the strong Confucian hierarchal values in Korea. Much of the appeal of these dramas was tied to nostalgia for a time that's been lost in Japan; a time when the family was central, gorgeous food was prepared at home, and people cared more for one another.

Many South Korean stars are more popular in Japan than in their own country. The most representative male stars are Bae Yong Joon, or "Yon-sama," Jang Donggeon, Lee Byung-Hun, and Won Bin, the "four kings of Korea" (a name given to them in Japan). Popular female stars include Choi "Princess" Ji Woo and the singer BoA. On August 14, 2007, around 18,000 fans attended the Kanryuu Expo FACE in JAPAN at Tokyo Dome.

Unfortunately not all people were happy with this Korean love-fest and there was a backlash called the *kenkanryuu* (Anti-Korea Wave).

Harajuku (原宿): A shopping district in Tokyo near Shibuya that's dominated by young girls interested in fashion. Fed by the discount and resale shops on streets like Takeshita-dori, it's famous for alternative street fashions—from gothic to punk to decora.

Like most of Tokyo, it was a barren wasteland after the war, but in 1947, Washington Heights, a living quarters for American soldiers, was erected just north of Yoyogi Park nearby. Shops moved to the location to target the foreigners, including Kiddy Land and the antiques store Fujitorii. During the Tokyo Olympics in 1964, Washington Heights was used as the Olympic Village and the area was suddenly full of foreign tourists. Curious Japanese teenagers flocked to Harajuku to see the latest fashions from overseas and the area was infused with new life. In 1970, fashion magazine *Anan* was founded, followed by *Non-no* in 1971, and both of them introduced Harajuku as an emerging chic area. In 1972, a subway station was opened by the park, increasing foot traffic. In 1977 some streets were closed off to vehicular traffic on Sundays, creating a "pedestrian paradise" that allowed shoppers free reign. The following year, the fashion building Laforet opened, followed by more and more fashion shops. Around 1978, kids in brightly colored baggy clothes showed up each weekend to dance in the streets and were labeled the *takenoko-zoku* (bamboo-shoot kids). They disappeared in the mid-1980s and dancing Elvis impersonators took over. Bands of wannabe pop stars began to rock the streets in the late 1980s and on weekends Harajuku was a riot of noise. During the 1990s, the area around Yoyogi Park also began to attract hundreds of Iranian men, who were in Japan as migrant workers but were suddenly unemployed after the recession. Among these men were some who sold drugs and fake phone cards, and from about 1992 the police began to actively patrol the area, making arrests. Many Iranians were deported. In a last-ditch effort to clean up the area the pedestrian paradise was suspended and has never been resurrected. The rock bands moved away; young GOTH-LOLIS moved to Jingubashi Bridge by JR Harajuku Station, and the remaining rockabillies shifted inside Yoyogi Park.

Harajuku is a major tourist destination for Japanese and foreigners alike. There are idoru stores for JOHNNY'S and HELLO! PROJECT, and a massive VOLKS store for doll enthusiasts.

Harem (ハーレム): A genre of anime, manga, and video game narratives that brings a large number of beautiful women together around a single man. The protagonist is typically hopeless with women, so suffers greatly from all the attention. He usually stumbles his way through humorously erotic encounters with all the characters before eventually choosing the one he really wants to be with. Just like dating simulators (see GYARUGE), the variety of female characters is a major selling point for viewers. See also GYAKU HAREM.

H

HELLO! PROJECT STORE IN HARAJUKU

Hatsune Miku (初音ミク): See VOCALOID.

Hayashibara Megumi (林原めぐみ): Born in 1967 in Tokyo. The "Queen of SEIYUU" and the most prolific voice actress of all time, with 236 credits to her name as of 2007. One of the pioneers of the Third Seiyuu Boom in the 1990s. After simultaneously completing her seiyuu training at Arts Vision and getting her nursing license, Hayashibara made her debut in 1986 playing minor roles in *Maison Ikkoku*. She has since played Hello Kitty, Faye Valentine (*Cowboy Bebop*), Lime (*Saber Marionette*), Urashima Haruka (*Love Hina*), Ayanami Rei (*Neon Genesis Evangelion*), Lina Inverse (*Slayers*), Canal Volphied (*Lost Universe*), Piyoko (*Di Gi Charat*), female Ranma Saotome (*Ranma ½*), and many others. She also played Momo from *Magical Princess Minky Momo* (1991), one of the shows credited with encouraging OTAKU to watch *SHOJO* anime. She hosts radio shows, writes books, and has an advice column appearing monthly in *Newtype* magazine.

Hello! Project (ハロー！ プロジェクト): The largest agency for all-female IDORU groups under contract with Up-Front Group. The most famous groups to come out of Hello! Project since it was founded in 1998 are Morning Musume and Berryz Kobo, both beloved by OTAKU. There is a store in HARAJUKU, with branches in Ueno, Osaka, Nagoya, and Kyoto.

NAGAI GO'S HENSHIN SHOJO CUTIE HONEY

Henshin shojo (変身少女): Transforming female characters; ubiquitous in contemporary anime since NAGAI GO's *Cutie Honey* in 1973. Female characters in anime are often depicted as gaining colossal powers through transformations that allow them to triumph over fierce—typically BISHONEN—enemies. A perfect example would be Takeuchi Naoko's girl-power-driven story *Sailor Moon*, or more recently, *Pretty Cure*. For male viewers, anime's portrayal of women's potential for change reflects some of the serious dislocations Japanese society has undergone over the past decades. Women are objectified but also empowered. This shares many themes with the "magical girl" precedent of cuteness and power set by shows such as *Majokko Megu-chan* (1974).

Hentai (変態): Perverted or abnormal person or behaviour; but adopted by English speakers to mean explicit or pornographic ANIME, MANGA, and games. This use is not prevalent in Japan, where erotic materials are usually categorized as *seijin*, AV, or JYUUHACHI KIN. The English use of "hentai" is closer to the Japanese word ECCHI. The original Japanese meaning comes from the 1914 translation of Richard von Krafft-Ebing's *Psychology of Abnormal Sexuality*, or *Hentai Seiyoku Shinri* in Japanese. When wanting to specify that the topic of discussion is media and not a person, the traditional *kanji* is often abandoned in favor of the *katakana* (ヘンタイ).

The first erotic anime in Japan was *Lolita Anime*, followed by *Cream Lemon*, both in 1984. In 1991, Central Park Media in the United States launched its Anime-18 label dealing in adult anime such as the tentacle-sex classic *Urotsuki Doji*. A.D. Vision followed in 1992, releasing some hardcore stuff for its Softcel line. Retailers and fans called this "hentai" to distinguish animated erotica from normal live-action pornography. Hentai anime typically has a bad image because the medium lends itself well to experimentation, private fantasy, exaggeration and fetishism. Some genres in hentai other than straight sex include incest with mother, father, or siblings, *futanari* hermaphrodites, *LOLICON*, rape, S&M, tentacle-sex (see SHOKUSHU-KEI), YAOI (gay), and *YURI* (lesbian)—as well as pretty much any fetish that you can imagine, no matter how disturbing.

THE HENTAI CLASSIC UROTSUKIDOJI

Hetare (ヘタレ): Loser; as in those hapless types we love to cheer on as they try to make it in love and life. Tenchi, the titular character of *Tenchi Muyo!* is an obvious example. See also DAMÉ-ELITE.

Heta-uma (ヘタウマ): Deliberately nonperfect style of drawing manga. So bad (*heta*) that it is good (*uma*). According to *heta-uma* grandmaster Terry Johnson (the alias of pop artist and vinyl record OTAKU Yumura Teruhiko), the aim is to achieve a kind of soulfully bad image,

Hijitsuryoku (非実力): Non-ability. A central OTAKU belief that someone or something is more endearing if it's flawed. It emerged in the 1980s among fans of the amateurish child-idoru comprising the Onyanko Club. Innocence and vulnerability have since come to be one of the core aesthetics of idoru who do their best and sing their hearts out despite their lack of ability and beg the fans to love them. In 1988, Moritaka Chisato would take this to the extreme, openly stating how bad she was and gathering a fanatic following.

There's actually a traditional Japanese fondness for tragic failures—a sympathy known as *hanganbiiki* (判官贔屓), which is like rooting for the underdog.

The concept of non-ability now goes beyond mere idoru and characters to encompass an entire art style (HETA-UMA). Film director and personality Kitano Takeshi also has a regular TV show called *Dare demo Picasso* (Anyone Is Picasso), where he often showcases such dubious talent.

Hiki (ヒキ): Cliffhanger. Nobody likes them, but you buy the next episode to find out what happens. *HENTAI* anime notoriously cut scenes off to force the frustrated viewer to buy the next installment.

Hikikomori (ひきこもり): A social shut-in who never leaves his or her room. This is understood by most to be a symptom of mental illness. Typically these people are bullied at school and are unable to cope with the outside world. Hikikomori can be supported for years by their parents and only communicate with the outside world via their computers. Hikikomori are not necessarily OTAKU and should not be mistaken as such. By definition they lack the ability to communicate and thus withdraw into a passivity that excludes them from even the most basic of tasks; otaku tend to be the opposite, using cultural products (ANIME, MANGA, FIGURES, MAID CAFÉS) for some form of activity. Hikikomori are also often confused with NEET (Not Employed, in Education or Training), social loafers who choose to buck the system by not participating in it fully. NEET, however, can be a badge of honor. People may say "I'm NEET!" but no one would ever say, "I'm hikikomori!"

YOU'RE NOT HIMOTÉ OR HIKIKOMORI ARE YOU ONIICHAN?

Himoté (非モテ): Unpopular, especially with females. Himoté guys believe that the status of women is built on the backs of men, who must slave to earn money and win female attention. In some cases, himoté have a political bent and gather to boycott Christmas, Valentine's, and WHITE DAY, when men are expected to make extravagant "offerings" in the name of romance. They spend a lot of time online, and it's a chicken-or-egg question as to whether they are unpopular because of the theory, or created the theory because they are unpopular.

Hinichijosei (非日常性): A feeling or experience of something odd or beyond the everyday. Many OTAKU see this as the key to any pleasurable response, including MOÉ, ZETTAI RYOIKI, and so on.

Hinnyuu (貧乳): See MUNYUU.

Hiroshima International Animation Festival: Established in 1975 by Kinoshita Renzo and Sayoko. *The Old Film* by TEZUKA OSAMU won the first grand prix. Held every second summer every two years in Hiroshima. Aside from feature screenings and competition, amateur film screenings and workshops are held.

Hiroshima Manga Library (広島市立まんが図書館): Founded in 1997, this is a massive MANGA collection inside the Hiroshima City Library. Hiroshima has a deep history with manga, such as the classic *HADASHI NO GEN*, and since 1985 the biannual

HIROSHIMA INTERNATIONAL ANIMATION FESTIVAL has been held. The library was the first, and remains the largest, public library for manga in Japan, on par with the private collection at the KYOTO INTERNATIONAL MANGA MUSEUM. It has around 137,000 volumes in stock.

Hitokomamanga (一コママンガ): A caricature, or a one-panel cartoon of the type found in news periodicals.

Hizamakura (膝枕): A "knee pillow," specifically a woman's lap when she is kneeling Japanese-style, legs tucked under. It's thought be the height of intimacy for a man to lay his head on his lover's lap. Lonely men, however, end up buying pillows designed to recreate this experience. See also DAKIMAKURA, MONOKATARI NO HITOBITO, and DOLLER.

Hokusai Manga (北斎漫画): Fifteen volumes containing approximately 4,000 humorous drawings and prints done by Ukiyo-e master Hokusai in the early 1800s. These celebrated the comic, the fantastic, and the joy of movement, and they provided the source for the word "manga," or "fanciful pictures."

Honeymation: A version of stop-motion animation employed by ANIME director ANNO HIDEAKI in his live-action adaptation of the NAGAI GO anime *Cutie Honey* in 2004. Anno shot numerous still photos of the main actress, Sato Eriko and then refilmed them as animation.

Host clubs: Clubs where good-looking men, primped-up like MANGA characters, fawn over women. The customers tend to be wives of rich men or are often women working as hostesses. First appeared in 1966. Bisco Hatori's shojo manga *Ouran High School Host Club* (2003–present) is a good reference for what goes down. See DANSO CAFÉ.

Hostess clubs (ホステスクラブ): A form of MIZUSHOBAI entertainment in Japan where good-looking women are hired to sit and talk with male clients. They fawn over the men, light cigarettes, pour drinks, tell amusing stories, and sing KARAOKE. These clubs can be very expensive, and it's not uncommon for the bill to be over $600 for only a couple of hours. Lower quality clubs are sometimes mistaken for hostess clubs. These include "snacks," or "*kyabakura*" (cabaret club), although the latter tends to imply a little more than dinner company is required of the female staff. In such cases, *dohan*, or paid dates, are brokered, and these can involve sex. The pay can be very good at both high- and low-class establishments, and many poor, young, or foreign women and men take up hostessing and hosting. Men called "catches" roam the streets looking for women to recruit for clubs. In 2007, the Japanese government cracked down on illegal employment, deporting many foreign workers and closing clubs. The customers at hostess clubs tend to be groups of SALARIMEN. See also MAID CAFÉ.

I

Ichi Maru Kyuu Biru (109ビル)**:** The 109 Building or Shibuya 109. A famous department store in Shibuya, Tokyo's fashion and club district. It was built not far from JR Shibuya Station in 1979, by the Tokyu Group. 109 is a pun on the company name, which sounds like 10-9, or *tou kyuu* in Japanese. The building is packed with small boutiques selling the outrageous fashions high-school- and college- age women in Toyko wear. It's the epicenter from which Japanese and in turn East Asian girl's fashion originates, and was essential to the formation of 1990's GYARU culture. The building, with its iconic cylindrical shape, is often featured in film, TV, magazines, MANGA, and ANIME.

THE 109 BUILDING IN SHIBUYA

Idol: See IDORU.

iDOLM@STER, THE (アイドルマスター)**:** Or *Aimasu*. An arcade and console rhythm game released by Namco in 2005. The player takes the role of producer, choosing girls from a pool of eleven wannabes, and trying to win fans by teaching the potential IDORU to sing and dance. *Idolm@ster* is extremely popular among OTAKU, who get to control cute girls who aim to please by performing offbeat numbers. In 2007, the game span off into an alternative TV ANIME series, *Idolm@ster: Xenoglossia*. It was produced by the creators of the BISHOJO hits *My-HiME* and *My-Otome*, and recreated the idoru as MECHA fighter pilots. A dream come true for pretty much every otaku—cute singing and dancing girls in giant robots!

Idoru (アイドル)**:** An idol. A highly produced, costumed singer, dancer, or performer who appeals directly to an adoring audience by pandering to their fantasies. They're not loved for their talent so much as their ability to capture the hearts of the audience. Japanese idoru most typically suffer from some kind of NON-ABILITY, perfom to DENPA- style music, and adopt

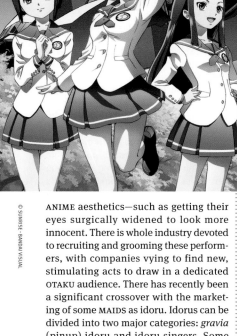

watching her daily activities. They are kind of creepy in a stalker-ish way and rely heavily on CHAKUERO and fantasy suggestion. Basically, no nudity is shown and no boundaries are crossed that would make this pornography; instead viewers are taken to the edge of fantasy by providing all the tools to identify with a dreamy time and place—such as a school or deserted beach—and create a relationship or encounter with the subject. What happens from that point on is all in the mind. Disturbingly, this means even underage girls can, and do, make idoru videos, skirting child protection laws and raising the question, "What the hell are their parents thinking?!" See also JUNIOR IDORU.

I.G: See PRODUCTION I.G.

Ikemen (イケメン): Hot hunks, beautiful boys or sexy men.

Image song (イメージソング): A song inspired by an ANIME, game, or drama, sometimes sung by the actors and actresses in character, and released as a tie-in to a popular series. The idea is to expand a character's personality and feed into the cult of the fans. These songs are not usually in the original work but offer insights into the character or series in question. SEIYUU HAYASHIBARA MEGUMI is likely the most successful image singer, releasing many CDs of character songs and character versions of the songs from popular anime she has appeared in. These songs can also be about a character or series but are not sung by the seiyuu or actors involved.

Imouto café (妹系カフェ): Little-sister café. A place where waitresses pretend to be your little sister—sometimes in school uniforms, other times in frilly get-ups.

ANIME aesthetics—such as getting their eyes surgically widened to look more innocent. There is whole industry devoted to recruiting and grooming these performers, with companies vying to find new, stimulating acts to draw in a dedicated OTAKU audience. There has recently been a significant crossover with the marketing of some MAIDS as idoru. Idorus can be divided into two major categories: *gravia* (pinup) idoru and idoru singers. Some representatives of the former are Ogura Yuko, Hoshino Aki, Koike Eiko; and the latter include Morning Musume (and members such as Fujimoto Miki) or AKB 48, MATSUDA SEIKO, and Koizumi "Kyon Kyon" Kyoko.

Idoru video (アイドルビデオ): Videos that center on idolizing a girl from afar, by

They play games, ask for advice, and have violent mood swings like every sibling does. The first and most famous is Nagomi Pash Café in Akihabara.

Impact lines: See SHUCHUSEN.

INNOCENCE: GHOST IN THE SHELL 2

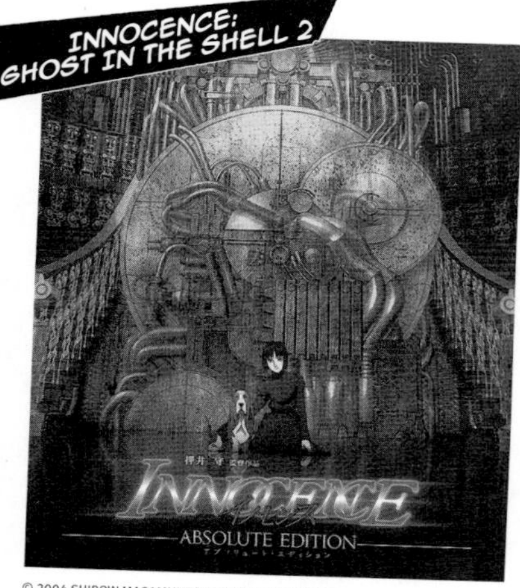

***Innocence: Ghost in the Shell 2*:** The 2004 sequel to the anime film *KOUKAKU KIDOUTAI* (*Ghost in the Shell*, 1995), written and directed by OSHII MAMORU and based on a chapter called "Robot Rondo" from SHIROW MASAMUNE's original *Koukaku Kidoutai* manga. The film cost $20 million to make and was co-produced by PRODUCTION I.G and STUDIO GHIBLI.

SPOILER ALERT!! STOP READING NOW IF YOU DON'T WANT TO KNOW WHAT HAPPENS!

The story follows the character Batou, and is set in 2032 after the events in the first film, when Major Kusanagi merged with the AI hacker known as the Puppet Master and disappeared. Batou is investigating the company Locus Solus and its *gynoid* sex robots. They have malfunctioned, or been tampered with, and killed several clients. These machines have "ghosts" (souls), which are mass-produced by an illegal "dubbing" process that kills human children once their "ghosts" have been copied. Batou is also suffering with memories of his unrequited love for the Major. He storms LOCUS SOLUS and is reunited with her in the form of a hacked gynoid. After Batou saves the children, the gynoid says, "I'll always be with you online," and the Major disappears again.

The film was a finalist for the Palme D'Or award at the Cannes Film Festival in 2004.

International Manga Award: *Kokusaimangashou*. Established in summer 2007 by special order of the Minister of Foreign Affairs at the time, Aso Taro. The award goes to a MANGAKA living abroad who has enhanced manga's popularity and subsequent reader respect for Japan. This is part of the COOL JAPAN movement by the Japanese government to promote pop culture. In 2008, veteran Hong Kong cartoonist Lau Wan Kit took top honors for his *Feel 100%* romance MANGA, which ran from 1992 to 2007 and has been translated into various languages and adapted into film and TV.

WINNERS AT THE 2008 INTERNATIONAL MANGA AWARD

Ishiba Shigeru (石破茂): Born in 1957 in Tottori Prefecture. A politician associated with the Liberal Democratic Party who has been the minister of defense. He is a military and PURAMO OTAKU, and a diehard fan of the IDORU group Candies. While in office, he was instrumental in getting the Self Defense Forces (SDF) to appear in the 2005 movie, *Sengoku Jieitai*, based on a book of which he was a fan. He also wrote the text for a MANGA about the SDF. He is called "*Kimo-ota*" by fans.

Ishinomori Shotaro (石ノ森章太郎): Born in 1938 in Tome, Miyagi Prefecture. Died in 1998. His original pen name was Ishimori, but he changed this in 1984 before writing *Hotel*. He was the "King of MANGA," responsible for such classics as *Cyborg 009*, *Kamen Rider*, and *Genma Wars*—from a novel by Hirai Kazumasa, and a major inspiration behind the apocalyptic beliefs of AUM SHINRIYKO. Ishinomori's mentor was TEZUKA OSAMU, whom he met in 1955 and assisted on *TETSUWAN ATOMU*. Ishinomori is credited with refining the temporal flow in ANIME, as opposed to the still shots and timelessness of many dramatic works. In his *Cyborg 009*—which became Japan's first superhero series in 1963—speeches overlap to represent a constant flow of time. While Hirai and artist Kuwata Jiro's *8 Man* was the first cyborg superhero in 1963, it was Ishinomori's MANGA cyborg *Kamen Rider*, released by Toei in 1971 as a live-action superhero show, that established the transforming, martial artist superhero genre. He also made *Himitsu Go Ranger* (1977), the first of the *Super Sentai* series. Aside from SENTAI, he did much to expand the genres of SF and educational GAKUSHU manga. His work spans 500 volumes and 770 works, noted in the Guinness Book of World Records as the largest corpus ever for a single comic creator.

Itai (イタい): Painful. Also used to describe "The Painful," a group of OTAKU who were deemed too deviant and expressive in their fandom in the early 1990s. At the time, otaku in general were under heavy fire following the MIYAZAKI TSUTOMU INCIDENT, and most went on the lam. Itai were thought to draw undue attention to the fandom at a time when it was shameful to be otaku. Present-day activities such as OTAGEI and objects such as ITASHA are descendants of this. An itai boom occurred in 2008, impetus for a new category of painfully uncool people, activities, and things: *Itai-kei* (itai-style).

Itasha (痛車): Painful car. A car decorated with designs from ANIME, MANGA, or games, usually of sexy female characters. Similar to muscle cars overseas that are decorated with airbrushed images of naked girls and flames. They often have matching interior decorations and are stuffed to the gills with figures, goods, and accessories that go along with the overall theme. The name literally means "it hurts car," (see ITAI) and is a pun on Japanese slang for "Italian car" that reverses supposed classiness into classlessness. Indeed you can't help but recoil when seeing these rolling shrines to anime babes.

idoru • 桜川ひめこ

SAKURAGAWA HIMEKO

SAKURAGAWA HIMEKO (22) MADE HER DEBUT as an Akiba-kei idoru in maid outfit and NEKOMINI in August 2005, just as the maid boom was in full swing. She's gained media attention with her single, "Goin' to Akiba," and in January 2008 she appeared with the actor Tommy Lee Jones in a BOSS canned coffee commercial set in Akihabara.

PG: Why did you start coming to Akiba?

SH: I always liked games, but it was embarrassing if anyone saw me buying them and called me an otaku. I kind of kept it hidden when I was at school. But when I came to Akiba I found that everyone here was like me, so it was OK. It's my favorite place in the world! I feel really relaxed here.

PG: So how did you start out as an idoru?

SH: Well, firstly I was scouted in Harajuku to be a photo idoru. But I wanted to be like my favorite singer, Matsuura Aya from Hello! Project, so when I got the chance to join the Marvel Yell agency and sing in Akiba, I took it. It wasn't my plan to be an Akiba-kei idoru at first, but being so attached to Akiba, it just kind of happened.

PG: What do you like best about being an idoru?

SH: The live performances. Singing and feeling the energy of the audience. You don't sing alone when you're an idoru. My support group, the guys I call "*oniichan*," have always been there. They sing and dance with me, and when I call out, they answer. That is the best thing ever!

PG: How are the fans?

SH: It's a warm relationship. A lot of the regulars have been coming to performances for years. I remember there was this DJ from California who was playing my songs on FM radio in the US, and my Japanese fans helped translate so he could talk to me. It was great!

PG: What is your life like now, after the Boss CM?

SH: Things are really busy! My single "Goin' to Akiba" was rereleased in November 2007, and I'm working hard to be able to sing this song on the *Kōhaku Uta Gassen* (Red and White Singing Battle) TV show on New Year's Eve. I want to spread the joy of Akiba across Japan!

PG: Why is Akihabara so special?

SH: It's such a fun place! If you don't come then you won't know, but everyone here is having fun. It's happy!

PG: How's it changed?

SH: When I debuted, the old station building was there—the Akiba Department Store was still open. There were lots of places to eat, more than now, I think.

PG: I see . . . I mean, how are the live street performances?

SH: To be honest, I've never actually done a live performance on the street. But for the "Goin' to Akiba" music video I wanted to capture a place everyone knows, so we filmed it on Chuo-dori street when it was still closed to traffic on Sundays. I'm a little sad when people say there's a gap between the ways things look in the video and the street now. But this won't last. Akiba will get back to the way it was.

Internationally renowned pop artist MURAKAMI TAKASHI has said that "Itasha is the desire to be seen and the joy of being embarrassed. It's like S/M play, with heavy emphasis on the M component." Drivers are typically between twenty and fifty years old and ride in packs, often gathering in carparks to show off. Due to media attention, there was a boom in 2008. Magi, the organizer of Fuji Speedway Itasha Meeting held in May 2008, reports that more than 300 itasha registered. *ItaG*, a nationally syndicated magazine, organized another "festa" in front of Fuji TV in Odaiba on November 2008. Aside from the increasing costs of cars and gasoline, some spend $10,000 or more on decorating their wheels. But others have taken to drawing and applying their own itasha decals. For those wannabes who can't afford a car, the solution has been the emergence a new kind of itai bike gang culture. *Itansha*, or itai motorcycles, are equipped with TVs tuned to anime and booming sound systems playing anime theme songs. Further down the food chain are *itachari*, or "painful chariots," pedal bikes tricked out with anime images in the spokes of the wheels. The itai boom extended even to *itumblers*, or "painful coffee mugs" (no joke) with printouts of BISHOJO babes inserted in the customizable image plates. Owners invade the chic café space, line up their cups, and take pictures.

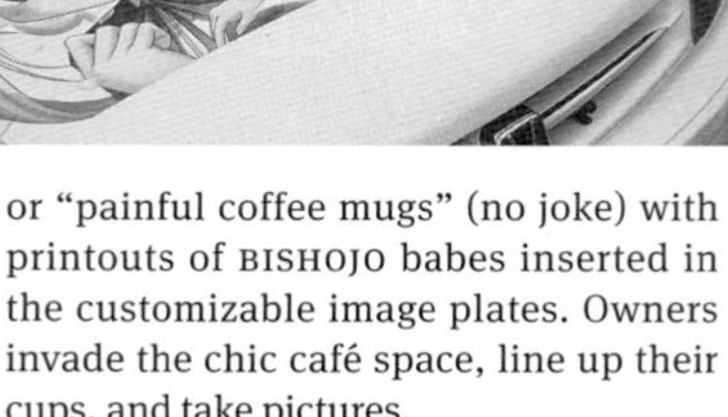

ITASHA AT COMIKET

ITASHA

Amid the current itasha boom, some OTAKU have taken to calling their cars *moésha*, or moé cars. They believe this sounds better than itasha, which has a negative meaning. The annual Moésha Meeting in Kanishi, Gifu Prefecture, drew 600 cars in 2008.

Iyashi-kei (癒し系): Healing; relaxing or soothing. One of the key things sought by OTAKU. This is also a form of MAID CAFÉ noted for the calming influence of the design and attention to atmosphere.

J.A.I.L.E.D.: The Japanese Animation Industry Legal Enforcement Division, formed in 1995 to combat the distribution of unlicensed anime series by tape traders at SF conventions in the United States. Central Park Media and US Manga Corps were the founders, and VIZ was its most active member. They had a lawyer on call and an anonymous 1-800 tip line. Some people actually ratted on fans and a few fan-subs were seized by VIZ. Its presence at conventions died down after 1997, and after 2000 its status was unknown. Most companies look out for their own products, making the organization irrelevant.

Japan e-Sports Association, The: See NIHON E-SUPOTSU KYOUKAI.

Japan Expo: Held annually in Paris, this is the largest event in Europe devoted to ANIME, MANGA, and OTAKU culture. As many as 70,000 people attend over the course of a few days.

Japanimation (ジャパニメーション): An American term for Japanese ANIME. It was popular in the 1980s when anime was making headway in the United States, but has since fallen out of fashion.

Jishu seisaku (自主製作): A privately funded and produced work. Director and creator SHINKAI MAKOTO's ANIME film *Voices of a Distant Star* is a good example.

Jisshaban (実写版): Live-action film version. Generally of an ANIME, video game, or MANGA.

Jitakukeibiin (自宅警備員): Home security guard. An OTAKU joke, said when asked what their job is, implying they spend all day at home holding down the fort.

Johnny's Entertainment (ジャニーズ・エンタテイメント): The top male talent agency in Japan, famous for producing beautiful, and disposable, boy bands. Famous alumni include Tokio, SMAP, Kinki Kids, Arashi, and News. Every weekend hundreds of woman line up in HARAJUKU to enter the Johnny's shop, a spectacle that is startlingly similar to OTAKU lining up to get into the HELLO! PROJECT store nearby or to get tickets for AKB 48 concerts in AKIHABARA.

Jojoga (抒情画): Lyrical pictures. Mostly pre-WWII illustrations of beautiful young girls and boys in idealized positions—boys being macho and fighting, girls being pretty and passive. Magazines such as *Shojo's Friend* came out of this tradition.

Josei no otaku (女性のオタク): A female OTAKU; distinct from FUJOSHI because these women don't read YAOI or BOYS' LOVE MANGA and tend to be interested in more general otaku things. A woman who collects FIGURES, for example, would likely be called "josei no otaku," not "fujoshi."

Joshiryo (女子寮): Girls' dormitory. A space decorated to look like a girl's boarding school bedroom. These are essentially lounges in areas like AKIHABARA that provide the fantasy of entering an all-girls' sleeping quarters. Female staff dress up in pajamas and are available to play tabletop or video games with in their "rooms."

JOSHIRYO CAFÉ CHEKI

Josoko (じょそこ): A guy who CROSSPLAYS as a female character.

J-Pop: Japanese pop music. Recently, J-Rock, J-Jazz, and many other distinctions have been made. There are similar terms for the music of other East Asian nations, such as K-Pop (Korea) and C-Pop (China).

Junai (純愛): Pure love. Images in which a loving but not explicitly sexual relationship is depicted or implied. The purity and innocence of the characters are the main appeal. This is the most innocent of the four major types of MOÉ.

Junior idoru (ジュニア・アイドル): Girls aged three to fifteen years old who appear in IDORU videos. The genre really took off in the 1990s, when columnist Nakamori Akio coined the term "*CHIDOL*" (child + idol) to describe the sudden influx of young models. The neologism was replaced by "junior idoru," which shifted the emphasis from children to the more acceptable idoru-in-training image.

It's hard to imagine that these don't explicitly target pedophiles, but as in the videos of older idoru, there is no sex, and the emphasis is on nostalgic settings and platonic relationships. As disturbing as these videos are, they're a recognized genre in Japan. Junior idoru are popular among LOLICON and MOÉ fans. For such men, there is a nationally syndicated magazine, *Moékko*, and an outlet store for videos, Oimoya in AKIHABARA. Of the junior idoru appearing at Oimoya, about 70 percent are from a company called Charm Kids, boasting a roster of around a hundred girls. A few of these young girls go on to be idoru, tarento, or AV stars, but most just disappear from public view. In March 2008, UNICEF Japan called for a ban on child pornography, in which they included junior idoru media. The issue has yet to be resolved.

***Jyanguru Taitei* (ジャングル大帝):** *Jungle Emperor*, a 1965 ANIME TV series by TEZUKA OSAMU adapted from his MANGA about a white lion that becomes the king of the African savannah. It's often rendered in English as *Kimba the White Lion* or *Jungle Emperor Leo*. It was one of the first anime to really capture a female audience in the United States, which can be attributed to the cast of cute characters and the deep emotional impact of the romantic epic. Startling similarities with Disney's 1994 film *The Lion King* caused a major controversy. Tezuka tells of Kimba, Disney of Simba. Entire splash panels, images, and angles from Tezuka's work are present in the Disney film, including the famous image of Mufasa on Pride

JYANGURU TAITEI BY TEZUKA OSAMU

Rock. Nonetheless, Disney's legal team claimed its animators were not influenced by Tezuka's work and all similarities are purely coincidental. The Tezuka estate never pursued legal action because Tezuka was a fan of Disney, and the issue was forever resigned to speculation.

Jyuuhachi kin (18禁): R-18; X-rated; banned for people below the age of 18. Used to mark pornography.

Kage animeshon (影アニメーション): Shadow animation. A type of animation in which shadows produced by black paper silhouettes are filmed. German silhouette animation was imported to Japan in the 1920s and flourished during the silent-film era. Some of the famous works are *The Dream of Madame Butterfly* (1940) and *Kujira* (1953).

Kageyama Hironobu (影山ヒロノブ): Born in 1961 in Osaka. The "God of ANISONGS." One of the most prominent performers of ANIME, and TOKUSATSU theme songs. Kageyama got his break when he was sixteen and by the early 1980s found major success. Kageyama went on to be dubbed the "Prince of Anime and Tokusatsu Songs." He was also given the nickname "Mr. DBZ" by fans of *Dragon Ball Z* when he did most of the songs for that insanely popular SHONEN ANIME. Over time, he rose to godlike status, thus his present nickname. He is an original member and the current leader of the popular vocal group JAM Project. Along with Endoh Masaaki, he hosts *Anipara Ongakukan*, a TV show aired on Kids Station Channel.

Kaiju (怪獣): Strange beast. A monster of the type seen in Japanese TOKUSATSU (special effects) films. They are similar to those in classic monster movies in the United States, but with more elaborate costumes and special effects. There are also subcategories, including *kaijin* monster men, *daikaiju* giant monsters, and *yokai* ghouls.

Kaiju movies feature these giants attacking cities in rages or flattening them while fighting other kaiju. Kaiju and the tokusatsu genre started with *Godzilla* in 1954. The film's director, Honda Ishiro, and special effects wizard Tsuburaya Eiji were inspired by the American film *King Kong* (1933) and formulated the Japanese genre. Their techniques included "suitmation," which was basically a human actor in costume playing a giant monster on miniature sets. Other kaiju include Gamera, Mothra, Anguirus, Rodan, King Ghidorah, and the *Ultraman* kaiju.

Kaiju are usually organic in design, being modeled after animals, insects, or mythological creatures.

Kaikai Kiki (カイカイキキ): An artists' collective created by MURAKAMI TAKASHI.

NOBODY DIES BY THE KAIKAI KIKI ARTIST, MR.

It was originally called Hiropon Factory and was founded in 1996 along the lines of Andy Warhol's Factory. It was renamed Kaikai Kiki in 2001. It manages Murakami's many assistants, collaborators, and protégés. There are 130 employees in offices in New York and Tokyo. The organization produces art for gallery exhibitions, merchandise, and puts on the biannual Tokyo art fair GEISAI. Kaikai Kiki has been successful in establishing young artists in Japan and drawing international interest in their work. Examples include Takano Aya, Aoshima Chiho, and Mr., an OTAKU who enjoys drawing LOLICON girls. Mr. released his first live-action film in 2008, *Nobody Dies*, about schoolgirls who are into survival games. Kaikai Kiki also has an animation studio and Murakami's first original animation feature film, *kaikai & kiki*, is being produced for a 2010 release.

Kaiyodo (海洋堂): A Japanese company established in Osaka in 1964 that pioneered SHOKUGAN, food or candy with toy prizes, and later became known for model FIGURES. It initially worked closely with various confectionary companies, but has been working independently since 1982. Its early products include the *Aqualand* and *Dinoland* diorama series, and it has also developed miniature city and countryside settings for movies. Kaiyodo was influential in the GARAGE KIT boom in the 1980s and now run WONDER FESTIVAL. It has produced over 2,000 items, including ANIME, MANGA, and game FIGURES. It is widely considered the world's best model maker due to its fetishistic attention to detail regardless of the subject's size, artistic difficulty, or content. In 2004, it began releasing the *Weekly Dearest My Brother* little girl figures, very MOÉ stuff. The Monsieur BOME collection of BISHOJO figures has been displayed in art spaces worldwide. Kaiyodo moved its Tokyo store from SHIBUYA to AKIHABARA in 1997, and has a museum in Nagahama, Shiga Prefecture.

FIST OF THE NORTH STAR FIGURES BY KAIYODO

Kaiyodo Figure Museum (海洋堂フィギュアミュージアム): Located in Nagahama, Shiga, near Biwako, Japan's largest lake. The museum was founded in 2005 and traces the evolution of the KAIYODO company. It's one of the largest repositories of model FIGURES and the first museum space for figures in Japan. An enormous Tyrannosaurus Rex head welcomes guests to the museum, and inside there are roughly 200 dioramas with several thousand figures. Major sculptors in the Kaiyodo stable are given space to strut their stuff, including BOME for BISHOJO, Kagawa Masahiko for classic ANIME and movies, Yamaguchi Katsuhisa for MECHA and anime, and Kinoshita Kashi for TOKUSATSU and SENTAI heroes.

Kaizoku-ban (海賊版): Pirated or illegal versions of a product. Bootlegs of Japanese MANGA in particular were popular in Korea before the 1990s—due to restrictive import laws—as are copies of Japanese movies and ANIME in China today.

Kakioroshi (書き下ろし): A newly written text or drawn work. A commissioned work.

Kamerakozo (カメラ小僧): Camera kids. Also known as *kameko* or *kamera-zoku*, these are the dedicated hobby photographers who take pictures of IDORU, COSPLAYers, and singers. Photographers of this kind were once stereotyped as older men, in their forties or fifties, who liked cameras and pretty girls; but that has been changing recently. In general they can seem creepy, but they are usually polite, if sometimes pushy and obsessive about getting the perfect shot. Much of an idoru, cosplayer, or singer's fame and publicity is generated by these fans. They often form friendships with the people they shoot, and provide them with high-quality photos as thanks for posing. They usually check with the subject to make sure the shot is OK, and may carry portable printers to give images over on the spot. The photo albums of street idoru and cosplayers are usually full of shots taken by kamerakozo.

Kami animeshon: See KIRIE.

Kamishibai (紙芝居): Paper drama. Narrating a story with illustrated plates, which are removed to reveal more images as the story progresses. It originated in the 12th century as a way for Buddhist monks to preach to the mostly illiterate audience, and it made a comeback in the 1920s, and after WWII, as a cheap form of entertainment. This popular form of amusement influenced the development of MANGA and ANIME forms of storytelling that center on images and are episodic.

Kan cosu (完コス): Complete COSPLAY. A highly intense approach to cosplay that borders on religious zeal. Someone into *kan cosu* doesn't put on a costume just to look good, have fun, or pose, but tries to actually become the character as accurately as possible in appearance, thought, and action. See also KIGURUMI.

KAMERAKOZO AT COMIKET

Kanno Yoko (菅野よう子): Born 1964 in Sendai, Miyagi Prefecture. Composer, arranger, and musician best known for her work on the soundtracks for many seminal ANIME and games. She's mastered a variety of musical styles and has a taste for unique musical fusions. She has written the scores for *Macross Plus* (1994), *Cowboy Bebop* (1998), *Vision of Escaflowne* (1996), *Ghost in the Shell: Stand Alone Complex* (2003), and *Wolf's Rain* (2003), and she is the most trusted composer by veteran and new-wave directors such as TOMINO YOSHIYUKI, WATANABE SHINICHIRO, and KAWAMORI SHOJI. Kanno has also composed music for J-POP artists, the most notable being Sakamoto Maaya and Koizumi Kyoko. She's also the front woman for The Seatbelts, who've performed Kanno's compositions on various anime soundtracks.

Kan-zume (缶詰): Canning; canned goods. Also slang for when editors in Japan attempt to control their MANGAKA by "canning" them away from outside influence and distraction, such as keeping them locked in a hotel room. This process means editors can force their artists to meet deadlines and micro-manage the content. This is one of the reasons editors carry such weight in the production of MANGA; they are the ones responsible for the polished product that goes to market.

Kaomoji (顔文字): An emoticon, or the faces and images—either textual or graphic—that convey emotional messages in text messages of e-mail. For example: (^3^). See also AA.

Karaoke (カラオケ): Empty orchestra. The wildly popular Japanese pastime of singing to hit tunes that've had the vocal track removed. The NHK TV show *Nodo Jiman* from 1946 to the present features karaoke enthusiasts competitively strutting their stuff on stage to a national audience.

KARAOKE BUILDING IN SHIBUYA

Kashihon (貸本): Rental books or MANGA. They were especially popular in the 1950s. At the time, story-oriented manga targeting adults tended to be found in books or anthologies rather than in manga magazines. But because these books were expensive they were rented rather than sold. The rental stores (KASHIHONYA) tolerated more experimental and offensive work than magazines, which was ideal for up and coming leftist, politically charged GEKIGA manga. Gekiga began to boom in the 1960s, and magazines specializing in the content, such as *GARO* (founded 1964), began to appear. This spelled the beginning of the end of the kashihon, though they persisted along into the 1970s.

Kashihonya (貸本屋): Rental libraries in the early days of MANGA fandom where youth would go to read the latest manga and rent them instead of making an expensive purchase. Kashihonya no longer exist but their spirit lives on in MANGA KISSA.

Kasou genjitsu to sennou (仮想現実と洗脳): Virtual reality and brainwashing. The classic media representation of the OTAKU mind; disconnected from reality by lascivious fantasy. This feeds the comparisons to cultists and psychos that began in the 1990s following the MIYAZAKI TSUTOMU

K

INCIDENT and fueled by the AUM SHINRIKYO cult.

Kato Tomohiro (加藤智大): See AKIHABARA INCIDENT.

Katsuta Seiyuu-Gakuin (勝田声優学院): Katsuta SEIYUU Academy. A voice actor and actress training center founded in 1982 by Katsuta Hisashi, the SEIYUU who voiced Dr. Ochanomizu in *TETSUWAN ATOMU*. Famous alumni include Mitsuishi Kotono, Yokoyama Chisa, and Imai Yuka.

Katyusha (カチュウシャ): A headdress. The lace headband maids wear. Possibly named after the character Katúsha from Leo Tolstoy's novel *Resurrection*.

Kawaii (かわいい): Cute. Because this word appears in almost every conversation among Japanese girls, it's often one of the first words picked up by ANIME fans. It may be the single most common word in Japan, and the constant squeals of "*Kawaii! Kawaii!*" used by girls to describe just about anything can at times be nauseating.

Since the 1970s, companies have created products that target the *SHOJO* (young girl) market and driven home the message that kawaii is good. Japanese women are now *supposed* to be kawaii. In Japan, kawaii is an almost universal cult that finds expression in everything from pet dogs and pop stars to cartoon mascots and merchandise. Official documents for the government and police are even kawaii to make them less threatening.

In March 2009, the Japanese Ministry of Foreign Affairs appointed three young female models to be Japan's international "ambassadors of cute" (*kawaii taishi*). Each of the girls will wear a different style of cute fashion: Lolita (Aoki Misako), Harajuku (Kimura Yu) and schoolgirl (Fujioka Shizuka). See also GOTH-LOLI, HARAJUKU, SEIFUKU, ANIME AMBASSADOR.

Kawamori Shoji (河森正治): Born in 1960 in Toyama Prefecture, and raised in Yokohama. Renowned mechanical designer who played a key role in such notable ANIME series as *The Vision of Escaflowne*, *Earth Girl Arjuna*, and *Genesis of Aquarion*. He is best known for his MECHA designs in the *MACROSS* franchise, including *Super Dimension Fortress Macross*, *Macross Plus*, *MACROSS Zero*, *Macross F*, and so on. He has also worked as a script writer and director. A graduate of the engineering department of Keio University, he is well known for his application of engineering and real science to sci-fi settings.

Kawanabe Kyosai (河鍋暁斎): Born in 1831 in Kogashi, Ibaraki Prefecture. Died in 1889. Often called the Meiji master of the gag MANGA, Kyosai was a student of the European comic style and one of the forefathers of manga style.

***Kaze no Tani no Nausicaä* (風の谷のナウシカ):** *Nausicaä of the Valley of the Wind*. A seven-volume MANGA series created between 1982 and 1994 by MIYAZAKI

HAYAO. In 1984 he adapted it into the landmark animated film that established STUDIO GHIBLI. Miyazaki's friend and mentor Takahata Isao produced the film, and Hisaishi Joe created the soundtrack. Among the many animators Miyazaki hired to work on the film was a young ANNO HIDEAKI of *Evangelion* fame.

Nausicaä takes place a millennium after the "Seven Days of Fire" devastated both humanity and the Earth's ecosystem. The humans that remain live in constant fear of the spreading Sea of Decay, a toxic jungle of giant plants and fungi swarming with giant, volatile insects. The protagonist is Nausicaä, a character inspired by Nausicaä from Homer's *Odyssey* and the Japanese folktale "The Princess who Loved Insects."

COURTESY WANI BOOKS

KEGADOL BY WANI BOOKS

Nausicaä seeks a cure to restore Earth's ecosystem but becomes involved in a war between the Kingdom of Torumekia and the Dorok Empire, who are fighting over the remaining inhabitable areas of the planet. Nausicaä has the ability to communicate with the giant Ohmu insects that roam the wasteland, and ultimately she's able to create a peace where humans and insects can coexist in harmony.

SPOILER ALERT!! STOP READING NOW IF YOU DON'T WANT TO KNOW WHAT HAPPENS!

Because of the film's strong environmental message, *Nausicaä* was supported by the World Wide Fund for Nature. It sold almost a million tickets when released and won the Animage Anime Grand Prix prize. However, the English-language dub of the film was a disaster. It was renamed *Warriors of the Wind* and heavily edited, causing Miyazaki to curtly suggest people put it "out of their minds." An uncut DVD version of *Nausicaä* made it around the world in 2005, thanks to Buena Vista Home Entertainment, Optimum Home Entertainment and Madman Entertainment.

Kegadol (ケガドル): Injured idol. An IDORU wearing bandages and an eye patch. It was a big boom in the darker corners of the GOTH-LOLI world before moving to idoru. It's similar to the *mask-musume* (girl in a surgical mask) and *megane-moé* (glasses moé) appeal of covering up the face and emphasizing the need to be protected. The most popular of these characters is Ayanami Rei from *Neon Genesis Evangelion* (1995), who is injured several times. Kegadol characters have also been seen in *Ikki Tousen* (2003), *Full Metal Alchemist* (2003–2004), *Bleach* (2004–present), *D. Gray Man* (2006–2008), and even Quentin Tarantino's film *Kill Bill* (2003). In 2008, Wani Books put out a photo album called *Kegadol* that featured the likes of GRAVIA idoru Nakamura Miu.

Keitai (ケイタイ): Abbreviation for "*keitai denwa*," or cellular phone. Because of their affordability, almost all working adults in Japan have keitai. According to a government survey in 2008, 31.3 percent of elementary-school students, 57.6 percent of middle-school students, and 96 percent of high-schoolers had keitai. Research from Net Asia, in the same year, adds that as many as 22.3 percent of Japanese see themselves as keitai addicts. And who can blame them? Standard features include photo and video camera, picture e-mail, games, GPS navigation, music players, 3G services, a barcode reader for QR CODES, credit card and pass ID functions, TV, and Internet. With so much to do on them, people in Japan seem to be constantly fiddling with their keitai, especially during long commutes to and from work. Talking on the phone is frowned upon in trains, so people tend to make use of keitai e-mail, using AA and KAOMOJI to have lively conversations. A single message can be 10,000 characters long, and some people literally write novels (*KEITAI SHOSETSU*). MANGA, games, and ANIME music are available for the keitai, and even older companies such as Toei Animation are releasing content for the keitai. In 2008, the anime *Count and Fairy*, suffering from poor broadcast coverage, became free to download for the keitai.

Keitai shosetsu (ケイタイ小説): KEITAI novels. Books written on mobile phones that are uploaded to sites for other keitai users to download and read. The use of keitai has become so habitual that text messaging is now a desired style of writing for some budding authors and has become a booming genre. In 2007, half of the ten best-selling books in Japan started as keitai novels. One of the most successful keitai novels so far is *Deep Love* by Yoshi, published in 2002 and since then adapted into MANGA, ANIME, and a live-action film.

Kenage (健気): Brave; gallant; manly. Someone who never gives up on dreams despite copious difficulties.

Kewpie (キューピー): A Cherub-like baby character created by Rose O'Neill in 1909 to run in comic illustrations in *Ladies' Home Journal*. With a cute face and "Keep Smiling" motto, Kewpie became a smash hit. O'Neill got wise and put out patented dolls and figurines in 1913, becoming the world's first case of comic character merchandising. The celluloid or ceramic products were made in Ohrdruf, Germany, famous for its toy manufacturers. Kewpies were highly collectible and sparked a global craze. Kewpee Hamburgers came to the States in 1923; the Q.P. Corporation's famous mayonnaise hit Japan in 1925; and Kewpie was enshrined in the Time Capsule at the World Fair in 1939. The first plastic versions came in 1949, making them more affordable and prevalent. Kewpie mayonnaise with the mascot logo is still very prevalent in Japan. KEITAI straps of this character are extremely popular, and there is a range that have the dolls dressed up in various costumes, ranging from schoolgirl uniform and OTAKU to an otaku dressed as a schoolgirl.

KEWPIE KEITAI STRAP

© ONLY-ONE

Key: One of the most successful dating simulator game (GYARUGE) makers in Japan, founded in Osaka in 1998. Key games are distinguished by their highly emotional and complex story lines, and lush soundtracks. Some of their most popular games include *Kanon*, *Air*, and *Clannad*. The male characters are allowed a personality, and their faces are shown, which is rare in dating sims. The player is therefore more passive than normal and ends up getting more emotionally involved than sexually involved. Because of that, these games are sometimes called "crying games." KYOTO ANIMATION is responsible for the popular anime versions of Key's games. See also NOVEL GAMES.

Kichijoji (吉祥寺): A suburb in western Tokyo. Sometimes referred to as the "Anime Town" due to the high density of studios in the area, including STUDIO 4°C, Studio Deen, and Studio Pierrot. This is a byproduct of its historical position as an artist colony. Artmic, the powerhouse behind *Megazone 23* and *Genesis Climber MOSPEADA*, was also located here before closing its doors in 1997; the building still stands, a sacred spot for MECHA fans. Kichijoji was a booming hobby town in the 1990s when resin kits were the rage. Be-j modelers, one of the best stores of its kind, still remains. Also of note are the playful and creative Ghibli Museum in Inokashira Park, the Capcom Plaza arcade, and the annual Anime Wonderland festival. Kichijoji is now home to a bustling MANGAKA community.

Kichiku (鬼畜): Brute. A cruel character who simply does not consider the feelings of others in pursuit of personal satisfaction. It's often applied to male characters in YAOI DOUJINSHI and BL MANGA. The *SEME*, or dominant male partner, is often kichiku because they must act as masters to break in the *UKE* submissive. Kichiku types are stereotypically tall, brooding, and stern, and wear glasses and suits—major MOÉ points for FUJOSHI.

Kichiku-kei (鬼畜系): Extremely brutal, or sexually violent, ANIME, MANGA, or games, often featuring all the worst stereotypes of HENTAI (rape, torture, and brutality). This term refers to both YAOI and straight contexts. An early example is NAGAI GO's *Devilman Lady* from 1997.

***Kido Senshi Gundam* (機動戦士ガンダム):** *Mobile Suit Gundam*. Japan's most popular MECHA ANIME, created in 1979 by TOMINO YOSHIYUKI and a changing group of creators at Sunrise working under the pseudonym "Yatate Hajime."

There are numerous series in seven different timelines and universes. What connects them all is the existence of space colonies and mobile suits such as

KIDO SENSHI GUNDAM

the Gundams, which are massive bipedal robots controlled by a human pilot from a cockpit in the torso. The planned title was *Gunboy*, but this was apparently changed to "Gundam" in reference to a 1978 commercial for the male cosmetics brand Mandom (human freedom), in which veteran actor Charles Bronson delivered the iconic line, "Mm, Mandom."

SPOILER ALERT!! STOP READING NOW IF YOU DON'T WANT TO KNOW WHAT HAPPENS!

Mobile Suit Gundam takes place in the Universal Century, when humans have colonized space and the Principality of Zeon is rebelling against the Earth Federation. Zeon has developed mobile suits, Zaku, for combat in space, and these prove to be far more powerful than anything the Earth can muster. The Earth has a weapon of its own, the super-powered mobile suit Gundam, but Zeon attacks colony Side 7 as the Earth Federation ship carrying the mobile suit is in dock. Amuro Ray, the angsty adolescent son of Gundam's inventor, reads the instruction manual and pilots Gundam to save the people he loves, including his female friend Frau Bow. The two get swept up in the One Year War, and aboard the flying fortress *White Base* it is revealed that Amuro is a NEWTYPE human. He is forced to grow up, but is in constant emotional and physical conflict with his family, friends, and shipmates. He has crushes on an older woman, Matilda Ajan, and an enemy pilot, Lalah Sune; he feels connected to his masked rival, Char Aznable from Zeon, but also despises him. Char's sister, Sayla Mass, is one of Amuro's shipmates, and Char is actually trying to destroy Zeon from within to avenge his murdered family and sweep away the corrupt monarchy.

The show was originally sponsored by the toy company Clover, which started funding anime in 1977 with *Zanbot III*, a super-robot series with samurai-style MECHA designs produced by studio Nippon Sunrise (later just Sunrise). But while it involved robots, *Gundam* was not a super-robot series like *Zanbot III*. Director Tomino Yoshiyuki changed the formula by not focusing on the mecha so much as the human drama of his space opera. The show struggled for realism in characters, technology, weaponry, and setting, and mecha robots were just tools in a brutal, political war that can't be simplified to good and evil. In fact, the samurai-style Gundam and other mecha designs changed late in production, and Clover ended up releasing toys based on earlier designs that were not popular with fans of the realistic mecha they saw in the show. The complex plot and characters attracted older fans who did not want toys made for kids. Ratings were sagging for Tomino's slow-moving anime too, exacerbating the problem for Clover. The series won the Animage Anime Grand Prix prize in 1979, but Clover pulled the plug on *Gundam* in January 1980 after just forty-three of

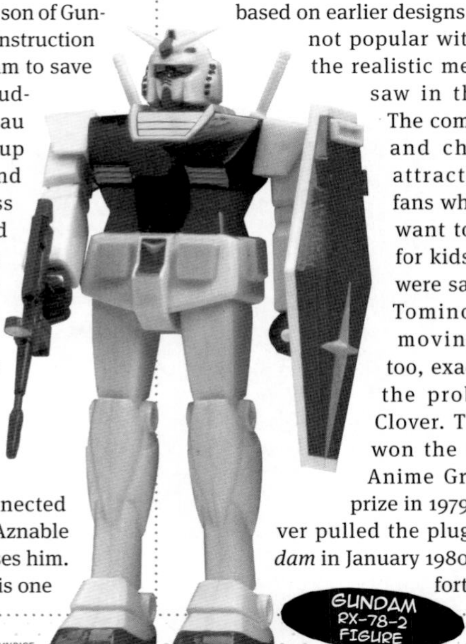

GUNDAM RX-78-2 FIGURE

the planned fifty-two episodes. Fans campaigned for the return of the show, impetus to Sunrise's three hit movie editions of the series (1981–82). While Clover struggled to push its toys, BANDAI acquired the exclusive rights to make highly detailed, standard-scale, affordable plastic models of the *Gundam* mecha. They hit the shelves in 1980, and fans went into a feeding frenzy fighting over limited stock. The realism of the plastic models changed the face of the toy industry and lured older, discriminating fans, that is, OTAKU. Many series in the 1980s featured realistic mecha tied to sponsorship by toy makers. Of course, various movies, sequels, OVAs, and spin-offs from the *Gundam* franchise were among these.

The show did well in Hong Kong and much of Asia. It was licensed to be shown in the US on Toonami in 2001, but met lukewarm reception. *Macross*, or rather *Robotech*, had hit the States first and had a strong following. The common image of *Gundam* is the US is *Gundam Wing*, a spin-off BISHONEN series that hit on Toonami in 2000.

The perennial series is by now a staple of Japanese culture, and when the original *Gundam* was released on DVD in Japan in 2007 it sold over 100,000 copies in a month. There are *Gundam* stamps at the post office, and both the Japanese Self Defense Forces and fire department have made *Gundam* references in the names of advanced projects. Both Isuzu and Mitsubishi have created concept cars based on Gundams, and Mitsubishi produced a recruiting video called, "How to Make a Gundam." There is a statue located in Kamiigusa, near Shinjuku, where Sunrise has its offices. The train station there plays the *Gundam* theme song as a boarding chime; the Bandai offices in Kuramae have elevators that speak famous *Gundam* lines; and the Bandai Museum, located in Tochigi Prefecture, boasts a 1:1 scale Gundam head. In 2008, an ink painting of a Gundam was sold at a Christie's auction for $600,000. The International Gundam Society was founded on August 24, 2008, the first academic organization based on an anime. To commemorate the 30th anniversary of *Gundam*'s original broadcast, an eighteen meter statue of the RX-78-2 Gundam was erected in Odaiba, Tokyo, in June 2009.

Kigurumi (着グルミ): Kind of creepy cosplayers who add full-head masks, gloves, and socks to their costumes so that not a single piece of flesh can be seen. Because of the uncomfortable costume the hobby is dominated by men, but they tend to dress up as female characters. Anikao Shizuka, an IDORU in AKIHABARA is known for wearing a kigurumi BISHOJO mask. Because she can't speak in the mask, she pantomimes and writes messages on a board she carries.

ANIKAO SHIZUKA WEARING A KIGURUMI MASK

Kimezerifu (キメゼリフ): A sound bite that sticks with viewers and brands a character, show, or product. For example: "For love and justice, the pretty soldier in a sailor suit, Sailor Moon! In the name of the moon, I'll punish you!" See also SOUND DROPS, which often make use of these.

Kimoi (キモい): Gross.

Kimokawaii (キモかわい): Gross but cute. A kind of cuteness where something repugnant somehow becomes alluring. For example, MIYAZAKI HAYAO's creepy character Ponyo is very kimokawaii.

I'D RATHER BE A KOGAL THAN A CYBORG ANY DAY!!

Kimoota (キモオタ): A gross OTAKU, or an otaku who goes far beyond the pale.

Kinsella, Sharon: Born in 1969 in Hampshire, England. A researcher based in Britain with a Ph.D. in sociology from Oxford University. She conducts cross-cultural research into emerging social trends among youth, the media, subculture, corporate culture, and new modes of governance. She was instrumental in early English definitions of KAWAII, OTAKU culture in the 1990s, and Japanese female subcultures. Her most important works include the book *Adult Manga* and the essays "Cuties in Japan" and "What's behind the fetishism of schoolgirls' uniforms in Japan?" Her second book, *Girls as Energy: Fantasies of rejuvenation in contemporary society*, focuses on SHOJO and GYARU images in Japanese media.

Kirie (切り絵): Cutout animation, also known as *kami animeshon*. Shapes made of paper or other material designed to be seen in different poses. When filmed, they appear to move, like the fabric characters of *South Park*. Basically, this is animation where the drawn CEL image is replaced by a paper or material one.

Kisekae ningyo (着せ替え人形): Dress-up dolls. Especially of the virtual variety downloaded and customized on the Internet. They were very popular in the 1990s under the name KiSS dolls. These were originally aimed at young girls but were appropriated by OTAKU who played with them as they did with ERO-GE.

Kishotenketsu (起承転結): Introduction-development-turn-conclusion. The classic narrative pattern of Chinese poetry adopted by early Japanese. It's also the basic narrative principle of four-panel comic strips, as well as most of TEZUKA OSAMU'S works.

Kiwameru (究める): To master or study thoroughly; to carry to extremes.

Kogal or kogyaru (コギャル): A young gal. A subculture of Japanese teenage girls that was particularly prevalent in Shibuya in the mid-1990s. The most stereotypical type were those in high-school uniform, who would hitch up their skirts to micro-mini lengths and wear baggy LOOSE SOCKS bunched around their ankles. They tended to have fake tans and hair bleached brown. Other must-have accessories included oversized wool cardigans and Burberry-brand tartan scarfs. "Kogal" became a media buzzword at the time and was often associated with ENJOKOSAI. They all but vanished in the early 2000s but remain a major fetish for some guys, and some sex clubs still have girls dressed as kogal. In late 2008 there also seems to have been a retro revival in kogal fashion among some girls in Shibuya. Kogal-type characters often pop up in MANGA and ANIME, and ANNO HIDEAKI's film *Love & Pop* (1998) was about kogal and enjokosai.

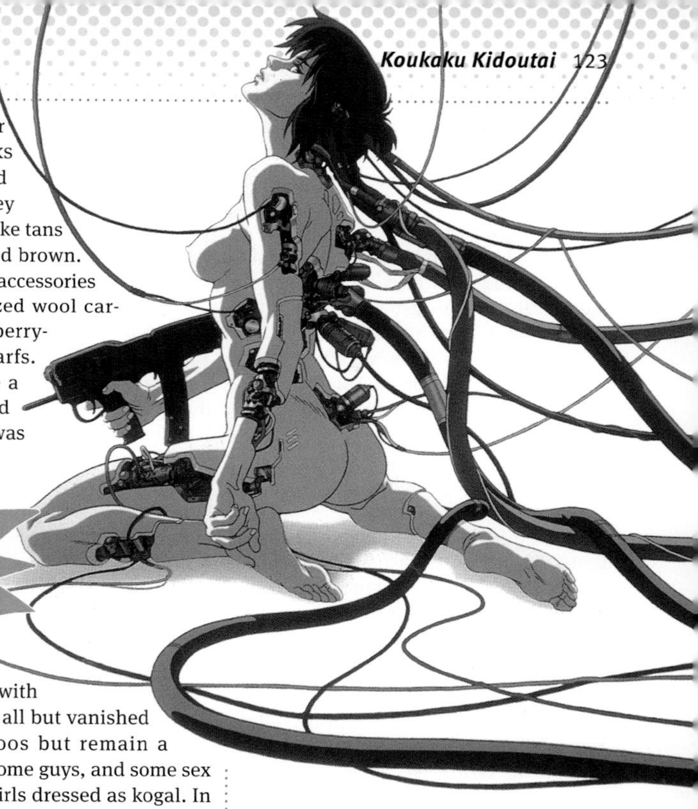

MAJOR KUSANAGI FROM *KOUKAKU KIDOUTAI* (GHOST IN THE SHELL)

Koha (コウハ): A "hard" man, who is undistracted by women.

Kokusaimangashou (国際漫画賞): See INTERNATIONAL MANGA AWARD.

Koma (コマ): Panel in a MANGA, or single frame in a film or video.

Koma manga (コマ漫画): Comic strip, usually a four-panel type. Some say koma manga are related to *setsuwaga*, didactic Buddhist paintings that are some of the first examples—from any culture—to employ pictures in panels.

Komatori (コマ撮り): Stop-motion animation. Those freaky animated sequences where each frame is an individually shot picture so things appear choppy and transform between frames. ANNO HIDEAKI used this process in his "HONEYMATION."

Komawari (コマ割り): Layout or transition. Panel layout, panel arrangement, panel transition. The way a comic unfolds visually across the page.

***Koukaku Kidoutai* (攻殻機動隊):** Literally "mobile armored riot police," but known as *Ghost in the Shell* or GITS outside of Japan. A CYBERPUNK MANGA created by SHIROW MASAMUNE that ran from 1989 to 1991. It was followed by *Koukaku Kidoutai 2: Man/Machine Interface* and *Koukaku Kidoutai 1.5: Human-Error Processor*.

SPOILER ALERT!!
STOP READING NOW IF YOU DON'T WANT TO KNOW WHAT HAPPENS!

The story follows Major Kusanagi Motoko, a cybernetic babe from Public Security Section 9, on her quest to stop the mysterious "Puppet Master," a criminal who "ghost hacks" and controls people's minds. A wide cast of characters support the Major's progress, including the cyborg Batou, the human detective Togusa, data diver Ishikawa, and section chief Aramaki. Although the Major thinks she is the hunter, the "Puppet Master"—an AI program that has achieved sentience and autonomy—is actually intent on merging minds with her.

In 1995, director OSHII MAMORU adapted this MANGA into an ANIME film that downplayed the sexual and humorous elements and stressed the philosophical, existential dilemma of a "ghost" soul in a digital and mechanical world. The result is more serious, atmospheric, and slow-paced than Shirow's manga. The setting also moved from Japan to Hong Kong. The Major's eyes typically remain unblinking, giving her a creepy, doll-like presence. The mood was amplified by the haunting musical score by Kawai Kenji. The animation was by PRODUCTION I.G, and it was one of the first films to seamlessly integrate CEL and digital techniques. A good example of this is the famous opening scene, where the Major assassinates someone, jumps off a building, and disappears with thermoptic camouflage (a digital cloak). The film ends with the cryptic observation, "The Net is vast and infinite."

The film was renamed *Ghost in the Shell* when it was dubbed into English in August 1996, and debuted on the Billboard Top 10 for US video sales. This was before the insanely popular *POKÉMON* franchise hit the market in 1998, and many thought it was impossible for an anime to go beyond the niche fan market and negative media stereotypes (see *MINNA AGECHAU* CONTROVERSY). The movie was critically and academically acclaimed, and it spread anime fandom in the United States. It also had a huge stylistic and visual influence on films that would follow, most noticeably on the Wachowski brothers' 1999 film *The Matrix*.

After the success of the first GITS film, there has been a sequel and a TV anime. The *Koukaku Kidoutai: Stand Alone Complex* TV series remained truer to the spirit of Shirow's work, was animated by Production I.G, and featured music by Kanno Yoko, making it a smash hit. The English title for the film, *Ghost in the Shell*, was introduced to Japan in 2008 and used in Oshii's renewal edition of *Koukaku Kidoutai*, which he named *Ghost in the Shell 2.0*. Also in 2008, DreamWorks and Steven Spielberg announced they had aquired the rights to produce a live-action 3D version of *Ghost in the Shell*.

See also *INNOCENCE: GHOST IN THE SHELL*.

Kuchi-paku (口パク): Mouth flap. The movement of an animated character's mouth in time with dialogue, especially when it doesn't match spoken lines. Since TV ANIME in Japan seeks to reduce the number of images, mouths are either open or closed. Dubbing by SEIYUU occurs after, and doesn't always synch. This is different for high budget films, such as *Macross: Do you remember love?* that allowed fans to sing along to realistic mouth movements.

Kurahi (蔵飛): Shorthand for "Kurama x Hiei," a coupling of the two studs in a DOUJINSHI version of the MANGA *Yu yu Hakusho* that became one of the most popular couplings in the world of YAOI. *Yu yu Hakusho* is known for bringing emotionally scarred characters together, and it started *trauma-kei* (as opposed to *macho-kei*) couplings. The SHOTACON genre really took off when the Hiei half of Kurahi was miniaturized and infantilized.

Kurobeta (黒ベタ): Black-ink drawing or inking. The lines or shades of a character or scene done in black ink, especially obvious in the GEKIGA style. See also BETA.

Kuso (クソ): Shit.

Kusoge (クソゲー): Shit game. Illustrator and commentator Miura Jun takes responsibility for creating the word. The first game to be called this was *Ikki* (1985), and by 1986 the word appeared in reviews in the gaming magazine *Famitsuu*. The opposite word is *kamige*, "god game," but a kusoge can be so bad that it comes to be worshipped as a kamige.

Kuuru (クール): Japanese for one season on TV. There are four kuuru per year, of three months or 13 weeks each. The length of a series is defined by the number of kuuru it was running on TV: effectively, 13, 26, or 52 weeks.

KY: Abbreviation of *kuki yomenai*, or someone who can't read the feelings of those around them, and goes off into flights of personal fancy. See GEEK OUT.

Kyara (キャラ): A highly stylized or simplified character that can be easily reproduced and consumed outside of its original narrative context. The rise of kyara is tied to studios using individual characters to appeal to niche markets after NEON GENESIS EVANGELION. Most MOÉ-based media is dominated by kyara.

Kyara song (キャラソング): See IMAGE SONG.

Kyonyuu (巨乳): Giant breasts. As in a female character with "huge tracts of land." Also called *bakunyuu* (bomb breasts), because they look as if they're about to explode. Women and girls with large breasts are pretty standard in MANGA and ANIME.

Kyoto Animation (京都アニメーション): Also known as KyoAni. A Japanese animation studio established in 1981 in Uji, Kyoto Prefecture. The company is affiliated with the noted studio SUNRISE. The two biggest shows of 2006 and 2007, *The Melancholy of Suzumiya Haruhi* and *Lucky Star*, were from KyoAni.

Kyoto International Manga Museum (京都国際マンガミュージアム): This museum opened in 2006 and was the first of its kind in Japan. Kyoto, the ancient capital of Japan and seat of much of its high culture, is also home to Seika University, one of the country's strongest centers for manga studies.

K

Ladd, Fred: Born in 1927 in Ohio, USA. The producer who brought *Astro Boy* to the US in 1963 and got it on national TV, starting the First Wave of international ANIME fans. He also is responsible for the American release of *Gigantor* in 1964, and *Kimba* in 1965.

Ladies' comics: See REDISU COMIKKU.

LARP: Live Action Role-Playing game. Pretending to be a game character and playing an RPG fantasy in the real world. Fans affectionately refer to the practice as "larping."

Laws of Robotics: The three laws written by ISAAC ASIMOV that govern the robots in his sci-fi fiction:

1. A robot may not injure a human being or, through inaction, allow a human being to come to harm.
2. A robot must obey orders given to it by human beings, except where such orders would conflict with the First Law.
3. A robot must protect its own existence as long as such protection does not conflict with the First or Second Law.

The laws were introduced in the short story "Runaround" in 1942 to mitigate the prevailing killer robot theme. These days as humanoid robots become more of a possibility, the three laws are considered by some to be too simplistic to actually ensure human safety.

Layout, transition: See KOMAWARI.

LD (レーザーディスク): Abbreviation of "LaserDisc." David Paul Gregg invented the process for making a video record disk and other optical disk technology in 1958. In the early 1960's Gregg sold his company, Gauss Electrophysics, and the patent to MCA. In 1978, MCA Discovision released the first commercial LD player in Atlanta, Georgia. This was two years after VHS and four years before the CD. LD had great storage capacity, visuals, and sound, but it was expensive. Despite its superiority, it lost to the cheaper, more durable, readily available VHS format, much like BETAMAX did. Unlike tapes, however, LD store well over time, so have always been popular with collectors in the same way vinyl records are. This is truer in Japan, where niche film and ANIME fans quickly adopted LD. There are still stores in places such as NAKANO BROADWAY that buy, sell, and trade LDs.

Leet (リート): Short for "elite" and usually written "l33t." Internet or gamer slang for an advanced or elite entity. Someone who is fully initiated into the protocols of the interaction or game and acts as an experienced leader. They speak in their own advanced language called "leet speak" to keep newcomers out. These outsiders are known as newbies or "NOOBS."

PHOTO: TAKARA TOMY

LICCA-CHAN

Licca-chan (リカちゃん): Or Kayama Licca, is a Japanese Barbie-like doll released by Takara in 1967. Created by SHOJO MANGAKA Maki Miyako and said to have inspired her husband MATSUMOTO LEIJI in his elegant, elongated character designs. The doll's face and persona are by now ubiquitous in shojo design and are said to mix the best elements of Japanese and Western sensibilities. Licca-chan's father is Pierre, a French cellist, and her mother, Orie, is a Japanese fashion designer. As of 2007, more than 53 million Licca-chan dolls had been sold.

Light novel (ライトノベル): Abbreviated as *rainobé* and sometimes called *seinen*, these are slightly more challenging than MANGA—that is, they have fewer or no pictures—but by definition cover material that isn't quite as hard as the standard literary work or serious literature. The first dedicated full-time author of light novels was Kanzaka Hajime, who wrote *Slayers* in 1989, now considered the archetype of the genre: easy to read, character driven, and appealing to middle- and high-school students. The original *Suzumiya Haruhi* novels by Tanigawa Nagaru are emblematic of the style—and were the basis for the hit ANIME *The Melancholy of Haruhi Suzumiya* (2006).

黄金の最終章
折原みと

MITO ORIHARA / KODANSHA

OUGON NO EPILOGUE LIGHT NOVEL BY ORIHARA MITO

Limited animation (リミテッド・アニメーション): Animation that is not fluid or realistic, be it for reasons of style or budget. This is what Japanese refer to as "ANIME," as opposed to the "full" animation shown in theaters. Limited animation (usually twelve frames per second) is more suited to low-budget productions such as TV anime and employs abstract art, symbolism, and camera tricks to create the illusion of movement. It is sometimes choppy and rough, but it is responsible for generating many alternative filming techniques, tricks, and creative use of space and time. For example, a climatic scene in *NEON GENESIS EVANGELION* (1995) is in episode twenty-four, when the protagonist, Shinji, sits unmoving in his MECHA, struggling with whether or not to kill an enemy who's become his friend. For over a minute, there's only one still frame of his mecha holding the tiny figure in its massive hand, but the scene is carried by the power of the narrative and the swelling orchestral score.

L

Lion King controversy: See JYANGURU TAITEI.

Little-sister café: See IMOUTO CAFÉ.

Live-action version: See JISSHABAN.

Lolicon (ロリコン): Lolita complex. Derived from Vladimir Nabokov's 1955 novel *Lolita*, which details a man's obsession with a twelve-year-old girl. In Japan, "lolicon" is used to describe either a sexual attraction to prepubescent girls or an individual with that desire; a desire that has, of course, been around much longer than the word itself.

For example, Kawabata Yasunari—winner of the 1968 Nobel Prize in Literature—described a lolicon-type desire in his short story "Izu Dancer" (1925), about a man who falls in love with a prepubescent girl but decides to treasure her innocence and leave her untouched.

The term "Lolita complex" may have first been introduced to Japan when Russell Trainer's book *The Lolita Complex* (1966) was translated. But MANGA artist Wada Shinji was the first to actually use and explain it in his 1974 manga *Stumbling Upon a Cabbage Field* (*Kyabetsubatake de Tumazuite*), which was a parody of *Alice in Wonderland*. The shortening of the term to "lolicon" came later, and in 1979 AZUMA HIDEO created the DOUJINSHI manga *Cybele*, the first blatantly lolicon work in Japan. That same year, MIYAZAKI HAYAO's *Lupin III: The Castle of Cagliostro*, was released and the innocent, young princess character, Clarisse, became a lolicon idoru. Miyazaki, however, has criticized lolicon artists and fans, differentiating his own female characters from those he says are treated "as pets."

OOH . . . THAT'S WHAT LOLICON MEANS!

Between 1980 and 1984 lolicon art peaked, with magazines like *Manga Burikko* (1983–86) and *Lemon People* (1981–88) carrying lolicon images. A backlash against this kind of art came after MIYAZAKI TSUTOMU, who murdered four little girls in 1989, was found to be a fan of lolicon, and a Japanese non-profit organization called CASPAR was founded to campaign for the regulation of lolicon.

The lolicon boom was displaced in the 1990s by the BISHOJO boom, and in the 2000s by the MOÉ boom, which combines elements of lolicon and bishojo.

Child pornography was outlawed in 1999 (see WAISETSU), although lolicon characters are legal in Japan. Despite the prevalence of this theme, instances of sexual abuse in Japan are low—only 762 sex abuse cases reported in 2000 (Ministry of Health, Labor and Welfare) compared to 89,500 in the US that year (Office of Juvenile Justice and Delinquency Prevention). This could be due to a reluctance to report abuse or because the legal age of consent in Japan can be as low as thirteen, depending on the prefecture.

The underage appearence of lolicon characters in ANIME is typically excused by the use of convoluted plot devices that suggest that these prepubescent-looking girls are actually much older. For example, Sasami from *Tenchi Muyo!* (1992) is a lolicon character, but she is also an alien who matures slowly; what appears to be a child is actually a being that's hundreds of years old. And Klan Klein from *Macross F* (2008) is a giant, voluptuous Zentradi woman, but due to a genetic defect she turns into a little girl when she shrinks to human size. Other famous idoru such as ten-year-old Chiyo from *Azumanga Daioh* (2002) or the elementary-school girls in *Ichigo Mashimaro* (2005) and *Alien Nine* (2003) are, however, simply young girls.

The biggest title recently that's been associated with lolicon is *Kodomo no Jikan* (2007) by female manga artist Watashiya Kaworu. Although the series was a hit in Japan, in 2007 it was deemed "inappropriate" for American audiences when the manga was due to be published under the name *Nymphet*. Watashiya responded to the controversy on her blog where she said the issues surrounding her work "made [her] realize the differences in cultures between the countries."

I THINK LOOSE SOCKS LOOK PRETTY CUTE WITH THIS OUTFIT!

Loose socks (ルーズソックス): A style of sock that comes up to the knee but flops down into baggy folds; generally worn as part of a school uniform by young fashionable girls in the mid-1990s (see KOGAL). They are so bulky that special "sock glue" is needed to paste them onto a girl's calves and keep them in place. Two prominent views are that the fashion originated in provincial towns like Sendai, Miyagi Prefecture, or Mito, Ibaraki Prefecture. In both stories it was to protect against the cold, but they became popular because they made fat legs seem thin and looked damn sexy. Around 1993—as Japanese high-school girls in Shibuya began to shorten the skirts of their uniforms—loose socks became an essential part of the kogal look and were infamous during the ENJOKOSAI scandals at the time. Loose socks are still highly fetishized by OTAKU and others who associate them with the vibrancy, innocence, and sexuality of teenage girls.

Love doll (ラブドール): The contemporary term for what Japanese call a "DUTCH WIFE," or an anatomically correct, humanoid sex doll.

LOVE HOTELS WHERE COUPLES CAN "REST" AND PLAY, OR "STAY" AND REST

PHOTO: GHP (KATO PLEASURE GROUP : GLOBAL HOTEL PRODUCERS)

Love hotel (ラブホテル): A hotel that's available for a "rest," of a few hours, or an overnight "stay," and are priced accordingly. They became popular after 1958, when prostitution was made illegal. They are also an essential part of any relationship in Japan, where many young lovers or couples still live with their parents until they are married, or even after marriage. They are often near train stations or highways for ease of access, and much of the hotel is automated to limit awkward interaction with the staff. Many are outrageously themed with incredible decorations and playthings inside. Each year love hotels in Japan rake in $42 billion and accommodate 500 million visits.

Lucca: Located in Italy's Tuscany region, this is the "City of Comics." Since 1966, the city has hosted an annual event every November dedicated to strip cartoons. International comic experts, publishers, authors, critics, and fans attend, and in 1993 the event changed to include illustrations, comics, animation, and games. The Lucca Comics and Games event, as it is now called, was an early adapter of OTAKU culture such as COSPLAY, and around 100,000 visitors from around the world gather in an 18,000-square-meter venue in the center of the historic town. The event teamed up with the Italian Museum of Comics in 2001 to become a sponsored cultural gathering.

ITALIAN GOTH-LOLIS AT LUCCA

PROPERTY OF LUCCA COMICS & GAMES SRL. SONIA MELONI

Ma (間): Empty space and time. Also a literary concept describing places in a story where the reader must fill in what's missing from the narrative. This is quite common in ANIME and MANGA.

Macek, Carl: Born in 1951 in Pittsburgh, Pennsylvania. The founder of Streamline Pictures and a controversial ANIME pioneer in the United States. While with Harmony Gold, he produced *Robotech* and *Captain Harlock and the Queen of a Thousand Years* (see CAPTAIN HARLOCK DEBACLE). Macek wanted to bring *Super dimension fortress macross* to the United States, but he could not sell the thirty-six-episode masterpiece to network TV at that length. The limit for a syndicated series at the time was sixty-five episodes (thirteen weeks at five episodes per week), so Macek spliced *Super Dimension Fortress Macross* with the unrelated *Super Dimension Cavalry Southern Cross* and *Genesis Climber Mospeada* to make *Robotech* in 1985. Right or wrong, this epic series was a vast improvement over much that had come before and was largely responsible for starting the Third Wave of fans in the United States. Macek has himself said he believes his hybrids and rewriting of the Japanese source material was superior to the originals.

Macias, Patrick: Born in 1972 in California, USA. Journalist, critic, and author of many books that introduced Japanese OTAKU culture to the US and American otaku culture to Japan. He got his start writing on Asian cult film for the *San Francisco Bay Guardian* and later *Pulp* and *Animerica* magazines. His blog is one of the most trusted sources of information on these topics. He was also a correspondent for NHK's syndicated TV show

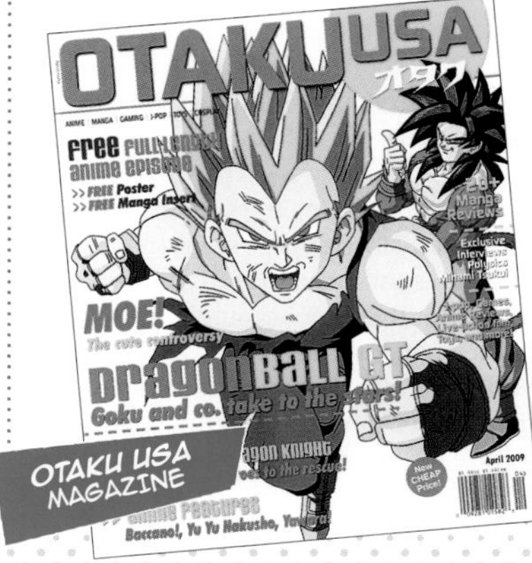

OTAKU USA MAGAZINE

"Tokyo Eye," and is editor-in-chief of *Otaku USA* magazine.

Macross (マクロス): Or *Chojiku yosai Macross* (*Super Dimension Fortress Macross*), a 1982–83 ANIME series from Studio Nue with mechanical designs by KAWAMORI SHOJI and characters by Mikimoto Haruhiko.

The story begins in 1999 when a city-sized alien spacecraft crashes on Earth. Over the next ten years, humans put aside their differences and band together to fix the ship. They reverse engineer the alien technology to create transforming fighter planes called "Valkyrie." As humans prepare to launch the rebuilt alien ship, SDF-1, a giant race of warrior aliens called "Zentradi" appear to reclaim it. A young civilian pilot, Ichijyo Hikaru, gets caught up in the conflict that follows. Outnumbered by the Zentradi, the humans, aboard SDF-1, use "space folding" technology to escape. As the Zentradi pursue them, the ship desperately struggles to survive.

SPOILER ALERT!! STOP READING NOW IF YOU DON'T WANT TO KNOW WHAT HAPPENS!

Hikaru joins the defense force, and is drawn towards his female commanding officer, Hayase Misa. Hikaru, however, also loves Linn Minmay, an IDORU, and becomes torn between the two women. Minmay's singing confounds the Zentradi which allows the humans on SDF-1 to prevail. They return to rebuild Earth along with the surviving Zentradi, who want to live in peace.

Despite having a surprisingly simply story of a love triangle set against intergalactic war, *Macross* is remembered as one of the best anime series of all time. The reason for this is quite simply the realism of the characters and an obsessive devotion to MECHA details. Not surprisingly, the transforming space fighter planes fed a craze for toys and figures. Takatoku was the first company to made *Macross* toys, including the complex, highly detailed VF-1 Valkyrie, dubbed "*kanzen henkei*" (perfect transformation). When Takatoku went bankrupt in 1984, BANDAI took over the kanzen henkei series. Another important aspect of the show was that, for the first time, bubblegum pop and idoru music accompanied the story and animation. The *Macross* movie *Do you remember love?* was the first anime where fans could sing along with the characters. Lynn Minmay, the strong central idoru figure, was an early sign of the shift from mecha to MOÉ anime.

When *Macross* ended its thirty-six episode run, fans were already hardcore enough to be called otaku. CARL MACEK of Harmony Gold brought the series to the US and cut it together with two unrelated series to form *Robotech* in 1985.

The fictional launch of the SDF-1 was February 7, 2009. A commemorative event was held at Akiba Square on February 22, 2009, with lots of tie-ins to *Macross F*, the anime made to commemorate the twenty-fifth anniversary of the series.

Madhouse (マッドハウス): One of the most in-demand Japanese animation studios. The company was started in 1972 by ex-employees of TEZUKA OSAMU'S MUSHI PRODUCTIONS, and the founders included such ANIME greats as Rintaro, Kawajiri Yoshiaki, Maruyama Masao, and Dezaki Osamu. At first, Madhouse worked on TV series for Tokyo Douga, which had given Madhouse start-up funds. This resulted in *Ace wo Nerae!* in 1973. In the 1980s, it moved to produce OVA and films directed by Rintaro. Hirata Toshio turned in the beloved *HADASHI NO GEN* in 1987. The company became truly sucessful with judo anime *Yawara*, a major TV hit in 1989. Soon after, Kawajiri directed *Ninja Scroll* (1993), which would become extremely

popular overseas. Entering into the TV business full throttle, Madhouse hit again with fan favorite *Cardcaptor Sakura* in 1998. That same year, it put out the internationally popular *Trigun*. Global accolades continued with *Vampire Hunter D: Bloodlust* in 2000 and *Animatrix* in 2003. In 2001, Rintaro directed an anime version of his mentor Tezuka's *Metropolis*. Madhouse didn't forget to feed its OTAKU fanbase and released *Di Gi Charat* (1999), and *Chobits* (2002). In 2006, it did the stellar animation for *The Girl Who Leapt Through Time*, a critical international success. It also animated *Death Note* and *Nana* (2006–2007).

Madhouse has also produced all four of director Kon Satoshi's films—*Perfect Blue* (1998), *Millennium Actress* (2001), *Tokyo Godfathers* (2003), and *Paprika* (2006)—and his TV series, *Paranoia Agent* (2004).

Mad movies: A general Japanese term for fan-produced or amateur videos put up on NICO NICO DOUGA and YouTube.

Magnificent 49ers, The: See NIJYUUYONNEN GUMI.

Mahoshojo (魔法少女): Magical girls. They also often "transform." These began following the ultra-popular Japanese dub of the American TV series *Bewitched* in the 1960s. At the time, studios were looking for an ANIME targeting the still largely untapped young female consumer market. Because *Bewitched*—with its sexy, kind-hearted witch was popular with girls, YOKOYAMA MITSUTERU, best known in the US as the creator of anime *Tetsujin 28-go* (*Gigantor*), decided to make *Mahotsukai Sarii* (*Sally, the Witch*). The result was one of the most popular and longest-running animation series in Japanese history. The genre became increasingly sexual and decorative with series such as *A-ko-chan, Akazukin Chaha*, and *Majokko Megu-chan*. The most popular mahoshojo among OTAKU are *Magical Princess Minky Momo* and *Magical Angel Creamy Mami*. See also HENSHIN SHOJO.

Maid (メイド): A girl in a maid outfit. The classic maid look is based on Victorian- or European-style housemaids from the late 1800s. They wear an ankle-length dark navy or black frock—with white lace edges on the sleeves and a stiff, high, white collar—with a long white apron that droops down to the floor. They also wear a distinct lace headdress called a KATYUSHA. Since the maid boom in 2005, variations on this classic costume have appeared, including a much shorter skirt, visible puffy bloomers, a form-fitting bodice, and more flexibility in color, theme, and maidol • ひとみ

HITOMI

HE UBIQUITOUS FACE OF MOÉ AND AKIHABARA, hitomi (spelled with a lowe case "h") is the most famous maid in Japan. Apparently born in a flowe garden and raised in a tulip, she's eternally seventeen years old. She began her career at @home Café in 2004, months after it was founded as he first entertainment-style MOÉ-maid café. Her frequent media appear ances, in which she performs as a "MAIDOL" (maid idol) have made her a maid legend. She was in the first maidol band, Kanzen Maid Sengen, and was the leader of the band Paletee. She now heads up the maid singing roupe @gumi, which is well known on online video-sharing sites.

PG: What are your hobbies?

HC: Recently I've become really hooked on riddles. I practice them and tell them o my masters* in the café, so they can have a good time! I also like doing my hair, nails, and makeup. Because being a maid means being seen by the public, it's mportant to take care of my appearance.

PG: Why did you decide to be a maid?

HC: Well . . . I was born a maid! I have a ittle brother, so I enjoy taking care of people, but it's only recently that I decided o work in a maid café. My dream is to make people happy, so I want to be both a maid and an idol—a maidol—and try even harder to spread happiness, one master at a time. I want to do my best at serving in he café and singing at live performances.

PG: What is a maid café? What do you do here?

HC: Basically, it's like, a café. Just a place o eat and drink. Although @home is more than that, it's a place to have fun with maids, people can enjoy a happy atmosphere, and we provide entertainment for the masters. There are other kinds of places that have maids, with massage and karaoke, but to me they're different. Rathe than simply wearing maid costumes, a @home the maids really work togethe to make our masters have fun! We don' just carry food and drinks. For example someone might be feeling a little dowr and come to the café after work, thinking, "I'd sure like someone to listen to me." By offering happiness we give them the energy to continue.

PG: What is the relationship like betweer the maids and masters?

HC: Of course it's master and maid right to the very end. But if a master isn't feeling well or something, a good maid is someone who can cheer her master up. Ou masters don't look at us as friends, bu rather as maids. And we don't look at them as men, either. They are always master in our eyes.

PG: What is the best part about being a maid?

HC: I do two things as a maid, serving in the café and live performances, and in my

* All good maids refer to their customers as *goshujinsama* (master) or *ojousama* (mistress).

case I have a lot of media appearances. But I think the thing that makes me happiest is getting a good response from my masters. When we're just talking in the café, it really excites everyone that I was on TV, and they mention it. What's most rewarding is not being famous, but knowing that when I perform many people can enjoy it. I really love that atmosphere!

PG: Is that what they call moé space?

HC: Yes! In the café and at performances the moé space spreads and enfolds everyone! I think maybe moé is not used outside Japan, and until very recently it only existed in Akihabara. The nuance of moé differs from person to person, and what is moé to one person is not necessarily moé to another. There are many different types of moé. When I say moé space, what I mean is a cute place where everyone can enjoy themselves, they feel excitement and a flutter of the heart. It's like, the inside of your heart is pink. But not pink in a weird way! When your heart is a bright, warm color, maybe that feeling is moé?

PG: What's best about maid cafés?

HC: In the case of @home café, I'm really happy that so many masters come! Even on weekdays the seats are full, and on weekends the lines are really long but people still wait. It's really hot in the summer and really cold in the winter, but they still come home*.

PG: Has the world of maids changed in your time?

HC: When I came, there were not many cafés and they were seen as kind of dark places in Akihabara where OTAKU gathered. They weren't "normal places" and the number of masters and mistresses who came to the café was much smaller. Since I started that's changed. Places like @home are bright, safe, and fun, nothing like the old image of maid cafés. I want to tell people who've never been to a maid café—who want to come but are a bit reluctant to—that it's such a fun place! Every time I serve or appear in the media that's the message I try to convey. Sometimes there's a tendency to view us in a lecherous way, like maids are from lewd stores, so I try to show that it's different. Compared to when I started, the customer demographic and way of thinking has changed drastically. Now, junior high-school girls and boys come on class trips, and even grandmas and grandpas are coming home. That makes me very happy.

Places like @home are bright, safe, and fun, nothing like the old image of maid cafés.

PG: What are your plans for the future?

HC: Of course my service in the café is most important, but there is an idoru unit called @gumi and I'm the lead vocalist. I feel that from now on I need to do my best to practice my singing and dancing so we can do bigger and bigger live performances. As a maid, well, I still have a lot of immature things about me, but I would like to become a more splendid maid. Right now @home café is only in Akihabara. If @home was like Starbucks and popped up all over, in various places, then when people say, "Let's get a coffee," you could answer, "Let's go to @home." It would be so great if that happened!

* Cafés are referred to as "home," and when customers arrive the maids greet them with a hearty "Welcome home, Master!" (*Okaerinasaimase goshujinsama!*)

design. Other accessories include droopy bows, frills, glasses, bowties, and thigh-high stockings. The sexy French Maid style, with a black miniskirt, white lace, and fishnet stockings, exists but is not incredibly popular in Japan.

Maids are usually found in cafés in areas such as AKIHABARA, where ANIME, MANGA and video games are popular. The different style of costume tends to signify what kind of persona the maid assumes. Girls who wear the classic Victorian style tend to roleplay as obliging servants and are categorized as *IYASHI-KEI*, or soothing style. All the others are called *MOÉ-kei* and are generally girls with colorful, bubbly personalities who act a little like ANIME characters. Moé-kei maids laugh and fool around with each other and create an infectious atmosphere of jubilant play that excites the customers, who are refered to as Master and Mistress. A café maid is usually a part-time worker between eighteen and twenty-eight years of age, but are eternally "seventeen" in the café. They make the minimum wage of about $8 per hour. They're often fans of anime, manga, and video games, so enjoy the work because they get to COSPLAY all day. For every maid position advertised in Akihabara there can be as many as 400 applicants. The really lucky ones may become maid idoru (MAIDORU) and appear in the media as the face of Akihabara and OTAKU culture.

Maids in some form or another have existed in Japan since the Meiji period (1868–1912), when servants were employed in wealthy, "modern" Japanese households. The number of housemaids declined with the closing income gap after WWII, the proliferation of nuclear families, and the appearance of companies offering cheap immigrant maids. However, maids reappeared in the popular imagination at the end of the 1990s.

Maids have been in anime since *Kindan no Ketsuzoku* in 1993, and in dating simulator games since *Bird in the Cage* and *The Song of the Chick* in 1996. All these, however, had sexualized and fetishized plot points to put women in a subservient role. This changed at the end of the 1990s with *Welcome to Pia Carrot*, about bright, cheerful girls working in a fictional restaurant. GAINAX's sci-fi romance comedy anime *Mahoromatic* (2001–2003) also centers on maids, and the manga *Emma* (2002–2006) is all about maids in Victorian England.

Maid café (メイドカフェ): Or maid *kissa*. Cafés with a syrupy-sweet atmosphere drawn from ANIME and video games where girls role-play in maid costumes.

Maid cafés basically started as rest stops for OTAKU tired after a hard day hunting rare DOUJINSHI and GYARUGE in AKIHABARA. They could go to a café and meet other like-minded people in an environment where women would not only actually *talk* to them but would say "Welcome home, Master!" when they arrived.

The cafés first appeared in 1998 at sales events for the game *Welcome to Pia Carrot*, and the first permanent maid café, Cure Maid Café, was founded by COSPLAY outfitter COSPA in Akihabara in 2001. The original concept was to create a place where people could relax, but it has since expanded to include childish coddling, playing board games, and song and dance entertainment.

The cafés' menus typically consist of the kind of food, drinks, and desserts that are usually found on kids' menus, and tend to be sweet and girly like the feminine, pink, decorative cafés themselves. Notably, the prices at maid cafés are inflated to reflect the services provided, which include talking to a maid, having one write messages with ketchup on your food, and sometimes a stage performance or game. Many cafés offer hand-to-hand games like "rock-paper-scissors" ($5 for three minutes) and personalized CHEKI instant photos taken with the maid ($5 per shot). The so-called "communication time" spent in the café can cost as much as $90 an hour.

The real boom in maid cafés can be traced to 2003 and 2004, when the media began to descend on Akihabara looking for the heart of COOL JAPAN. Maids were simply the most visually appealing aspect of the area, so many news reports commented on maid cafés. Public interest in the cafés reached a peak in 2005, when the hit Fuji TV drama *DENSHA OTOKO* consistently featured a maid café called Pinafore as a setting. Many non-otaku fans of the show began to flock to the area, and Akihabara's four cafés in 2002 ballooned to some forty establishments in 2006.

The wait to get into popular cafés, such as @home Café, can now reach as long as two hours, despite the fact that the time limit for a visit is sometimes only an hour. The first professional tour to include a maid café, operated by Akiba Map, appeared in 2006, followed by governmental JTB and private H.I.S. offerings.

Cafés can make around $45,000 a month. Ono Tetsuya, owner of Candy Fruits maid optometry, makes nearly $200,000 a month, according to his book *Dos and Don'ts of Starting a Moé Business*. Many entrepreneurs, former hostess club owners, and even gangs are muscling into the maid business. A glut of new cafés means cafés can only survive if they diversify and offer bizarre and niche characters, costumes, and services. In many cases, cafés only last a month. However, there are now maid cafés as far afield as Thailand, Taiwan, South Korea, China, France, Canada, the United States, and

INSIDE THE @HOME MAID CAFÉ

Mexico. As maid cafés have proliferated, maids have diversified, and these days "maids" in the loosest sense of the word can be found in various types of establishments where they cut hair, massage, sing and dance, act like bratty kid sisters or obliging mothers, pretend to be pious nuns or nurses, gamble, cross-dress, and so on. To combat the supposed "degeneration" of maids, in 2007 the Maid Cooperative (MAID KYOUKAI) created a Maid Standards Test (MAID KENTAI).

Maid gari (メイド狩り): Maid hunting; as in attempting to pick up, or date, a maid in AKIHABARA. After the AKIBA Boom in 2005, young men started flocking to Akihabara hoping to find easy women. In one particularly well-noted incident in October 2006, a young man lost it outside a maid café, threatened a maid with a knife, and fondled her. In June 2007, police began preventive surveillance. Along with OTAKU GARI (otaku hunting), maid gari was an issue many commented on in 2007 and 2008 in conjunction with the "slummification" of Akihabara.

Maid Kentei (メイド検定): The Maid Standards Exam given to maids to make sure they're the genuine article and are nice, clean girls. The test is made up of five sections covering the history of maids, cleaning, cooking, washing clothes, and most importantly, maid manners. The test is four pages long and contains forty questions; half are multiple choice and half short answer. Almost 90 percent are dedicated to maid manners and history. For example, "A customer at the café says, 'This coffee is too hot! I've burned my tongue.' What should a good maid do?" The correct answer is, "Check the customer's all right and, after apologizing, stay with them, engaging in soothing conversation, until the coffee has cooled down."

A BIRTHDAY CHEKI FROM THE MAIDOL HITOMI

The exam was dreamed up in December 2007 under the supervision of Daimon Taro, chief editor of *Cosmode* magazine and a prominent figure in the MAID KYOUKAI (Maid Cooperative). Daimon and others see true maid values as vastly different from what has evolved due to the intervention of commercialism, sex, and tourist interest in maid cafés. Sabashi Kunihiko, who opened the Maid Training Academy in February 2007, has said, "In a Japan where communication is getting ever weaker, the relations and intimacy established between the gentle maid and customer are crucial."

Maid Kyoukai (メイド協会): The Maid Cooperative. Formed in April 2007 and responsible for managing the overall trends and standards of maids and related establishments. As of June 2007, it had about 1,200 members.

Maidol (メイドル): A maid idol: those glamorous girls in maid cafés who are not only sensationally cute but can sing and dance too. The first maidol were the eleven-member Kanzen Maid Sengen, which appeared at @home Café in the summer of 2005 and is still the standard for the many copycat groups that followed. This group—which produced quintessential maidol and TV star hitomi—became defunct in February 2007 but returned as Paletee on July 21, 2007, a high-energy, DENPA, group of eight maids with hitomi at the center. This was reformed in 2008 as the massive @gumi unit, which all the maids at the café try out for. MIA, another café, also has a band called SKB 48—an obvious reference to the idoru group AKB 48.

Makuhari Messe (幕張メッセ): A massive convention center located on Tokyo Bay in Chiba Prefecture. Many OTAKU-oriented events are held here, including C3Hobby, Tokyo Motor Show, Tokyo Game Show and the Jump Festa.

Mandarake (まんだらけ): Established in Nakano Broadway in 1980, this was one of the first and most successful retailers of used MANGA in Japan—growing out of a desire for affordable and interesting reading material. The name literally means "covered with manga," an apt name for a company bringing so much manga to the masses. The owner, Furukawa Masuzo, claims his store will "take over the world." So far Mandarake has stores in Los Angeles and Bologna, in addition to Japanese locations including a veritable fortress-like bunker in the middle of Tokyo's Shibuya district. Furukawa's office is decorated to look like that of Shocker, the villain of long-running TV show *Kamen Rider*. He is intent on preserving the long history of manga in Japan, which has until recently been ignored by museums. The store only sells second-hand goods, including manga and DOUJINSHI, FIGURES, toys, ANIME, COSPLAY, CDs, games, and so on. It is a treasure-trove of rare and collectible goods.

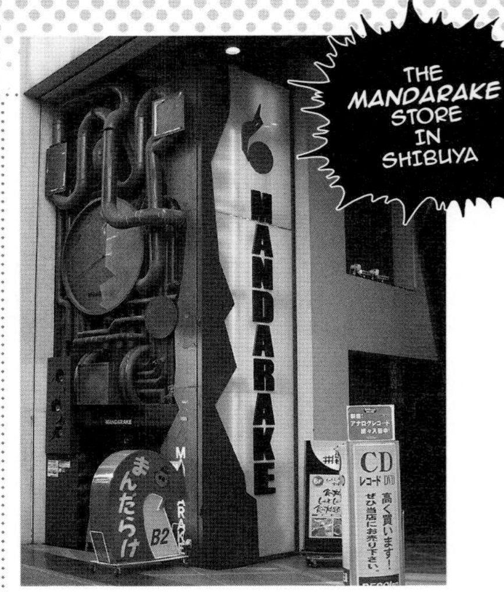

THE MANDARAKE STORE IN SHIBUYA

Manga (漫画・マンガ): Japanese comics and graphic novels. The term literally means "fanciful pictures" and was used to describe the comic works of the Edo-period (1600–1868) Ukiyo-e artist Hokusai. The basic aesthetics of manga are often traced back to the Buddhist *CHOJUGIGA* of the 12th century—illustrated scrolls that featured animal characters, sweat drops, speed lines, and so on—but this theory is often questioned. Modern manga began after WWII as a cheap source of entertainment. Manga artist TEZUKA OSAMU, often called the "God of Manga," innovated a cinematic and symbolic style he called "hieroglyphics" to tell a written story in pictures. His use of large eyes, ellipses, snot bubbles, bloody noses, and so on, came to define the look that is still associated with manga today.

Manga appeals to a wide range of readers with subjects from action to romance, sports to comedy, sex to historical drama, learning materials to sci-fi and fantasy, and everything between. These are roughly divided into SHONEN (for boys) and SHOJO (for girls), depending on the target audience.

Manga are typically printed in black and white and read right to left. Many are serialized in telephone book–size weekly or monthly manga magazines. These massive magazines are printed on cheap paper and are considered disposable. Manga magazines often contain serial episodes from several manga competing for readers. Popular manga can become ANIME, TV series, film, and so on. Sometimes manga are inspired by other media.

Manga are economically, socially, and politically of great significance in Japan. Manga mediate social issues such as sexuality and violence out of political discourse, because they are dismissed as popular, youth, or subcultural entertainment. This was clearly the case with the magazine *Garo* and the student movements in the 1960s and 1970s. After the student movements failed, many radicals became manga and anime creators. Manga also serves a political purpose as the cultural product of COOL JAPAN, as demonstrated by the devotion of official museum space in the 1980s. From an economic standpoint, manga claimed $6 billion in sales in 1995, which was forty times more than the US comics market. Circulation of manga peaked in 1996, when *Shonen Jump* sold 6 million copies a week, roughly the same amount of comics sold in the entire United States that year.

Things are slowing down, but according to the Information Media White Papers released by the Japanese government in 2004 and 2005, manga still makes up 40 per-cent of print publications, or 200,000 new titles and 300 weekly magazines (some with 2.5 million copies in circulation), and constitute about $4.5 billion in annual sales. As of 2007, some 46 million paperbacks of *Bleach* had been sold in a country of 127 million people. There are 3,000 *manga kissa* (reading rooms) in Japan, some of the richest people in the country are mangaka, and there is an International Manga Award and a Manga Museum

Despite this, manga didn't fare well in the United States at first. Manga series came to the US in the 1980s, but they were

confined to specialty comic book shops and largely ignored. The first blockbuster series was *Lone Wolf and Cub* in 1987, which had covers drawn by American artist Frank Miller. It sold 100,000 copies a month when *X-men* sold 400,000. But the comics industry collapsed in the 1990s, taking manga with it.

This all changed with the arrival of SHOJO and romance manga that appealed to women in ways comics didn't. *Mixxzine* released *Sailor Moon* in 1997, and suddenly girls were coming to comic shops and conventions. In 1998, millions of copies of the *Pokémon* manga flooded Toys "R" Us stores, drawing in kids and mainstreamers. TOKYOPOP started releasing unflopped "100% Authentic Manga," which were more affordable and faster to market, as there was no need to fix the inconsistencies in manga flopped to read left to right (see FLOPPING). Manga retailers and publishers flourished. In 2002 when VIZ released the 300-page weekly *Shonen Jump* in English for $5, an American comic book at 32 pages for $3 looked like a ripoff. *Shonen Jump* had a circulation of 250,000 in 2007, while *Spider-Man* was at 100,000. From 2003, the manga industry overseas continued to grow annually by 100 percent, with 1,000 new titles making $207 million in 2005. The saturated market has since slowed down however.

Manga eiga (漫画映画): Old term for animated films. First used in the 1930s, and due to the popularity of American animation at the time, the term tended to mean animation produced in the US. Japanese animation was called *senga eiga* (line-drawing movie).

Manga-izamu (漫画主義): Manga-ism. A group and magazine dedicated to promoting a better image of MANGA (1967–78). It was associated with art critic Ishiko Junzo and philosophical manga by greats such as Mizugi Shigeru. See also GEKIGA.

Mangaka (漫画家・マンガ家): Manga author or manga artist. They are treated as celebrities in Japan when they achieve success, but rookies make around $20 per page and live in constant fear of falling out of favor in reader polls and being canceled. If successful, a MANGAKA gets to do color pages of his or her work or the cover of the magazine and even have the chapters of their work republished in a higher quality TANKOBON anthology (about the height and width of a paperback novel, but thinner). This sometimes involves color, although this takes more time and assistants—which most mangaka don't have until they are famous enough to run a small studio. Mangaka TAKAHASHI RUMIKO is one of the richest people in Japan, with an annual income of over $3 million.

Manga kissa (マンガ喫茶): A manga coffee shop; a place to read rental comics. Something like an Internet café, these library-like, homey manga cafés have sprung up all across Japan. Customers are provided with a comfy chair in a private cubicle and pay by the hour to have unlimited access to the Internet, every

MANGA KISSA

m

manga title imaginable, and sometimes games, drinks, and even showers. As they are usually open twenty-four hours a day, they are also a cheap place to stay for people who miss the last train home. There is even a significant section of urban youth and working poor who use these establishments as a home base when they can't afford rooms. The population of these "Net café refugees" was estimated by government officials in August 2007 to be at least 5,400. Many OTAKU also spend their nights in manga kissa in order to be the first in line for events, or to read away the lonely nights.

Manga Koshien (まんが甲子園)**:** A nationwide manga competition for high-school students held every August in Kochi. Its full name is the "National High School Manga Championship Conference," but it is called Manga Koshien in a somewhat humorous reference to the famous national baseball tournament also called Koshien. It was founded in 1992 as an outlet for high-school manga circles and a way to compare work and exchange ideas in friendly competition. Cynics, however, simply describe it as a regional promotion to fight a shrinking population and the sluggish economy. Teams of three to five people, from thirty schools, have a day to make a work on a given theme. It's produced many manga talents, and winners receive prizes for their school. In 2007, the Minister of Foreign Affairs, Aso Taro—who became prime minister in September 2008—delivered the opening remarks.

AN ENTRY FROM THE MANGA KOSHIEN

PHOTO: MANBOO

Manga-manbun (漫画漫文)**:** Words and pictures together on the same page in manga. This is the common format now, but prior to WWII there was a discourse that the arts should be "pure" and not mix with each other. The pure-artists felt pictures were one thing, words another, and both must be kept isolated to maintain their artistic value. The move to integrate text and images in manga started as an experiment by avant-garde creator Okamoto Ippei (1886–1948).

Manga no Kakikata (マンガの書き方)**:** *The Manga Technique*. A bible-like textbook on the fundamentals of creating narrative stories, or manga, written by TEZUKA OSAMU.

Manga-shi (漫画誌)**:** Pulp monthly or weekly manga magazines that are read by millions of Japanese. Most popular series get their start in magazines such as the venerable *Shonen Jump, Ribbon*, and so on. The first manga-shi was *Japan Punch* (see PONCHI-E), actually started by an Englishman in 1862, and *E-Shimbun Nihonchi* in 1874.

Manhwa (만화)**:** South Korean comic books. South Korea and to a lesser extent China are emerging powers in the world of MANGA and ANIME due to their experience and interactions with Japan. For years Japanese pop culture has been filtering into the rest of Asia (see COOL JAPAN), and to lower production costs many Japanese anime studios have been outsourcing tweening (in-between frames) and other grunt work to South Korea and China. Now artists, in South Korea especially, are using what they've learned to create their own content with its own unique flavor. Some manhwa are adaptations of popular Korean computer games such as Lee Myung-jin's *Ragnarok* and Kim Jae-hwan's *Warcraft: The Sunwell Trilogy*, but the original material is where manhwa shines. Examples include Lee So-young's *Model*, Kang Full's *Apartment*, and Park Kun-woong's *Massacre at Nogunri*, which tells of misconduct by US soldiers during the Korean War. Hyung Min-woo's *Priest* was so popular that it was going to be adapted into a film directed by Sam Raimi and starring Gerard Butler, but the project fell through in 2008. Manhwa can also refer to animated works, for example *My Beautiful Girl, Mari* (2002), which won the Grand Prix (Best Feature Film) at the 26th Annecy International Animated Film Festival; *Wonderful Days* (*Sky Blue*), which took seven years and $12.28 million to turn into Korea's most ambitious anime project in 2003; and *Empress Chung* in 2005.

I HAVEN'T SEEN YOU SINCE PAGE 133! DID YOU MISS ME?

Mania (マニア): Functionally equivalent to the term OTAKU—for example, train-mania, muscle-mania, he's a mania—but with the connotation of more expertise. People referred to as mania might be thought of as acceptable otaku types. This is reinforced by the fact that "a mania" is usually a person obsessed with socially valued, physical objects such as motorcycles, or vinyl records and so on, meaning they are not wasting their time dreaming about deviant fantasy worlds, as many commentators claim otaku do with ANIME and MANGA.

Maniac (マニアック): Crazy, extreme, underground, or hardcore.

Manpu (漫符): Symbolic speech: specifically, the comic symbols such as HANAJI (nosebleeds) and sweat drops, that add an extra layer of meaning to the speech of MANGA and ANIME.

Manzai (漫才): Traditional stand-up comedy groups usually made up of a clown (*BOKE*) and a straight guy (*TSUKKOMI*). The basic structure of boke and tsukkomi pops up again and again in characters across all forms of media.

Matsuda Seiko (松田聖子): Real name Kamachi Noriko, born 1962, in Fukuoka. An idoru singer who ruled the

m

charts in the 1980s with twenty-four consecutive No. 1 hits. She unsuccessfully attempted to break into the US market and is best known there for "The Right Combination"—a duet with Donnie Whalberg from New Kids on the Block. She will forever be remembered in Japan as the first BURIKKO, or youth faker, because she extended her career into middle age while maintaining a girlish idoru image.

Matsumoto Leiji (松本零士): Born in 1938 in Kurume, Fukuoka Prefecture. Sometimes called Matsumoto Reiji in English. A prominent MANGAKA who pioneered the space opera genre. Matsumoto made his debut in 1953 drawing SHOJO MANGA. He had his big break writing WWII stories, which would later be collected and rewritten as *The Cockpit* (OVA in 1993). *Space Battleship Yamato* (1974), *Captain Harlock* and *Galaxy Express 999* (both 1977) made him a legend. The shared universe of *Captain Harlock* and *Galaxy Express 999* is often called the "Leijiverse." Many fans such as OKADA TOSHIO have drawn inspiration from Matsumoto's romanticism, his epic narrative, and his ethereal designs.

Matsuri (祭り): Festival. This is also used as slang among OTAKU to describe a situation where many people come together and experience the same event, which they then share online. It became a popular term in June 2003 when an online group planned and executed a matsuri entailing hundreds of fans—dressed as "agents" from the *Matrix* movie—marching across the famous intersection in front of Shibuya train station. Now a matsuri is used to describe any time mobs convene, including attending events, conventions, street performances of OTAGEI and idoru dances, and even waiting en masse for something to occur.

Mazakon (マザコン): Mother complex; Oedipus complex. An intense longing for a mother figure, which often manifests itself in preferred character types or even sexual preference. For example, Belldandy from the manga *Oh My Goddess!* cooks, cleans, and cares for the protagonist like a nurturing mother but is also his number one love interest; Ayanami Rei from the anime *Evangelion* is a clone of the protagonist's mother but also his primary attraction; and maids are both pampering caregivers and sexy idoru. Anthropologist Anne Allison has suggested fixation on large, inviting breasts in pop culture is also connected.

***Mazinger Z* (マジンガーZ):** Or *Tranzor Z* in North America. The first of the super robot genre of ANIME, based on the 1972 MANGA by NAGAI GO. His ultra-masculine piloted robot is considered a template for super robot series. Nagai named the robot after "*majin*," which means "demon god."

In this melodramatic story, Mazinger Z is a giant robot built of Chogokin Z, a fictitious super

SPOILER ALERT!! STOP READING NOW IF YOU DON'T WANT TO KNOW WHAT HAPPENS!

alloy mined from Japan's iconic Mt. Fuji. Its creator, Dr. Kabuto Junzo, employs the robot, based on a forgotten Grecian titan design, to repel the megalomaniacal German scientist Dr. Hell and his terrible Mechanical Beasts. Hell's henchman, the hermaphrodite Baron Ashura, kills Kabuto, but not before he entrusts Mazinger Z, and the fate of the world, to his grandson Kouji. Kouji and a lovable supporting cast fought evil for ninety-two episodes from 1972 to 1974, and *Mazinger Z* became one of the highest rated anime series of all time. Due to this success, the story naturally continued in the sequel *Great Mazinger*. Many other movies, OVA, and so on followed.

Thirty years after the start of the original program, Nagai's company, Dynamic Planning, released a *Mazinger* OVA. Nagai also made a self-parody in *Panda Z*, where anthropomorphic animals duke it out in cutesy MECHA. *Mazinger Z* spawned all sorts of merchandise, most notably CHOGOKIN die-cast toys. Aside from being the first super robot series, *Mazinger Z* also featured one of the first female robots, Aphrodite A, with breasts that could fire missiles. Furthermore, Nagai may well have created the first transforming robot in that Kouji had to fly a hover vehicle into Mazinger Z's head and shout "Pilder on!" to get the machine moving.

The connection between man and machine is also an important precedent. From the 1980s, *Mazinger Z* went on to be one of the most beloved anime outside of Japan. It was generally faithfully localized, with the exception of the United States, where 3-B Productions edited it for a young audience and shortened it to sixty-five episodes, the standard of TV syndication packages. Key episodes such as Aphrodite's destruction were cut, and forget about the breast missiles! In 1977, Toei commissioned a more faithful redub by Frontier Enterprises, but it was only twenty-nine episodes long.

SUPER ROBOT MAZINGER Z BY NAGAI GO

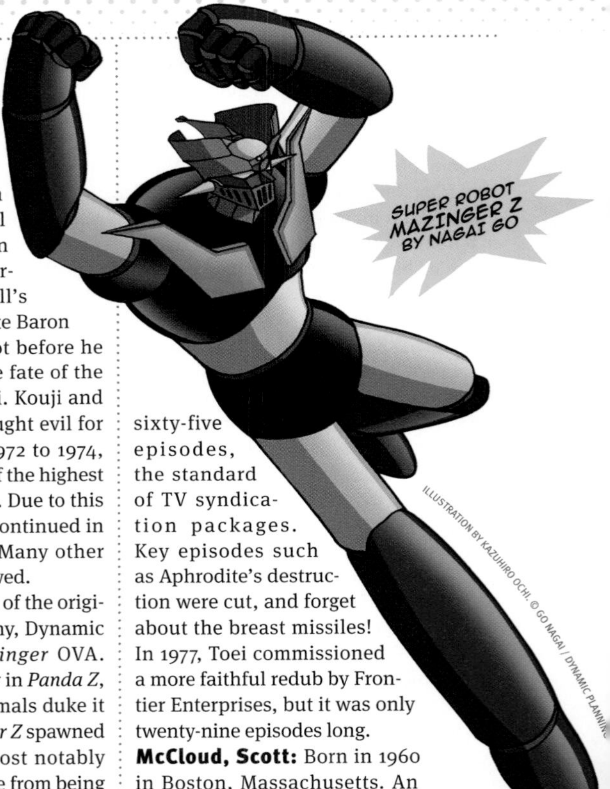

McCloud, Scott: Born in 1960 in Boston, Massachusetts. An American cartoonist and comic theorist who wrote *Understanding Comics* in 1993. Responding to the dark themes and economic woes of American comics in the 1980s, McCloud wrote comedic works such as *Zolt* (1984) and authored the "Creator's Bill of Rights" in 1988, which aimed to protect comic-book creators against exploitation in the dominant work-for-hire practices. He actively creates online WEB-COMICS which explore unique panel layouts in the "infinite canvas" of the web, as opposed to the two-dimensional pages in a book.

He is best known for this critical thinking on the medium of comics. In his discussion of MANGA, for example, McCloud identifies many critical concepts, including the "masking effect." He describes this as when manga provides sumptuous, realistic environments in the story and backgrounds, but then knowingly shows characters as cartoons to allow them to be both easily identified and suppressed by the consumer as he or she takes their place in the narrative. One example is the TEZUKA OSAMU technique of identification: where he shows the character's face, and in the next frame draws what the character is seeing to imply that the reader is actually seeing things from the same point of view.

Mecha (メカ): Also called *meka*. An abbreviation for mechanism, or any mechanical vehicle used in ANIME, MANGA, or video games. In non-Japanese usage, mecha can be limited to piloted, walking, armored fighting machines. The Japanese usage, however, is much broader, including all sorts of robots, spacecraft, exoskeletons, cars, bikes, and so on. "Robo" can be used to distinguish humanoid machines from general mecha.

An early example of mecha is YOKOYAMA MITSUTERU's *Tetsujin 28-go* (*Gigantor*) in 1963, in which a boy controls a giant robot via remote. The first piloted mecha and first of the masculine and stylish super robot genre, was NAGAI GO's anime series *MAZINGER Z* in 1972. Nagai, with Ishikawa Ken, also invented transforming or combining mecha with *Getter Robo* in 1974. *MOBILE SUIT GUNDAM* ushered in the real robot genre in 1979, which feature realistic mecha. This was taken to new heights by *Super Dimension Fortress Macross* (1982–83), and later shows such as *Bubblegum Crisis* (1987). Overseas fans were exposed to mecha in *Robotech* (a localized and syndicated retelling of *MACROSS*) in 1985, and other videotapes of "mecha anime" from Japan. Note that in Japan there is an established category of robot anime but not for mecha anime.

Mecha is extremely popular in the US. For example, the giant robot anime *The Big O*—only a minor series in Japan—met with huge success when it aired on Cartoon Network. The network was then able to co-produce a 2003 sequel with Sunrise.

In anime and manga, mecha are a particularly common metaphor for adolescence and maturity. Humanoid machines piloted by humans—usually angst-ridden teenagers—create a temporary cyborg amalgam of pilot and battle suit.

COME TO ME
YOU SEXY
MECHA !

The young pilot enters into the robotic womb, fights impossible battles, and grows into an adult. *Gundam 00*, *Macross F*, and *Tengen Toppa Gurren Lagann* are all recent additions to the genre.

In 2005, the Sakakibara Kikai company created a real-life walking "mecha," called Landwalker.

Media mix (メディアミックス): Media franchise. A character or story appearing in many different mediums to extend its popularity. In Japan, this began in the 1970s with Kadokawa, which published books, then made movies out of them and sold related merchandise. Other companies followed to market their products aggressively across various media outlets. In the 1980s, minor MANGA magazines such as *Shonen Captain, Comic Comp*, and *Comic NORA* appeared on the scene with media mix business models in mind. Kadokawa continued to lead the way in the 1990s with the *Slayers* media mix, and was involved in *Neon Genesis Evangelion*. It's now fairly standard practice for a popular series like *The Melancholy of Suzumiya Haruhi* to appear in some combination of novels, manga, ANIME, games, music CDs, films, and merchandising.

Meeting of the Animation Three: See ANIMATION SANNIN NO KAIGI.

Meganekko (メガネっ娘): A girl (*ko*) in glasses (*megane*). Any character or IDORU who's rocking a pair of specs is a meganekko.

Meruhen (メルヘン): Sounds like "Merlin," and sure enough this magical design concept indicates an element of romantic fantasy. It comes from the German, *märchen*, for fairytale.

Mihiraki (見開き): Double-page spread. Also describes an artistic rendering across two pages. This is the artist's chance to grab the reader or viewer with their best work, stunningly presented and sometimes in color.

Mimikaki (耳かき): A traditional Japanese spoon used to remove ear wax. Japanese women may sometimes clean their lover's ears using mimikaki, something that's considered the height of intimacy. This is also one of the stranger services offered by maids at certain establishments called mimikaki, or *HIZAMAKURA*, lounges.

Miniskirt police (ミニスカポリス): A type of uniformed policewoman that became a popular motif after the look appeared on *Shutsudou!*, a late-night TV show in 1996. The thought of authority figures in short skirts unsurprisingly became a major fetish for a lot of men, and alongside the costumes of other "women in uniform" such as flight attendants and RACE QUEENS, these often show up as erotic costumes. There is also a chain of restaurants in Japan called "The Lockup" where waitresses dress as sexy cops and put customers in prison cells.

MEGANEKKO AT THE CANDY FRUITS MAID OPTOMETRY

m

***Minna Agechau* ♥ Controversy (みんなあげちゃう♥ 問題):** In 1991 Central Park Media, one of the first companies in the United States to import and localize ANIME, announced the release of the mildly erotic romance comedy *Minna Agechau* ♥, at ANIMECON '91. The series, which has some exposed flesh and PANCHIRA (panty flashes), was not really that much more sexual than other 1980s anime. However, the box art had a rather racy design, and Sony packaged the set with a pair of pink paper panties. The outraged *L.A. Times* and Fox News were quick to use the show's images of exposed flesh and bawdy gags to denounce this new anime trend as a scandalous "assault on American morals." Treating anime as "Japanese pornography" was a dominant theme for some time after. Due to the extreme pressure from lobbyists, Sony dropped the title and it was never released in the States. Central Park Media went on to start its Anime-18 label specializing in extreme adult series such as *Urotsuki Doji*, changing the way people viewed anime in the United States. A.D. Vision entered the market in 1992 and quickly started the Softcel HENTAI division, said to account for a quarter of the top-selling series in the 1990s.

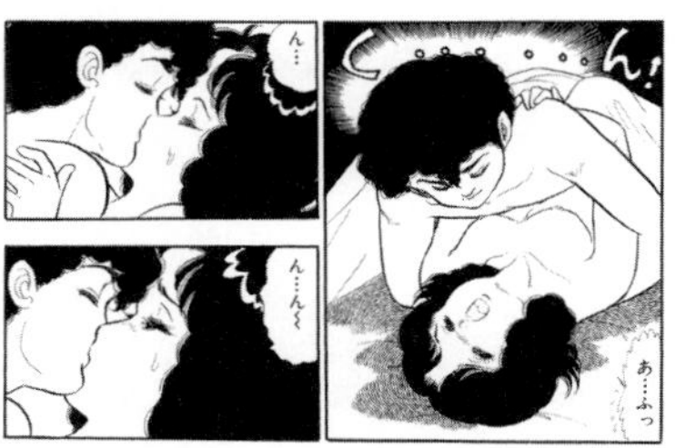

A PAGE FROM THE MANGA OF *MINNA AGECHAU* ♥ BY YUZUKI HIKARU

Misemonogoya (見せ物小屋): Theaters showing amazing things; freak shows and nonsense. These were a popular form of entertainment in the Edo period (1600–1868). There are still a few of these shows around today.

Mixi (ミクシィ): Founded by Kasahara Kenji in 2004, this is the largest online social-networking site (SNS) in Japan. In 2008 it had 10 million users, 2 million page views a day, and an 80 percent share of Japan's SNS market. The name is a combination of "mix" and "I," reflecting the idea that users can be themselves and mingle with others. Only those over eighteen are supposed to join. Each person is allowed 1,000 "my Mixi" friends. Most groups are made up of Japanese, as a Japanese cell phone is required at registration, but other than that the demographic is quite diverse. A high percentage of active users are women.

Mixi-tsukare: Mixi fatigue. Getting tired of keeping up with the demands of your online friends and finally terminating your Mixi account.

Miyamoto Shigeru (宮本茂): Born in 1952 in Kyoto. A world-renowned Japanese video game designer who put the magic and character into games. He's often called "the father of modern video games" or "the Walt Disney of electronic gaming," and is also know as "Miyahon." His 8-bit pixel character Jumpman, now known as Mario, has become a iconic maid ・ 葉月あこ

HAZUKI AKO

HAZUKI AKO (23), A TARENTO AND ACTOR FROM THE QUIET TOKYO SUBURE of Kanagawa, has become well known among Akiba-kei otaku. She was a maid at @home Café in Akihabara for one and a half years before playing the maid that made Tommy Lee Jones get all *moé* in a Boss Coffee commercial* that aired in 2008.

PG: How did you get your start in this business?

HA: I've been interested in drama since unior high school, but it was when I was at a school studying childcare that I began acting in educational plays. Eventually I thought I should join a talent agency, and that's when things really got started. I still sing songs for children and appear in play productions for grade schools held across the country.

PG: How did you go from that to working as a maid?

HA: A maid's job is to make people happy, so it's not so different from performing for children. It's similar in the way you feel the energy of the audience and feed off of it. My friend thought my personality would suit being a maid, so I gave it a try.

PG: Did you enjoy being an Akiba-maid?

HA: I didn't really have any idea about Akihabara or OTAKU. But Akiba is a such a fun place with so many different stores for hobbies. My favorite part about being a maid was playing rock-paper-scissors, because the customers and I could play together. They taught me so much.

PG: What was it like playing rock-paper-scissors with Tommy Lee Jones?

HA: I was really nervous, but it was fun. He's a very nice person and seemed to be enjoying the maid café! But I don't speak English so it was hard to communicate. want to study English so I can talk to more people.

PG: Have you been busy since starring in the commercial?

HA: Yes! I released a DVD, called *Kyun Kyun,* in July, started introducing products on the online auction site Rakuten, and am an image girl for online games. I get to do so many different things, it's not just GRA-VIA, or singing, or acting. Every day is different and interesting.

PG: What are your fans like?

HA: They're very enthusiastic! I like that they get so excited. I was in a pop group Pure Romance, for six months and we sang songs for otaku. The OTAGEI was great! I was amazing to see. We were creating the performance together.

PG: What do you want to do from now?

HA: Well, I've only been acting for children up to now, so I'd like to try some more mature stage plays. I hope everyone will watch and support me.

* These TV commercials for Boss canned coffee feature Tommy Lee Jones as "Alien Jones," an alien investigating Earth. The series features the actor trying his hand at various jobs, including a host in a host club, a construction worker, a supermarket employee, and a sound man for a film crew visiting Akihabara. He visits a maid café where he is fed OMURAISU by Ako, whom he declares is "*MOÉ.*"

SERT
VINDUJOUR
SYRAR
PINO NOIRE
CHARDONNAY
RIESLING

game character and has appeared in more than one hundred games since the seminal arcade smash *Donkey Kong* in 1981. Miyamoto is the lead designer for NINTENDO and is responsible for hits such as *Mario Bros.*, *Donkey Kong, The Legend of Zelda, Star Fox, Pikmin*, and *F-Zero*. His works are characterized by refined control mechanics, intuitive game play, simple story lines, and imaginative worlds that players are encouraged to explore and discover. Miyamoto has criticized Sony and Microsoft for focusing on hardcore gamers. In the mid-2000s he started a popular renaissance in gaming with a return to simple themes, nostalgic characters, and intuitive play that broadened user demographics. Examples include *Nintendogs* for the Nintendo DS, which is popular with women who make use of the stylus to pet virtual animals, and *Wii Fit* for the Nintendo Wii, which is popular among adults and families.

Miyazaki Hayao (宮崎駿): Born in 1941 in Tokyo. Japan's most famous living animator. A graduate of the elite Gakushuin University with degrees in politics and economics. In 1963 Miyazaki joined TOEI ANIMATION, then the biggest studio in Asia. By 1966, his work already stood out and he was chosen as a key animator for *Sally, the Witch*, a hit TV ANIME based on the MANGA by Yokoyama Mitsuteru. While at Toei, Miyazaki met Takahata Isao. The two were involved in the labor demonstrations and the student movement of the early 1970s, and as early as *Future Boy Conan* in 1978 began to introduce sophisticated social messages in their animated works. In 1979, the up and coming Miyazaki was awarded a well-funded project featuring the popular Lupin III characters from Monkey Punch's MANGA, and what emerged was *Lupin III: The Castle of Cagliostro*, a ground-breaking, perfectly executed action-romance-comedy beloved by the likes of Steven Spielberg. Among OTAKU, *Lupin III: The Castle of Cagliostro* is said to have defined LOLICON with Lupin and the villainous Cagliostro fighting over the affections of the little girl protagonist, Clarisse. This was followed by the award-winning *Nausicaä of the Valley of the Wind* in 1984, which was based on a manga drawn by Miyazaki himself during what some people call his "otaku days." He continued to expand the manga until he completed fifty-nine episodes in 1994. Fans say the MECHA and monster designs, Nausicaä's PANCHIRA, and the apocalyptic story line are proof that he was not that far removed from the body of core anime otaku at the time.

Following this success, Miyazaki co-founded Studio Ghibli with Takahata. Over the years, Miyazaki has turned out a string of hits, including *Laputa: Castle in the Sky* (1986), *Kiki's Delivery Service* (1989), *Porco Rosso* (1992), *Princess Mononoke* (1997), *Howl's Moving Castle* (2004), and *Ponyo on the Cliff by the Sea* (2008). Miyazaki shifted from otaku fantasy to

MIYAZAKI HAYAO
WITH THE GOLDEN BEAR TROPHY HE WON FOR HIS FILM ***SPIRITED AWAY*** AT THE 2002 BERLIN INTERNATIONAL FILM FESTIVAL

family fare with *My Neighbor Totoro* in 1988, which features the pastoral and elegiac anime for which he is now famous.

Studio Ghibli's parent company Tokuma signed a distribution agreement with Disney in 1996, and Miyazaki became an international sensation. In 2003, his *Spirited Away* took the Academy Award for Best Animated Feature.

Miyazaki Tsutomu Incident (宮崎勤事件): Often abbreviated as the "M-Case." Miyazaki Tsutomu was a young man who in 1988 and 1989 abducted and murdered four little girls aged four to seven years old. After killing them, he mutilated and sexually molested their corpses and ate portions of his third and fourth victims. The crimes—which, prior to Miyazaki's arrest, were called "The Little Girl Murders"—shocked Japan, which was generally considered a safe country and had a low record of crimes against children. Miyazaki claimed that he and the victims were friends but that the "rat man" had hurt the girls. When the police raided his house they found a massive collection of videocassette tapes. The majority were a variety of TV and movie productions, but they included videos taken of his victims along with some BISHOJO ANIME, porn, and extremely disturbing slasher films—including the horrific *Flower of Flesh and Blood*, which he reportedly used as the model for one of his crimes. Among the 5,763 pieces of media in the room—enough to literally block out his window—was a sealed copy of *Ultraseven* episode twelve ("From a planet with love"), which was aired only once in 1967 and released in 1975 as a rare BETAMAX. Insular and disturbed, Miyazaki was considered to be the epitome of OTAKU at the time, and his "typical otaku room" was broadcast all over Japan with the understanding that *this* was where the otaku fantasy life leads. Miyazaki was called the "Otaku Murderer" and became the symbol of moral outrage against otaku.

Being an otaku in the 1990s meant being associated with Miyazaki, effectively killing all high-profile activity in the otaku community (see ITAI). Throughout the 1990s, Miyazaki remained incarcerated and was put through a battery of psychiatric evaluations, ending with the 1997 conclusion by a team of psychiatrists from the University of Tokyo that Miyazaki—though suffering from dissociative identity disorder and extreme schizophrenia—was still aware of the consequences of his crimes and was therefore accountable for them. Miyazaki was sentenced to death by hanging, upheld by the Supreme Court of Justice on January 17, 2006. He was executed on June 17, 2008, nine days after the AKIHABARA INCIDENT.

Mizushobai (水商売): "The water business," meaning night life. This term was first used during the Edo period (1600–1868) when cheap, non-licensed prostitutes would wait by the river outside the Yoshiwara brothel district to sell themselves, then do the deed in boats away from prying eyes. Today "mizushobai" refers to all kinds of entertainment from gambling and prostitution, to clubs including "snack" bars and hostess clubs.

MMORPG: Massively multiplayer online role-playing games.

Moblogging: Mobile blogging. Most bloggers in Japan post from their mobile phones. MIXI, the number one social networking site in the country, reported in September 2007 that posts from phones exceeded those from computers.

Mode Gakuen Cocoon Tower (モード学園コクーンタワー): An iconic tower which resembles an alien-like cocoon, located outside the East Exit of Shinjuku Station in Tokyo. It was designed by Tange Associates and was completed in late 2008. It's over 203 meters tall and houses three schools, including the HAL Tokyo College of Technology & Design. HAL mainly focuses on the development of high-tech games and 3D computer graphics. It also offers courses in car and robot design, multimedia, music, and general information processing.

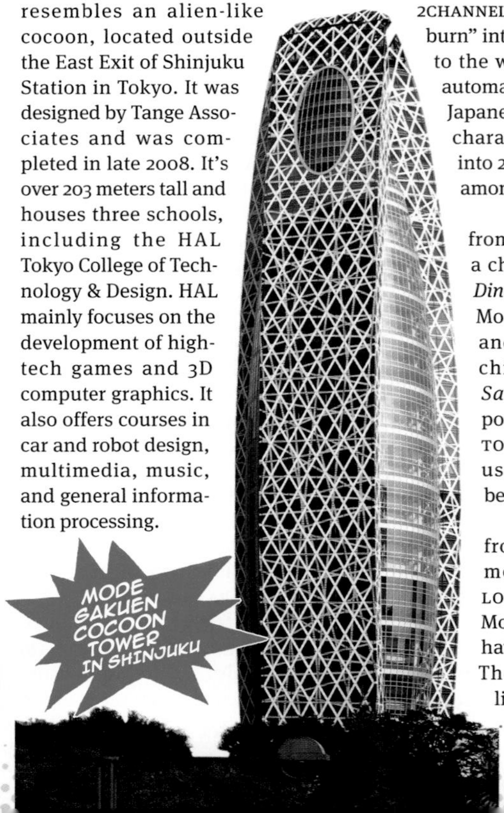

MODE GAKUEN COCOON TOWER IN SHINJUKU

Moé (もえ・萌え): Literally meaning "to bud" (萌える; *moéru*) and a pun on the homonym "to burn" (燃える; *moéru*), moé is used among OTAKU to mean getting fired up for budding young beauties. It can be used as an adjective (e.g., "*sore ga moé*," or "that is moé") or a verb (e.g., "*Rei ni moéru*," or "I burn for Rei"). It can further describe moé in, or the moé response to, an object ("*Rei-moé*," or "[I] feel moé for Rei").

Although moé has been a part of the Japanese vocabulary since the *Man'yoshu* in the 7th century, precisely why the word has entered contemporary use in this way remains unclear. One story has it the term came from a mistaken keystroke on 2CHANNEL, changing the character for "to burn" into "to bud." This is possible due to the way Japanese word processors automatically turn the *hiragana* of the Japanese alphabet into *kanji* (Chinese characters). The word was adopted into 2chan-speak and spread quickly among otaku.

Another possibility is it came from Sagisawa Moé—the name of a childish character in the ANIME *Dinosaur Planet* (1993)—or Takatsu Moé from *Taiyo ni Smashu* (1993); and later spread to include the child-like Tomoé Hotaru from *Sailor Moon S* (1994). One last possibility is suggested by OKADA TOSHIO, who says moé was first used to describe the budding beauty of childlike GRAVIA idoru.

Regardless of where it came from, a character described as moé today is an amalgam of LOLICON and BISHOJO features. Most are infantile and bright and have massive, wet, dog-like eyes. They can seem almost animal-like, alien, or androgynous. The appeal of moé relates to childlike purity, so it should come as no surprise that moé characters tend to be younger than KAWAII BISHOJO schoolgirls. The lolicon image is now considered too "real," and too sexual, so moé is used instead to define a fantasy love or desire.

Taking this a step futher, MANGA artist Akamatsu Ken of *Love Hina* fame believes that moé is the latent mothering instinct in men who want to protect and raise these imaginary characters but at the same time are sexually drawn to them. Similarly, FUJOSHI read YAOI manga as moé when a pure friendship between male characters becomes transgressively and sexually intimate. In both cases, sex with the moé character is the opposite of the fetishized purity fans say they seek, and often takes the form of abuse. As weird as this may be, psychologist Saito Tamaki has suggested that without the fantasy outlet of moé a significant portion of the Japanese population would actually become deviant.

SO THAT'S WHAT MOÉ MEANS!!
萌え

Popular online theorist Shingo—author of a report on moé for the Heisei Democracy website—identifies four types of moé characters based on imagined access to, or distance from, the character: JUNAI (pure love), OTOME-KEI (maiden-style), DENPA (kinetic) or EROKAWAII (erotic-cute).

The meaning of "moé" is slowly becoming less and less clear as the word enters the popular lexicon. It was used as a catch phrase in *DENSHA OTOKO* (*The Train Man*), a popular television drama aired on Fuji Television in 2005, and became one of the top choices in You Can's survey of the ten most influential words in Japan. That same year, the moé market of anime, manga, and video games was estimated at $888 million. In March 2007, *Newsweek Japan* ran a cover story describing the global impact of moé. By 2008 the national tourist agency had jumped on board, with a book teaching Japanese how to explain moé to foreigners in English. The Imperial Household Agency also issued a reprimand for a popular *doujin* anime called *Mako-sama moé*, which was based on His Imperial Majesty, the Emperor Akihito's granddaughter, Princess Mako, demonstrating the reach of the once humble term.

PUT YOUR HANDS TOGETHER, MAKE A HEART, AND SAY MOÉ!

Moébanashi (萌え話): The discussion of MOÉ. Moébanashi is typically a form of play in which participants try to pin down the appeal surrounding a given character, relationship, interaction, or scene by probing "moé points." Participants in the discussion can discover a lot about the tastes and personalities of each other based on what they do and don't describe as moé. This is aided by a shared language they call their "moé dictionary" (*moéjisho*).

Moékyara (萌えキャラ): A character in ANIME, MANGA, games, and so on, that's designed to be MOÉ. Ever since the success of *Di Gi Charat* (1998), with its moékyara cat-girls, there's been a strong tendency for anime to have moékyara. Those who get hooked on these characters have come to be called "moé otaku."

Moésha: See ITASHA.

Mong Kok, Hong Kong (旺角): The OTAKU area of Hong Kong. Ten minutes from the station is Nathan Street, where the Sino Centre is located. This is sometimes introduced in Japanese guidebooks as the "Otaku Building." Many idoru events take place there, and ANIME, MANGA, magazines, FIGURES, EROGE, and other goods are abundant. On the other side of Hong Kong harbor is Wan Chai, a similar otaku haven dominated by the Oriental 188 Shopping Centre. There is computer stuff there, though Sham Sui Po's Golden Computer Arcade and Golden Computer Center are the best bets.

Monokatari no hitobito (モノ語りの人々): People who talk to objects. Typically people who have problems maintaining human relationships, so instead turn their attention to physical objects such as FIGURES and DOLLS. They can form very deep relationships with these things and may even abandon human contact. See also DOLLER.

Mootoko (喪男): Unpopular man. Similar to HIMOTE. The female version is *mojo*.

Mori Hiroshi (森博嗣): Born in 1957 in Aichi Prefecture, raised in Nagoya. An engineer, researcher, and mystery writer who won the Mephist Award in 1996 for his debut work, *The Perfect Insider*. He loves models, especially locomotives and airplanes, and claims to have become a writer to support his hobby. He was a fan of MANGA in high school, especially the works of *SHONEN-AI* giant Hagio Moto, and says she is the only artist to inspire him. Some of his work has been made into manga, and his novel *Sky Crawlers* was adapted into an ANIME by OSHII MAMORU in 2008. Mori's writing contains lots of computer jargon, which makes him a favorite with OTAKU techies. His *M* and *Z* series of novels are particularly popular.

Morikawa Kaichiro (森川嘉一郎): Born in 1971 in Hyogo, Japan. A design theorist and associate professor at the School of Global Japanese Studies at Meiji University. He studied architecture at Waseda University, where he taught for the Advanced Research Center of Science and Engineering. He's also taught at the Kuwasawa Design School. He is internationally famous for his research on otaku style and design and has lived in Washington, DC, London, and Sydney. He has published several books, including *Evangelion Style* (1997), *The Impact AUM Had on Architecture* (1996), and *The Architecture of the Private Room* (2000). His best-known book is *Learning from Akihabara* (2003), where he suggests private otaku hobbies have taken over public space. Also see the INTERVIEW WITH MORIKAWA ON PAGE 14.

Mosaic (モザイク): A design made of small pieces of colored material. Or more commonly in Japan the enlarged pixels used to cover genitalia in AV. This is done in accordance with obscenity laws (see WAISETSU). Some people actually claim to prefer this pixilated porn to the uncensored stuff. See CHIRARI-IZUMU.

Moyashikko (もやしっ子): Bean sprout. Slang for a pale, thin, weak youngster who doesn't go outside to play and grows up unexposed to the light of day. The word became popular in the 1960s to describe city-dwelling youth of the era. Geeks, nerds, and OTAKU could have been described as moyashikko, but the word is now rarely used.

Munyuu (無乳): No breasts. As in a girl without any. It's similar to an older word, *pechapai*. If they have ever-so-slightly larger breasts, then the correct term is *binyuu*, not the homonym "beautiful breasts," but rather "barely breasts." The final distinction is *hinnyuu*, or "poor breasts," meaning below average. Preference for munyuu or related chest-types is deeply tied to LOLICON, KAWAII, and fetishized innocence. It also appeals to people into androgyny and FUTANARI.

A STILL FROM THE ANIMATED FEATURE KAIKAI & KIKI BY MURAKAMI TAKASHI

Murakami Takashi (村上隆): Born in 1962 in Tokyo. A prolific, high-profile contemporary Japanese artist who draws inspiration from OTAKU culture. Murakami is a painter, but, also works in digital and commercial media. He draws no distinction between high and low art and borrows from mass media and pop culture. He studied traditional Japanese painting (*nihonga*) at Tokyo National University of Fine Arts and Music.

In 1996, Murakami founded a production house and promotion company called Hiropon Factory. Soon after, he pioneered a style called "Superflat," which entails flat planes of color, slick graphic images, and characters of the kind seen in ANIME and MANGA. Murakami is often compared to Andy Warhol because he uses pop culture as art. But he's taken this a step futher by selling products and merchandise based on his artwork. His collaboration with Louis Vuitton is legendary. Some of his work has even been mass-produced as small vinyl figures and sold in convenience stores. These FIGURES are now highly collectible. Murakami's most famous characters are Mr. DOB and the rabbit-like Kaikai and Kiki—who appear in the artist's first animated film, *kaikai & kiki*.

In 2001 he renamed his studio as KAIKAI KIKI Co., Ltd., and in 2003 *Miss ko2 (Project ko2)* (1996), a life-size fiberglass figure of an anime-style girl in a waitress uniform, sold for $567,500 at a Christie's auction. Since then Murakami's work has gone on to fetch higher and higher prices, and in 2008 *My Lonesome Cowboy* (1998), a sculpture of a boy twirling a semen lasso, sold for $15.2 million at a Sotheby's auction. That same year, Murakami was the only fine artist in *Time* magazine's list of the top 100 most influential people in the world. See INTERVIEW ON PAGE 182.

Mushi Productions (虫プロ): Or Mushi Pro. A film studio founded by TEZUKA OSAMU in the 1960s to produce ANIME for television. Tezuka established Tezuka Productions in 1968 to make MANGA, leaving Mushi Pro to focus on anime. Mushi Pro went bankrupt in 1973, and Tezuka stepped down as president. The company reformed in 1977 and has since not been related to the founder, Tezuka.

m

Naeru (萎える): To wither; to lose all strength. Literally the opposite of MOÉ.

Nagai Go (永井豪): Born in 1945 in Wajima, Ishikawa Prefecture. Renowned "bad boy" MANGAKA who in the 1970s single-handedly changed ANIME with grotesque, violent, and sexual content, setting the groundwork for more serious and adult themes. In series such as *Devilman* he pioneered anime that was heavy on blood and guts. In *Mazinger Z* he introduced piloted super robots that battle one another, transforming robots in *Getter Robo* (with Ishikawa Ken), and with *Cutie Honey* he dreamed up girls who wield secret powers through transformation. Nagai is also credited with started KICHIKU-KEI, or violent and sexual anime, with *Devilman Lady*.

DEVILMAN BY NAGAI GO

Nakano Broadway (中野ブロードウェー): Longtime OTAKU hangout in Nakano, Tokyo. Far more eclectic than Akihabara due to the concentration of all types of stores in one large, mazelike, old shopping mall. The third floor is a veritable den of otaku businesses and home to the original MANDARAKE store that sprawls across the building. Here you can find many vintage goods from overseas, as well as collectibles from rare Japanese series and FIGURES whose molds were broken long ago. It's not as crowded as Akihabara and is definitely worth the trip for connoisseurs. Aside from the usual MANGA, ANIME, FIGURE, and COSPLAY fare (stores and cafés), one thing that should not be missed here is Taco Che, a counterculture manga shop specializing in individually produced works. This was once the outlet for GARO magazine.

n

NAKANO FUJOSHI SISTERS

Nakagawa Shoko (中川翔子): See SHOKO-TAN

Nakano Fujoshi Sisters (中野腐女子シスターズ): Pronounced "Nakano Fujosisters." A seven-girl IDORU band. They were formed in 2006 and mainly appeared on the Internet TV website *GyaO@ShowTime*. They also appeared in live-houses around Nakano, building up their OTAKU fan base. Their debut hit, "GO! FIGHT! Fujoshi Sisters," was released for mobile phones in 2007. They had much greater success dressed as *DANSO* and performing as Fudanjuku, whose first mainstream CD was *Otokozaka* (2008). The group originally consisted of Inui Yoko, Kyan Chiaki, Kyomoto Yuka, Ura Erika, Konan Yuka and Suzanne, who became a famous TV TARENTO and left the band.

Nanpa (ナンパ): Slang for picking up girls. Can also describe a "soft" skirt-chaser, the opposite of a "hard" man (KOHA).

Napier, Susan J.: Born in 1955 in Boston, Massachusetts. An expert on Japanese literature and culture who explores the cultural elements of ANIME and MANGA on both sides of the Pacific. Her book *Anime: From Akira to Princess Mononoke* (2001) was among the first to investigate the impact of anime.

***Nausicaä of the Valley of the Wind*:** See *KAZE NO TANI NO NAUSICAÄ*.

NEET: Not in Employment, Education or Training. A government classification, first used in the United Kingdom. It's become common in Japan as a new way to criticize youth, especially OTAKU, PARASITE-SINGLES, and HIKIKOMORI. See also NON-SHAKAIJIN.

Nekama (ネカマ): Someone who acts gay online. Internet *okama*.

Nekomimi (猫耳): Cat ears; especially as costume pieces or charm points on ANIME and MANGA characters. Also refers to the sex kittens who wear or have them. Nekomimi characters often make a cute little "*nya*" (meow) sound when speaking. They've been popular since Oshima Yumiko's *Wata no Kunihoshi* series began in 1978. The fact these characters are not quite human is appealing to folks who desire the unusual.

Nekura-zoku (ネクラ族): The Gloomy Tribe. An early name for OTAKU prior to the 1980s. Basically, people defined as

NYAN! NEKOMIMI ARE SO KAWAII!

n

such were thought to be eccentric, brainy, weak, ugly, lacking fashion sense, lurking in shadows, and obsessive. Pretty much how a lot of people now view otaku.

***Neon Genesis Evangelion*:** See *SHIN SEIKI EVANGELION*.

Neo Tokyo (ネオ東京): A reconstructed, fictional version of the Japanese capital, usually following a catastrophe. One of the most common themes in ANIME and MANGA and typified by works such as *AKIRA*, the Neo Tokyo ideal reflects immense urban insecurity and the growing pains of a nation that went from under developed to First World in a matter of decades, only to have its efforts dashed time and time again by poor planning, war, and natural disasters. The fires of old Edo, the 1923 Great Kanto Earthquake, Allied firebombing in WWII, and the shared cultural memory of the atomic bombings, have reinforced a powerful collective memory of total destruction. The insecurity and dreams of Tokyoites are mixed with the city's imaginary destruction and reconstruction, as can be seen in films such as *GOZILLA* where Tokyo is destroyed. The twin pressure to move forward and rebuild is reflected in the Neo Tokyo ideal.

Neraa (ネラー): 2CHANNELer. Someone who uses 2channel often. There are many subcategories, for example VIPPERs, who write personal stuff when other topics run out.

Neta (ネタ): Online slang for "topic," although it's now also used in spoken OTAKU language. It can mean the discussions that crop up around anything from pictures and video to blogs and text. It's also used somewhat incorrectly to mean "online creator of fan fiction." Neta-*bare* means giving the story away

Netamikko (妬みっ娘): A jealous girl. An angry, sulking character type.

Neta-moto (ネタ元): Based on a NETA.For example, *DENSHA OTOKO* is neta-moto.

Net café nanmin (ネットカフェ難民): Net café refugees. A term for Japan's urban young working poor and homeless who use twenty-four-hour Net cafés and MANGA KISSA as a home base when they can't afford rooms. In August 2007 the number of people living like this was estimated to be at least 5,400.

Net idoru (ネットアイドル): An IDORU who appears mainly, or debuts, online. They tend to be amateurs with blogs or websites or are just starting their careers by promoting small companies. The first major Net idoru in Japan was Tsurumi Kaori in 1996, with her blog "A seventeen-year-old's Room." She became incredibly popular and appeared across magazines, TV, and radio. She was followed by Koga Rie and Michiko, which led to the establishment of Justnet Idoru TV, a site that fed the Net idoru boom in 1999. The site closed in 2002, but not before starting a major trend. Today, many Net idoru, such as Amane Ramu, can be seen on dedicated sites and communities such as YouTube or NICO NICO DOUGA.

AMANE RAMU
NET IDORU

New Age of Anime Declaration: See ANIME SHINSEIKI SENGEN.

Newtype (ニュータイプ): The next stage of humanity promised in the *Mobile Suit GUNDAM* series. Newtypes have a heightened mental awareness and have naturally adapted to life in space. The magazine *Newtype* takes its name from here and was launched in 1985, a week after *Zeta Gundam* began airing.

都合により、番組を変更してお送りしています。
ナイスボート
Nice Boat
最終話「素晴らしき舟」

THE "NICE BOAT" COMMENT HAS BECOME AN INTERNET MEME

Nice Boat: The day before the last episode of the *School Days* ANIME was scheduled to air in September 2007, a sixteen-year-old girl killed her father with an axe in Kyoto. The anime was known to have violent scenes, and TV Kanagawa and most other stations airing the show decided to replace the episode with thirty minutes of a ferry in a fjord scored by classical music. This was ostensibly to avoid association with the murder. The sudden swap of the final episode with scenic footage came as a shock to many fans, and a 4CHANNEL member made the ironic comment "Nice boat." The phrase became an Internet meme and was ranked tenth in Yahoo! Japan's keyword search in September 2007. Overflow, the creators of the game the anime was based on, named its booth "Nice boat" for Comiket 73 in 2007 and sold "Nice boat" merchandise.

2channel (2ちゃんねる): Ni-channel. Pronounced "nee-chan-ne-roo" and sometimes abbreviated as 2chan (nee chan). It is an anonymous online bulletin board system (BBS) frequented by OTAKU types who let loose with scorching criticisms and wild new ideas. Many of the most innovative otaku ideas, from ZETTAI RYOIKI to MOÉ, can be traced back to here. It was the bright idea of Nishimura Hiroyuki, the founder, infamous for the many lawsuits against him. In January 2009, Hiroyuki relinquished ownership of 2channel to Packet Monster Inc. in Singapore, ostensibly to limit his personal liability.

2channel-ers are known for the emoticon images they create with keystrokes (see AA) and their slang (see also LEET). The otaku idoru SHOKO-TAN uses 2channel-speak to denote her belonging to this subculture. 2channel and its activities were featured in *DENSHA OTOKO* (2005). It is the largest BBS in Japan.

Nico Chuu (ニコ厨): NICO NICO DOUGA plus *Chuugakusei*, or middle-school student. Slang for a hardcore Nico Nico Douga addict and enthusiast. The use of *chuu*, written with the wrong *kanji* (not 中 but 厨), gives the name an impression of youthful bliss and idiocy.

Nico Nico Douga (ニコニコ動画): A video-sharing website, similar to YouTube, where fans get together and post written comments on streaming video in real time. The comments are not below the video, but on top of the image, and the words unfold as they are written and at the tempo they are thought. It's the equivalent of having a room full of critics shouting comments out as the film is still rolling. The result is both confusing and brilliant, but always amusing as the anonymous fans let loose and reveal their thoughts about what they would normally be viewing alone.

Nihon e-Supotsu Kyoukai (日本eスポーツ協会): The Japan e-Sports Association

(JESPA). Founded in 2007 as part of the global drive to establish video gaming as an Olympic sport by 2016.

Nijigen fechi (二次元フェチ): Two-dimensional fetish. Someone who is sexually excited by, or only interested in, things that are drawn or animated. On October 22, 2008, a man named Takashita Taichi filed a petition on the Shomei TV website, asking the government to recognize two-dimensional marriages. Within two weeks, 2,443 others had signed on to his cause. There are still debates raging over how many men could theoretically marry one ANIME character.

Nijigenhatsukoi (二次元初恋): Two-dimensional first love. The first animated character an OTAKU or FUJOSHI falls in love with. Ask what someone's nijigenhatsukoi was if you really want to hit it off with another otaku.

Nijisosaku (二次創作): Second-generation creation. Roughly equivalent to DOUJIN MONO. These are works based on, or about, existing stories, usually done in homage or to explore variants. There are also "third-generation creations" that borrow and take off on tangents from nijisosaku.

Nijyuuyonnen gumi (花の24年組): The Magnificent 49ers. Collective name for innovative SHOJO MANGA artists (born around 1949, or Showa 24); first used in manga criticism in the early 1970s. With their multilayered page layouts, elaborately girly designs, and androgynous characters, these women are considered to be the founders of shojo manga, as it is known today. YAOI manga owes much to their pioneering work. Members include the legendary MANGAKA Hagio Moto, Takemiya Keiko, and Oshima Yumiko.

Nintendo (任天堂): A leading Japanese video game company and the longest surviving console manufacturer in the world. The company was founded in Kyoto in 1889 by Yamauchi Fusajiro, who was handcrafting colorful *hanafuda* playing cards. His grandson, Yamauchi Hiroshi, wanted to expand the company and tried to diversify into other areas such as LOVE HOTELS, taxis, a TV network, and instant rice, but none of these were successful.

Nintendo moved into the toy business in 1963. Led by developer Yokoi Gunpei, it made successful products including the Ultra Hand, Ultra Machine, Love Tester, and light gun games. In 1973 it produced the Laser Clay Shooting System, which made use of its light gun technology and became popular in arcades. Nintendo started making home systems in 1977 with the Color TV Game console. MIYAMOTO SHIGERU was hired as a developer and worked with Yokoi.

In 1980, Yokoi developed a hand-held game system after seeing bored salarymen playing with calculators on the train. The Game & Watch featured an LCD display and a "control-cross," or D-Pad, which allows for motion left, right, up, and down. This was an incredible global success. In 1981 Nintendo released the smash hit *Donkey Kong*. The game's protagonist "Jump Man," later became known as "Mario" and has become one of the world's most recognizable characters.

PHOTO: NINTENDO

The much-beloved Family Computer, or "Famicon" console, hit the shelves in 1983 along with versions of arcade favorites. It was released as the Nintendo Entertainment System (NES) in the United States in 1985. This was followed by *Super Mario Bros.*, one of the best-selling games of all time. Yokoi struck gold again in 1989 with the portable Game Boy system that dominated hand-helds until the advent of PlayStation Portable and Nintendo DS in 2004. Game Boy sold 118.69 million units worldwide. It was bundled with *Tetris*, one of the most popular Game Boy games, and was the home to the *Pokémon* franchise in 1996, which sold 76 million copies. Nintendo continued to innovate with Super Famicon (or SNES) in 1990, the Nintendo 64 in 1996, and Nintendo GameCube in 2001.

Developers, including Miyamoto, responded to Japan's aging population with intuitive console game-play targeting families. In 2007 Nintendo released the Wii system, which uses motion-sensing controllers so players can manipulate the game just by moving; this has led to a rash of fitness-driven games such as the WiiFit and Wii Balance Board.

Nintendo is now one of the most valuable companies in Japan and the tenth largest software developer in the world. By 2008, Nintendo had sold over 485 million console systems and 2.8 billion games.

THE NINTENDO WII

Nipponbashi, Osaka (大阪日本橋): A massive pocket of OTAKU activity in Osaka, Japan's second largest city, and one of the five otaku holy lands along with AKIHABARA, NAKANO BROADWAY, and OTOME ROAD in Tokyo, and OSU in Nagoya. It's most famous for FIGURES, toys and collectibles, but has its share of MAID and DANSO CAFÉS. Several blocks on either side of the 700-meter Sakaisuji street are peppered with great stores and hidden places, making it far larger and more diverse than even Akihabara in Tokyo. The main strip is sometimes called Den Den Town or "Otaroad," the Otaku Road. It's here that a massive festival for COSPLAY and street performance has been held since 2004, drawing some 170,000 people. It's often held in conjunction with other events such as the Japan SF Convention. Other than these special times, however, cosplay and street IDORU are not so common. Like Akihabara, it is suffering from an apartment building boom and a shifting demographic of non-otaku visitors.

Nomura Institute report (野村総合研究所オタク消費者層): The common name for a 2004 report lead by researcher Kitabayashi Ken that points out that OTAKU are "enthusiastic consumers" who get hooked on hobbies and spend a fortune to feed their addictions. The major claim was there are 2.85 million otaku in Japan spending \$2.5 billion a year on their hobbies. A follow-up study in 2005 re-evaluated the core otaku group at 1.72 million but claimed they spend \$3.5 billion a year on hobbies. This was the first detailed report on the scale of the otaku market, and it fueled the move of many government and business ventures into AKIBA, MOÉ, and otaku territory.

n

Non-ability: See HIJITSURYOKU.

Nonai kanojo (脳内彼女): Literally "girlfriend in mind." A relationship that exists only in fantasy but is taken very seriously by the lonely OTAKU involved.

Nonke (ノンケ): A man who does not consider himself gay and likes women, but somehow gets caught up in a homosexual relationship. Nonke are a common character type in YAOI and BL as a way to include non-gay characters in these stories.

Non-shakaijin (non社会人): Antisocial people. A common way to criticize someone who is not a working adult and therefore not a full-fledged member of society (*shakaijin*).

N00b (ヌーブ): Internet or gamer slang for a newcomer, or "newbie." Someone who's not yet used to the rules and protocols of online interaction or game-play, so tends to act like an inexperienced boob. The opposite is "l33t," pronounced "LEET."

Nopan (ノーパン): Abbreviation for "no pants," meaning "no panties" or a girl without knickers on. Nopan cafés were popular in the 1980s.

Nosebleed: See HANAJI.

Novel games (ノベルゲーム): Dating sims, BISHOJO games, and GYARUGE that are extremely text heavy and feature few, if any, images of sex. The focus in these games is to work through the narrative—which changes according to the player's choices—and experience the emotional roller coaster of romance and growing up. The works of game company KEY are particularly good examples.

Nozoki (覗き): Peeping. Japan has a long history of peeping Toms, and one even appears in the world's first novel, the 11th-century *Tale of Genji*. In the story, Kashiwagi, the son of a friend of Prince Genji, peeps through a curtain at Genji's second wife and falls in love. At the time noble women did not show their faces to people outside their families, so peeping was a necessary way for men to see what they were in for before starting a serious relationship. Sometimes this was even intentionally staged by women who came of marriageable age to spread rumors of their beauty. These days the same kind of enjoyment is found in CHAKUERO, FAN SERVICE, and even nozoki cafés.

AH! DON'T NOZOKI!! I HAVE NOPAN!

OA: Abbreviation for "on air." Especially used when a new TV ANIME is released. The more standard Japanese term is *hoso*.

Oden-kan (おでん缶): Oden—the hardy Japanese soup of fish, eggs, vegetables, octopus, sausages, and various other bits and pieces—available in a can. This first started in chilly northern Japan where hot canned oden is sold from vending machines; a pleasant side-effect of which being the heated cans keep you warm. Oden-kan was imported to AKIBA in 1990, when the owner of Chichibu Electronics started it dispensing from machines in front of his shop. He claims he did it so that OTAKU—waiting for events and sales during winter—could warm their hands. There were also few other dining options at the time, making fast food like this quite popular. Today, almost every store in AKIHABARA has some kind of character-branded oden-kan to sell to tourists. Chichibu has since expanded its range of hot canned food to include, *yakitori* chicken skewers, *ramen* noodles, and puddings. In 2007, the store reported over $800,000 in annual revenue from its vending machines.

ODEN-KAN A HOT MEAL IN A CAN!

Ofukai (オフ会): Offline meeting. Meeting people you normally deal with online in an offline, face-to-face context. Among OTAKU, this usually occurs in groups at events.

Okada Toshio (岡田斗司夫): Born 1958 in Osaka. Prominent authority on OTAKU culture and history. Okada was a mover and shaker at the DAICON conventions and a co-founder of GAINAX. Gainax transformed the ANIME industry and otaku culture in Japan, with Okada writing the OVA *Gunbuster* in 1988 and producing *Otaku no Video* in 1991. He was forced to resign as the president of Gainax in 1992 after partners accused him of neglecting the company. He was adjunct professor at the prestigious University of Tokyo from 1992 to 1997 and founder of "*otakugaku*" (study of otaku). Okada is often called the "OTAKING" (king of otaku). However, after losing fifty kilos in weight and writing a best-selling book on weight loss, he has now retired from theorizing on otaku. See INTERVIEW ON PAGE 174

Okashii (おかしい): Ridiculous; comical.

(W)okashi (をかし): Emotional attraction. A literary concept from the Heian period (794–1185) meaning an attraction to something that's slightly unusual or special. See also HINICHIJOSEI.

Okashi-kei (お菓子系): Candy-style. Saccharine sweet, sugary, and kind. Used especially when describing IDORU and AV stars.

Okoge (お焦げ): Burnt rice or rice that sticks to the pot. Slang for girls who like gay boys and stick to them because they fantasize about being with someone kind and unthreatening. This is roughly equivalent to the English term "fag hag," but it is distinct from FUJOSHI, who are fans of fictional romances between men rather than real gays.

Okui Masami (奥井雅美): Born in 1968 in Itamishi, Hyogo Prefecture. A prolific ANISONG performer responsible for many hit theme songs, including those from *Slayers*, *Revolutionary Girl Utena*, *Bakuretsu Hunter*, and *Soreyuke! Uchuu Senkan Yamamoto Yohko*. She was formerly signed to King Records, but now has her own record label, evolution, which is part of the Geneon group.

Omake (おまけ): A freebie; an extra; a bonus. These include supplementary ANIME segments on DVDs, behind-the-scenes shoots, and other goods that come free with a purchase.

Omocha (おもちゃ): A toy, or something that can be played with. Usually toys for kids, rather than the stuff that OTAKU buy. Japan was a leading force in the toy industry for a long time, taking the best of European models such as German tinker toys and creating high-quality and unique artifacts such as tin toys. The history of craftsmanship associated with Japan and its artisan class comes through in toys and dolls collected and revered around the world. John Lasseter of Pixar Animation famously loved Japanese toys so much that he centered his first 1988 short film, "Tin Toy," on them. There is a Tin Toy Museum in Kyoto and a Toy Museum outside Himeji.

Omuraisu (オムライス): An omelette with rice inside. A favorite item on the menu at MAID CAFÉS because maids write special messages on them with ketchup.

OMURAISU: A MAID CAFÉ CLASSIC

109 Building: See ICHI MARU KYU BIRU.

1 World Manga: Started in 2007, this is a cooperative effort by the World Bank and VIZ Media to produce MANGA for the 85 percent of the world's youth who live in developing countries. The manga are donated to public libraries to assist in education. Topics include HIV/AIDS, poverty, and corruption, a little different from the high-school romances and bawdy humor favored in Japan and the United States.

Oniichan (お兄ちゃん): Big brother. Also the way of choice for some IDORU and MAIDS to refer to their close circle of fans.

Only (オンリー): An abbreviation for "only event." A small, intimate convention devoted exclusively to a single interest, story, or character. For example, "*Prince of Tennis* only," "*Dragon Quest* only," or "NEKOMIMI only"). They can be found at various places around Japan throughout the year and are alternatives to the bigger events. The basic idea is that it's easier to relax and create a positive atmosphere among people who share a specific interest.

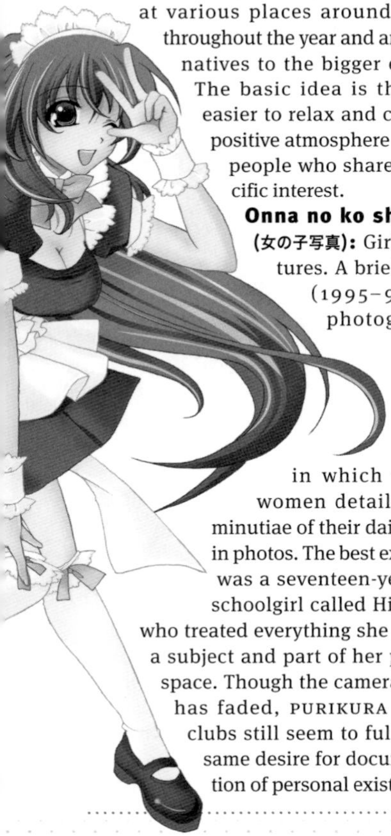

Onna no ko shashin (女の子写真): Girls' pictures. A brief boom (1995–96) in photography in which young women detailed the minutiae of their daily lives in photos. The best example was a seventeen-year-old schoolgirl called Hiromix, who treated everything she saw as a subject and part of her private space. Though the camera craze has faded, PURIKURA photo clubs still seem to fulfill the same desire for documentation of personal existence.

Ookii otomodachi (大きいお友達): Big friend. Used to describe adults who like kid's stuff, including types of ANIME, MANGA, toys, and so on. The guys alone in the theater watching DISNEY films or at theme parks watching SENTAI shows are good examples. The term became popular when SEIYUU Hisakawa Aya described an OTAKU fan this way at a *Sailor Moon* event.

Oppai-porori (おっぱいポロリ): Term used by gossip hounds to denote a boob-shot or incident in which the breast is exposed. Most famous might be Janet Jackson's "wardrobe malfunction" during the 2004 Super Bowl half-time show.

Osananajimi (幼なじみ): Childhood or lifelong friend. Like the girl-next-door scenario, this is sometimes used as a narrative device to bring two characters together and make them close without the need for an explanation. This is especially good for romantic angles, as in osanajimi of the opposite sex, and is often found in romance MANGA and ANIME, and EROGE. In such cases, the girl is typically a TSUNDERE-type or little-sister character who is bossy and bratty in her secret desire to be near her crush.

Oshii Mamoru (押井守): Born in 1951 in Tokyo. Director famous for his philosophical storytelling. He graduated from Tokyo Liberal Arts University in 1976 and was part of the student protest movements at the time. Oshii's animated and live-action films are often influenced by his experience in the later stages of the failed student demonstrations against the US-Japan Security Treaty during the 1960s and 1970s.

In 1977, he entered Tatsunoko Productions to work as a director. In 1980, he moved to Studio Pierrot, where he met screenwriter Ito Kazunori and character designer Amano Yoshitaka (who did the early *Final Fantasy* art). Oshii's work as director and storyboard artist for the wildly popular gag romance ANIME *Urusei Yatsura* (1981–86) put him in the spotlight. He directed two films, based on TAKAHASHI RUMIKO's *Urusei Yatsura: Only You* in 1983 and *Urusei Yatsura: Beautiful Dreamer* in 1984. The later was rewritten by Oshii to meet his more moody philosphical agenda, and Takahashi almost didn't approve. The animated dolly shots, a distended sense of time, and structural repetition created a dreamlike atmosphere the director would come to be known for.

After he finished the first OVA in Japan, *Dallos* (1983), Oshii left Studio Pierrot and went solo; he has remained so ever since. In 1985, he released *Angel's Egg*, a stunning art film inspired by his loss of faith in religion. Amano did the character designs.

Oshii joined up with his old friend Ito, and along with Yuki Masami, Izubuchi Yutaka, and Takada Akemi put out the *Patlabor* OVA (1988–89), TV series (1989–90), and films (1989, 1993). This was a huge MECHA hit, with plenty of comedy and drama, but it still touched on the issues of government and environment in a near-future setting.

Starting in 1986, Oshii penned a MANGA evoking his experience in the protest movements, the *Kenro Densetsu*. Many of his live-action films come from this work, including *The Red Spectacles* (1987) and *Stray Dog: Kerberos Panzer Cops* (1991). Oshii approached BANDAI about producing an animated version in the early 1990s, but as these films did not fare well at the box office, Bandai agreed only if Oshii did not direct. They offered him another project, which he took. It wasn't until 1999 that *Kenro* made it to ANIME directed by Okiura Hiroyuki; *Jin-roh: The Wolf Brigade* became the most well-loved of the *Kenro Densetsu*. Oshii would return to *Kenro* in 2006 with the live-action *Tachigui: The Amazing Lives of the Fast Food Grifters*.

In the meantime, the animated film Oshii directed for Bandai instead of *Jin-roh* was *GHOST IN THE SHELL*, released in

1995 and surely his most famous work. This landmark animated CYBERPUNK film is based on the sexy girl meets mecha action-comedy manga by SHIROW MASAMUNE, but Oshii made it his own. In his typical way, Oshii raises the question of humanity's place in an increasingly posthuman, technological world.

THE FILMS AVALON AND THE SKY CRAWLERS DIRECTED BY OSHII MAMORU

After a five-year directing hiatus, he returned in 2001 with the live-action Polish and Japanese film *Avalon*, which questions the bounds of online games and reality. In 2004, Oshii put out *INNOCENCE*, a sequel to *Ghost in the Shell* and one of the most pain stakingly rendered anime to date; it took a year to complete one sequence that took place in a doll house. STUDIO GHIBLI and PRODUCTION I.G co-produced the film. In 2004 *Innocence* became the first animated film to compete for the Palme d'Or prize at the Cannes Film Festival. In 2008, Oshii's anime film *The Sky Crawlers*, about ageless adolescents who eternally fight pretend wars at the behest of capitalist companies, competed for the Golden Lion in the Venice Film Festival and won the Future Film Festival Digital Award.

Osu, Nagoya (名古屋大須): A pocket of OTAKU activity in central Japan and one of the five otaku holy lands along with AKIHABARA, NAKANO BROADWAY, and OTOME ROAD in Tokyo, and NIPPONBASHI in Osaka. It has COSPLAY cafés of varied and interesting themes.

Ota (オタ): A suffix used to indicate OTAKU-like interest. For example, "John is such a Gun-ota" (*Gundam* otaku). Some fans prefer this to being called "otaku," which they say has become too diluted to describe any one fan group, whereas "ota" describes exactly what kind of otaku they are.

(W)ota (ヲタ): Contraction of (W)OTAKU and used the same way as OTA.

Otagei (オタ芸): A combination of the words "OTAKU" and "*geinou*" (art). This term is used among IDORU fans to describe the dance and cheerleading moves they use at idoru concerts to excite the crowd and the performer. Some practitioners, called "*otageishi*," train daily to sharpen

OTAGEI AT A SAKURAGAWA HIMEKO SHOW (SEE INTERVIEW P.106)

weeks. Tens of thousands applied to be officially certified as "otaku."

The test stopped in 2006 and now exists only in private circles and online. The Otaken has in some ways been revived in recent years by the regular ANIME KENTEI exam held at the Tokyo Anime Center in AKIHABARA.

Otaking (オタキング): The King of Otaku. The comical goal of the characters in GAINAX's *OTAKU NO VIDEO*. OKADA TOSHIO, a former producer at Gainax, has been called the otaking.

Otakkii (オタッキー): Adjective to describe OTAKU-like people or activities. It was mostly used in the '90s by non-otaku people to mean "gross" or "gloomy," but it has since fallen out of use.

Otaku (おたく、オタク): Nerd; geek or fanboy. A hardcore or cult fan. Originates from a polite second-person pronoun meaning "your home" in Japanese, allowing the speaker to refer to the listener indirectly. Since the 1980s it's been used, much like the term "geek" in the US, to refer to people who are really into ANIME, MANGA, video games, and technology.

The etymology of the word is complex, but there are several possibilities. The explanation preferred by cultural commentators is that because young nerds stayed home a lot, they were unable to manage social interactions and referred to one another indirectly as "otaku" the way their mothers did with each other. However, otaku themselves tend to stress that they imitated other fans who used the word, not their parents.

For example, some of the founders of the anime studio GAINAX—among the first

their skills, and they become as important to the fan community as the idoru herself. Basically these otakus' MOÉ levels have reached a point where watching is no longer enough, and they feel a need to become part of the show.

Otaken (オタ験): The Otaku Certification Exam. Developed in 2005 by Biblos publishers with the intention of separating ANIME and MANGA fans from "authentic" OTAKU. It basically consists of extremely challenging questions on the minutiae of geekdom. For example:

Which two statements about the COMIKET events between 1996 and 2002 are false? (Two points each)

1. All were held at Tokyo BIG SIGHT.
2. There was an incident in which a timed incendiary device was planted at the venue.
3. Visitors to the event surpassed 200,000 for the first time during the period.
4. The event was held for three consecutive days for the first time during the period.
5. One event held during the period was on Christmas Eve.

When Biblos released news of the test on its website, it got 500,000 hits in two hardcore anime aficionados—hail from Tottori Prefecture, where "otaku" is commonly used as "you." It's possible that fans who encountered the Gainax crew might have adopted the dialect as slang. The word "otaku" was also used by the characters in Studio Nue's seminal anime *MACROSS* in 1982, and the vernacular was quickly disseminated among fans.

In 1983 the essayist and humorist Nakamori Akio came across fans at DOUJINSHI markets calling one another "otaku." Shocked by their numbers, behavior, and appearance, he penned an unflattering article titled "Otaku Research" that ran in the magazine *Manga Burikko*. Anime fans moved to abandon the word, but it came back in the media frenzy surrounding the MIYAZAKI TSUTOMU INCIDENT in 1989 when a man who killed four little girls was found to have a massive collection of VHS tapes, including anime. This was the impetus for the media to call him the "Otaku Murderer." The same year, Nakamori turned out a book called *The Generation of M*, discussing otaku and the crime; and journalist Machiyama Tomohiro also released his *Book of Otaku*. The formerly innocuous word took on a taboo tone for many Japanese and was banned on one network TV.

OKADA TOSHIO, a producer at Gainax, responded to all this criticism by releasing a mock documentary called *Otaku no Video* in 1991 and giving lectures on otaku at the University of Tokyo in 1992. Unfortunately, the negative image stuck when, in 1995, AUM SHINRIKYO, a cult with apocalyptic beliefs influenced by anime, released sarin gas on the Tokyo subway, a horrendous tragedy again described by the media as perpetrated by otaku.

At the same time, "otaku" was entering the English vocabulary. It gradually gained traction at anime conventions in the early 1990s, and spread like wildfire with AnimEigo's translation of *Otaku no Video* in 1993. That year, the word was established enough to appear on the cover

of the premiere issue of *Wired* magazine. In 1994, the annual convention Otakon was formed, referencing otaku in its very name. This spread to sci-fi with mention in William Gibson's 1996 novel *Idoru*, and then a slew of news articles on anime fandom in the late 1990s and early 2000s. Otaku was popularly adopted to mean a specialist of Japanese anime, manga, and video games, and extensions of these such as COSPLAY, FIGURES, and IDORU.

Back in Japan, "otaku" still had negative connotations until the early 2000s. However, the acceptance of anime overseas led the Japanese government to start actively promoting anime, manga, and video games (see COOL JAPAN). Research firms ran the numbers and found otaku are ultra-consumers whose enthusiastic spending on hobbies didn't decline during the recession. Otaku were suddenly a bright spot for recessionary Japan.

In 2005, Fuji TV's *DENSHA OTOKO* heralded the beginning of the good-guy otaku image that changed the face of AKIBA. Today it's not uncommon for celebrities like SHOKO-TAN, or politicians such as ASO TARO, to associate with otaku.

(W)otaku (ヲタク): An alternative way to write or say "OTAKU," adopted by third generation otaku as a way to distinguish themselves.

Otakugaku (オタク学): The academic study of OTAKU. This includes work in cultural and media studies. OKADA TOSHIO pioneered this in lectures at the University of Tokyo from 1992 to 1997.

Otaku gari (オタク狩り): OTAKU hunting. The practice of finding otaku and mugging them. People target otaku for three reasons: 1) otaku have money to spare to fund shopping sprees, 2) they are considered weak and won't fight back and 3) they are too shy to tell the police and are unpopular with authority anyway.

Otaku gari gari (オタク狩り狩り): Hunting OTAKU hunters. Dressing like an otaku and beating the snot out of would be predators.

Otaku Murderer (オタク殺人事件): See MIYAZAKI TSUTOMU INCIDENT.

"'Otaku' no Kenkyuu" (『おたく』の研究): "'Otaku' Research." The first media exposé on OTAKU, published in LOLICON magazine *Manga Burikko* in 1983. The author, Nakamori Akio, identified otaku as eccentrics who are weak, ugly, unfashionable, shadowy, and obsessive, lumping everyone previously known as MANIA, fan, NEKURA-ZOKU, or just a plain "loser" into this new conceptual frame of "otaku." He was inspired to write the article by watching 10,000 geeks "freaking out" at COMIKET. In later installments of the column he labeled fans of ANIME, MANGA and games "otaku."

***Otaku no Video* (おたくのビデオ):** A semi-true mockumentary by GAINAX on the history of OTAKU and the company itself. It combined ANIME with live-action documentary sequences. The anime tells the tale of Kubo, who is led off the path to the top of Japanese society when he falls in with Tanaka and his otaku circle. Kubo decides to become the Otaking and create a place where otaku can belong. He starts an "otaku" company and fights for the right to be otaku. His big plans includes "otaku-izing" the world, building an otaku theme park, and journeying into space to find the planet of Otaku. The comedy of comrades struggling for success is juxtaposed with documentary interviews called "A Portrait of Otaku," which satirize the dark parts of otaku culture. It's believed all the subjects in these segments were Gainax employees, including OKADA TOSHIO, Sato Hiroshi, and Craig York, an

SPOILER ALERT!!
STOP READING NOW IF YOU DON'T WANT TO KNOW WHAT HAPPENS!

otaku · 岡田斗司夫

OKADA TOSHIO

ONCE KNOWN AS THE *OTAKING* (KING OF OTAKU), Okada Toshio (50) was one of the organizers of DAICON III and IV and a founder of Gainax who made the word "*OTAKU*" popular with his otaku studies books and seminars at the University of Tokyo. Now a lecturer at Osaka University of Arts, he claims otaku are culturally dead.

PG: Is otaku a purely Japanese thing?

OT: No, France, the countries of Southeast Asia, Italy, and so on are into otaku culture now, so I don't think it's purely Japanese anymore. However, it probably started in Japan.

PG: Why did it begin here?

OT: In Japan, a lot of entertainment targeting kids isn't the sort of thing one would normally want to show children. Take, for example, the 1974 TV anime *Heidi, Girl of the Alps*. There's a scene where Heidi's grandfather says that the people of the village are making a fool of him. In American or European animation this scene would be explained and resolved quickly. But in *Heidi* the resolution takes time, the issue is only gradually resolved over the course of fifty-two episodes. This is not something that a child watches and understands but is something an adult can relate to. It's not for kids, but it is packaged for children.

PG: How did this kind of entertainment evolve?

OT: The student protest movement occurred in Japan in the 1960s and '70s, and at the time, many job-hunting university graduates were not interested in first-tier corporations, or jobs associated with the government or other institutions. Instead they chose to work in TV, to make films, and maybe anime shows for kids. They thought they could teach the youth of Japan the ways of society through this media. The result is entertainment aimed at children but also interesting for adults to watch.

Even TEZUKA OSAMU covered adult themes in a format that was said to be for children. His work may look like it's for kids but he wrapped it in the destructive, erotic, and violent desires he held and expressed them in manga. At the time, again and again, educators and critics said manga was vulgar and blamed it for problems, but the creators didn't stop. That is another thing that contributed to the rise of otaku in Japan. In the United States, comics that had violent and adult themes were regulated.

PG: So why wasn't it regulated in Japan?

OT: Well, in Japan kids have a generous allowance. But in the United States kids don't have that much money of their own. If they want something, they have to ask their parents to buy it for them. The parents filter things so kids can only get what their parents allow. On the other hand in Japan, from preschool or grade school on, children have a daily allowance. If they want something, they can buy as much as they want within their budget and kept it secret from their parents. So, whether it's

SATURN
MONORAILS
宇宙時代

anime or manga, kids can get their hands on things that perhaps their parents don't want to show them.

PG: And that set of circumstances has helped otaku culture spread around the world?

OT: Yes. One thing that's necessary for the spread of otaku culture is interesting anime that hooks people when they discover it. But it's equally important that from an early age kids have the funds and freedom to purchase it of their own volition. One reason France was particularly quick to pick up on otaku culture is that parents often leave their children to be looked after by grandparents, who then give the kids an allowance. Kids use this disposable income to buy whatever they like. When they become university students, they still like anime and manga, and continue on into adulthood. That is the basis of otaku culture.

PG: But what does it really mean to be an otaku?

OT: An otaku is someone who is smarter than average people but chooses to divert their mental ability to childish hobbies. It's about *not* quitting the things that enthralled you as a kid. It isn't childish. An otaku is not a loser or someone who can only understand childish things. They understand high culture such as fine art but nonetheless insist that anime and manga are better. That is otaku.

PG: You wrote that otaku are already dead. What did you mean?

OT: In the beginning otaku were interested in various genres. For example, I like manga, but I also know about anime. In other words, otaku weren't limited to just one genre but had a set of knowledge that was shared among all otaku. But now the number of anime, manga, and games has drastically increased, and appears to be specifically aimed at otaku. It used to be stuff for kids that could be enjoyed by adults, but over time the software and content were tuned so that otaku could enjoy it more and more. For example, cute characters, what are known as MOÉKYARA, have appeared. Normal people have stopped watching. Only otaku enjoy this stuff and discuss *moé* with one another. More and more the things that were shared among older otaku, those things that made us aware of a connection, are gone, and we think, "I can't understand these otaku. They're different from us." There is a divide between us. I often use the United States as an example, because the US has many people of different backgrounds, values, and beliefs, but they still recognize that there's something that binds them as Americans. The same was true for otaku, with various genres and interests connected by some common ideas. But somewhere along the line these things were lost. All that remains are the divided groups. I'm not saying that otaku and their activities today are bad, not at all, just that the thing we all shared as a culture has been overthrown. What that means is we are no longer *otaku* sharing something, but *mania* involved in our own personal pursuits.

PG: For the record, what is the difference between a mania and an otaku?

OT: In this instance, I use "otaku" to mean someone with general knowledge and a shared culture, and "mania" to mean someone so enthralled with a single thing that he or she can't see beyond it.

PG: Is there anything left of the original otaku culture today?

OT: It's in the midst of disappearing. There are a few people left who are out to gain knowledge on otaku topics. The Internet is contributing to this, because it's easy to gather and share information. But then again, people are only gathering informaion on the things they like, and sharing with people who like those same things. If you want to talk all day long about moé characters, there's going to be someone out there who's into that. It's the same around the world. There is no more reason to go out of one's way to talk to people who are different from you.

> **An otaku is not a loser . . . They understand high culture such as fine art but nonetheless insist that anime and manga are better.**

PG: What about overseas—mania or otaku?

OT: People overseas still believe there's a lot to learn about Japan and they study and absorb as much as they can. So, actually, I think foreigners are more otaku than Japanese these days. What they see in anime and manga is a mysterious culture. They want to know what *kotatsu* (tables with heaters), *bento* (lunch boxes), and middle-school trips are. That desire to study and learn is very otaku. Japanese otaku just want to enjoy tomorrow the way they enjoy today. In Japan, real otaku are vanishing, but otaku goods are as abundant as ever. Overseas, these goods may be rare, but otaku are on the rise.

PG: What is the future of otaku?

OT: In Japan the people who want to create new work are decreasing, but the people who want to consume and watch things as cheaply as possible are increasing. They download or watch shows for free on YouTube. They think that watching as much as possible is the right way. If you act so selfishly, the common culture we all supported is eroded, just as products you don't pay for disappear from the market. Foreigners who are hot to learn and willing to invest will grow as otaku.

PG: Isn't the desire to create prevalent in DOUJINSHI and visible at Comiket?

OT: Yes, there still seem to be otaku there. Japan has the merit of being small. So people can gather in Tokyo and buy and learn from one another. But in the US, you couldn't possibly travel across the country just to sell a few doujinshi and see friends.

PG: How was it back in the Gainax days?

OT: Back then otaku watched anime and wanted to make anime. So they studied the techniques and mimicked every detail. Now, as I've said, many people may *like* anime but no one wants to *make it* any more. In the last twenty years or so, creators have been replaced by consumers. They don't go beyond that stage. The creators are all overseas now. Is there any creator in Japan in their twenties? Those at the top, people such as MIYAZAKI HAYAO, OSHII MAMORU, TOMINO YOSHIYUKI, are in their fifties or sixties now. Below that, people who understand anime, such as ANNO HIDEAKI, are in their forties. That there is no one I can name in their thirties or twenties suggests we've reached the limit. Japanese anime will disappear in the next twenty years.

PG: So things will move overseas? Who are the creators to look out for there?

OT: John Lasseter, the creator of *Cars*, or Peter Jackson, who did *Lord of the Rings* and *King Kong*. I can really smell the otaku on those guys. Also, Steven Spielberg is making a movie called *Interstellar* about the first galactic journey of mankind. If he makes that, I get the feeling that he might return to our side of the fence.

employee at General Products USA. They were given pseudonyms and had their faces covered by digital MOSAICS. The foreign otaku's name, Shon Hernandez, was adapted from two of York's coworkers, Shon Howell and Lea Hernandez. The interview was unscripted, and York was reportedly very earnest with his thoughts, but the comedic "translation" of his words is not even close to what he is actually saying. This became a point of contention when AnimEigo licensed the OVA for US release.

Despite allegations of discrimination, *Otaku no Video* is considered the first anime to comment on what it means to be an otaku and walk the hard path of a lost soul. The show was successful because otaku viewers could really relate to the characters. This set the foundation for otaku anime to become full of insider information and nostalgic references. More recent examples include *Genshiken* and *Lucky Star*.

©YOUMEX/GAINAX

OTAKU NO VIDEO BY GAINAX

Otaku talk (**オタクトーク**)**:** Equivalent to the American concept of "geeking out," but with a little more pepper to it in Japan. OTAKU discussions are deep and intense, but the less diplomatic describe them as obsessive and anal retentive to the point of shutting all others out. See also KY and CORE.

Otaku typology: Also known as The OTAKU 5. The five major types of OTAKU (*itsutsu no otaku zo*):

1. Masked Otaku with Family (25 percent)
2. "I will go my own way" Legacy Otaku (23 percent)
3. Information Super-sensitive Multi-Otaku (22 percent)
4. Social Chameleon Otaku (18 percent)
5. Doujin Female–Loving Otaku (12 percent)

These were isolated by the Nomura Research Institute otaku team in 2005 in a follow-up to their ground-breaking 2004 report. The team claims Masked Otaku display a wide range of interests but tend to focus on computers and audiovisual equipment and never "come out" as otaku to their families. The Legacy Otaku are said to display a spirit of independence and a penchant for data collection and analysis. They are typically between twenty and thirty years old and have an affinity for computers and audiovisual equipment, IT gadgets, vehicles, cameras, MECHA, and IDORU. Multi-Otaku are open and easily adaptable, showing little preference for any one thing and often coming out as otaku to others. There appear to be many women in this category. They worship connection and communication, frequenting community sites such as 2CHANNEL, and often start their own websites. The Social Chameleon Otaku is the type who has a great deal of independent spirit and wants everyone to know it, often involving others in play or antics. The typical member of this category is in his or her thirties and likes *Gundam* and *Dragon Quest*. The Doujin Female–Loving Otaku loves the characters that appear in ANIME and MANGA and pursues them in creative expression such as DOUJINSHI or GARAGE KITS. This type includes adult woman who are FUJOSHI and love BL, either secretly or among friends, and their male AKIBA-KEI and MOÉ-fan counterparts.

***Otaku wa sudeni shindeiru* (オタクはすでに死んでいる):** *Otaku Are Already Dead*. A book written in 2008 by OTAKU expert OKADA TOSHIO in which he announces the death of otaku culture as he defines it. The title is a pun on the *Fist of the North Star* line, "You're already dead" (*Omae wa mou shindeiru*). In the book Okada divides otaku into three generations: the Aristocrats (early adapters) from the 1970s, the Elites (savvy recruiters) from the 1980s, and finally the current MOÉ group (weak, isolated, and burned out). The early otaku are the archetypal role models. Okada writes that in the 1980s, individuals chose to pursue childish hobbies to intellectually and emotionally isolate themselves from society; and they sought to better understand the world through the communal pursuit of hobbies. In contrast, he says, today's otaku are self-absorbed by personal interests, have no community, and abandon society. Okada believes that if being an otaku is based on the shared understanding of core materials, then the mainstreaming of otaku fandom in the 2000s and its privatization in Internet groups effectively killed the core.

新潮新書 Brevity is the soul of wit, and tediousness the limbs and outward flourishes.
岡田斗司夫
OKADA Toshio
オタクはすでに死んでいる
新潮社 258

OTAKU WA SUDENI SHINDEIRU BY OKADA TOSHIO

Otaku-zoku (オタク族): OTAKU tribe. This is often used to describe a cohesive, core community of otaku.

Otapple (オタップル): OTAKU couple; a couple made up of two hardcore fans. Recently, it has become popular for an otaku male and a FUJOSHI, or a female otaku, to pair up (see the long-running series *Tonari no 801-chan*). This is in stark contrast to the image of otaku as lonely losers who can't get girlfriends.

Otemba (お転婆): Tomboy; rough and rowdy girls. Any lively minx with an attitude can be called an otemba, including Candice "Candy" White Ardlay (*Candy Candy*), female Ranma (*Ranma 1/2*), and Lina Inverse (*Slayers*).

Otome-chic (乙女チック): Maiden (*otome*) plus the "tic" of dramatic or romantic. The name of a type of SHOJO MANGA that was popular from the 1970s to the 1980s and mostly ran in *Ribbon* magazine. MANGAKA such as Mutsu A-ko, Tabuchi Yumiko, and Tachikake Hideko were especially popular. Their manga had young female protagonists with lots of heart and were distinct because of their dramatic romance, dreamy settings and a flowery, frilly, and ornate design style with lighly drawn lines. The editors at *Ribbon* noticed these attributes and pushed the style they described as otome-chic in the pages of their popular MANGA magazine. Many issues came with special giveaways, most often otome-chic drawings or accessories. The otome-chic style ended in the '80s when lines became bolder and the designs less flowery.

Otome-kei (乙女系): "Maiden-style" art. The male presence is de-emphasized to allow women to take center stage in stories set in an idyllic time and space;

for example the medieval past, or a high-school drama. The purity and innocence of the characters is the main appeal. This is one of the four major types of MOÉ.

Otome Road (乙女ロード): The "Maiden Road" and seat of FUJOSHI culture. A strip of shops on the street in front of the Sunshine City complex in east Ikebukuro, Tokyo, where female fans of ANIME and MANGA gather. It's the site of core DOUJINSHI stores, DANSO CAFÉS (such as B: Lily-Rose), and BUTLER CAFÉS (such as Swallowtail). For doujinshi and fujoshi goods, K-Books dominates the area with four locations, but MANDARAKE, VOLKS, Animate, and others are also present. Otome Road is quite small but is generally thought of as more progressive than AKIHABARA.

Otomo Katsuhiro (大友克洋): Born in 1954 in Hasama, Miyagi Prefecture. A Japanese MANGAKA and director best known for his works *Doumu* (1980–81) and AKIRA (1982–93). The ANIME film version of his MANGA *Akira* (1988) about disenfranchised biker teens and political unrest was a major force in establishing "JAPANIMATION" in the United States and putting gritty sci-fi anime on the popular and academic radar. Like many creators of his generation, he was greatly influenced by the student, labor, and anti-government demonstrations that raged in Japan in the 1960s and 1970s. He wanted to be a film director but instead debuted as a mangaka in 1973. He was influenced by America's culture of sex, drugs, and rock-n-roll in the free-wheeling 1970s, and these elements find their way into his works. Otomo finally found his stride making sci-fi manga in the 1980s.

He was praised for his ultra-detailed art, use of white space, rendering of realistic Asian-looking people, and photo-realistic backgrounds. As a whole, Otomo's style came to be called the "non-TEZUKA OSAMU method." By 1983, he

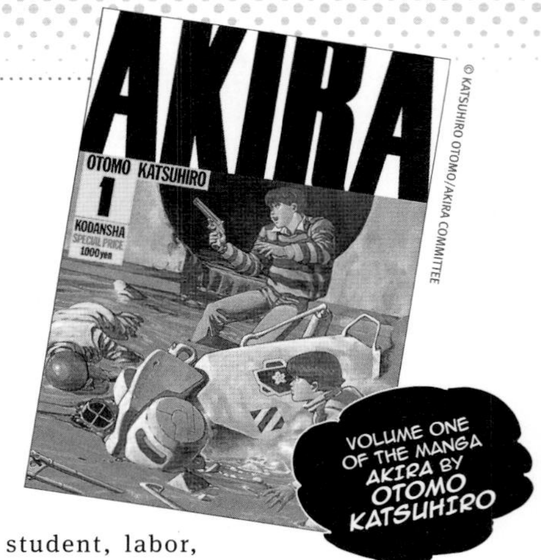

VOLUME ONE OF THE MANGA AKIRA BY OTOMO KATSUHIRO

was famous enough to do the character designs for the anime version of ISHINOMORI SHOTARO's *Genma Wars*. After the manga and anime *Neo-Tokyo* (1987) and *Akira*, he directed the collection of short anime films called *Memories* (1995), produced the anime film *Spriggan* (1998), and did the storyboards for the superb anime film *Metropolis* (2001). He returned with the unique steampunk film *Steamboy* in 2004, and in 2006 did the character and MECHA designs for the *Freedom Project* series of TV commercials for Nissin Cup Noodle, and the seven-part *Freedom* OVA that followed. In 2007, he directed the live-action version of Urushibara Yuki's manga *Mushishi*.

Otonagai (大人買い): Adult buying. Kind of like impulse shopping. For example, an adult who buys several boxed figures for their collection. Some adult buyers buy up whole series of MANGA, ANIME or merchandise in one go.

Oudou (王道): The rule of right, the main path. Generally used to mean the most popular characters in a series or genre but also used by FUJOSHI to describe the most common homosexual coupling of characters in YAOI DOUJINSHI.

OVA: Original video animation. Direct-to-home video ANIME. Sometimes called OAV, or original animation video. This should not be mistaken with the US direct-to-video market, which is basically stuff not worthy of mainstream release. In OVA the lack of TV broadcast rules, and higher budgets than TV anime, allow the creators more creative freedom, more frames per second, higher quality, and more-diverse themes. There are no restraints except money, so productions can be daring, niche, and take more time. The first OVAs appeared in the 1980s with the advent of the VCR and the increasing popularity of niche anime works. BANDAI's direct-to-market treatment of OSHII MAMORU's 1983 *Dallos* was the first OVA in the world, but it was overshadowed by the epic *Megazone 23*, four ninety-minute films from Artmic. *Bubblegum Crisis* and *Iczer 1* followed, both of which were only forty minutes long but featured outstanding art and animation by Hirano Toshihiro and Sonoda Kenichi. These two examples are closer to contemporary OVA, which are usually one to three episodes inspired by a popular TV series and running an hour or less.

Overnighter: Someone who camps out, usually unsanctioned, before an event to be one of the first ones to get the limited goods on sale.

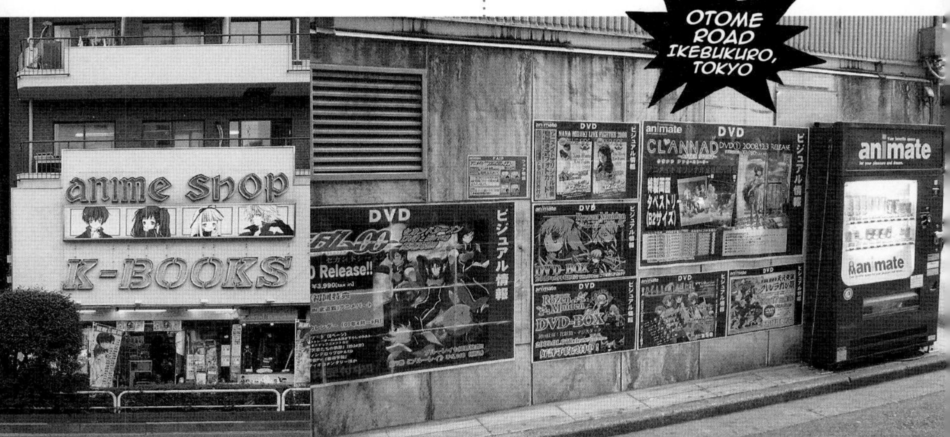

otaku • 村上隆

MURAKAMI TAKASHI

MURAKAMI TAKASHI (47) IS A JAPANESE CONTEMPORARY ARTIST influenced by otaku aesthetics. He is internationally famous for his "Superflat" exhibitions and his collaborations with both Louis Vuitton, and the musician Kanye West. In 2008, he was listed in TIME magazine's "100" list of the world's most influential people.

PG: When did you become interested in otaku culture?

MT: When I was young I was into *Space Battleship Yamato*. I'm a first-generation otaku and was seriously heading down the otaku path, but I kind of lagged behind my friends when it came to memorizing things. When *Gundam* got big it was really popular to memorize lines, but I couldn't keep up. So I'm an otaku dropout. I quit being an otaku then, but now I make otaku art from a critical point of view.

PG: Why focus on otaku?

MT: Otaku are like hippies. In some ways they're probably a social problem, but American hippy culture encouraged the development of music and computer science. People who desire independence struggle with themselves, but I think they have the power to change the world.

PG: Are otaku a Japanese thing?

MT: Otaku are part of Japanese culture. The very foundation of our impotent nation created otaku culture. Consider the American presidential election for a minute. If people believe they can control a country's future by voting, then they engage. But it doesn't work that way in Japan. We, as individuals, can't determine the future of the nation. Otaku are people struggling with the pent-up frustration that Japan is a puppet nation controlled by America. Just look at how many anime have themes of war, of people liberated from the dominant nation, of re-creating the world. Otaku are fighting in the fictional world. The Japanese nation does not function, so otaku seek alternatives.

PG: How do Japanese view otaku? Is it different from the vision overseas?

MT: I think Japanese view otaku as a self-portrait. People overseas don't understand this, so only see otaku culture as something crazy. But creators around the world are taking notice of otaku. Probably because they empathize with the cry for freedom embedded in otaku culture.

PG: Some have said that you criticize otaku, for example with your scuplture *My Lonesome Cowboy*. How do you respond?

MT: I once read a novel about an artist who loses his job because his portraits are too real. Even if the subject smiled, his or her sadness would come out in the portrait. So, rich patrons rejected the artist. My position is probably much the same. I'm an artist. It's my job to make expressions of truth. It's not criticism, it's just my observations.

PG: What will become of otaku from now?

MT: Sadly, or maybe not so sadly, as long as Japan is a puppet nation of America and there is no image of the future, otaku culture will grow and develop.

Pachinko (パチンコ): "Pachinko" is a combination of *pachin*—the onomatopoeia for "slap"—and *ko*, which means "ball." A Japanese form of amusement gambling. Similar to an upright pinball game, metal balls are shot up and fall though pins into holes to win more balls, which are then exchanged for prizes. Because money does not exchange hands, this form of gambling is legal. However, kiosks located near pachinko parlors buy back the prizes, at set prices.

The first pachinko parlor opened in Nagoya in 1930, but it wasn't until after the war that the pastime took off. At the time, ball bearings were in excess and cigarettes were rationed. But it was possible to win cigarettes gambling with metal balls at pachinko parlors, which were often run by Korean immigrants. Today, pachinko parlors are garishly decorated, bright, smoky, and obnoxiously loud. The video displays on the machines often depict ANIME characters and themes and deafen players with pumping ANISONG remixes. For example, an *Urusei Yatsura* machine will have Lum-chan saying "Keep trying, darling!" and engaging in antics from the series. Many game developers are making a name for themselves amid the current pachinko renaissance by attracting devoted players with cute GRAVIA and pop idoru, the promise of easy money or prizes, and obedient staff in sexy costumes.

PACHINKO MACHINE

SANKYO

Pakuri (パクリ): A rip-off; copy; taking somebody else's idea and passing it off as one's own.

Panchira (パンチラ): An upskirt or panty shot. Panchira is one of the most common forms of FAN SERVICE and has been around as early as TEZUKA OSAMU's upskirt shots of TETSUWAN ATOMU's sister Uran, and *Doraemon*'s Nobita flipping up Shizuka's skirt. Tezuka's *Marvelous Melmo*, released in 1971 as a kind of sex education, was the first panchira ANIME. MAHOSHOJO anime have also had an abundance of panty goodness since the 1970s. Contemporary panchira anime include *Maitchingu Machiko-sensei* (1981) and *Agent Aika* (1997).

Pan-Pee (パンピー): Abbreviation of *ippan* people, or "common people." It came into use in the 1970s when YANKIIS were all the rage and non-yankiis were called "pan-pee." It was then used by celebrities to describe people who are not in the "in" group. DOUJINSHI and VISUAL-KEI fans also used it to describe outsiders.

Panty thief: See SHITAGI DOROBO.

Para para (パラパラ): A popular form of synchronized group dancing in Japanese clubs, especially clubs in and around Shibuya. It's mainly performed by girls and arose in 1980s club culture. It is basically consists of stepping or hopping to the beat and waving your arms in frantic patterns. Different songs have their own unique moves and the music is of the speedy Eurobeat, techno, and trance variety. Many ANISONGS also have para para versions.

Parasite singles (パラサイトシングル): Single Japanese in their late twenties, thirties, and older who still live with their parents, pay no rent, and have huge disposable incomes. As their numbers increase amid job insecurity, they have become the target of public criticism for not forming families. The term was coined by the scholar Yamada Matsuhiko.

Parody kei (パロディー系): Parody style. Often seen in DOUJINSHI, YAOI, and ANIME that borrows from other anime and MANGA, and reinvents it—which often means putting famous characters into highly erotic situations that were never intended by the original creators.

Pasera (パセラ): A Japanese KARAOKE company known for its massive song selection system, Sigma, offering some 150,000 titles. Since 2002, it has worked to gain exclusive rights to numerous song catalogs. It is especially well known for carrying an extensive library of ANIME, TOKUSATSU and SEIYUU songs, making it the destination for OTAKU parties. The Pasera in AKIHABARA has a famous VIP room devoted to *NEON GENESIS EVANGELION*, complete with Unit 01 coming through the wall.

Pasu (パース): Perspective. The point from which an image, scene, or story is drawn.

Patten, Frederick Walter: Born 1940 in Los Angeles. A pillar of the early OTAKU community in the United States and one of the five founding members of the CARTOON/FANTASY ORGANIZATION. Trained as a librarian, he is best known for his substantial work as a historian of ANIME, MANGA and FURRY fandom with books such as *Watching Anime, Reading Manga: 25 Years of Essays and Reviews*, and *Furry!: The World's Best Anthropomorphic Fiction*. He wrote on these subjects for almost thirty years and first entered the fan community in 1960 at the Los Angeles Science Fantasy Society, soon after publishing in fanzines. He encountered manga in 1970 at Westercon and in 1972 co-founded Graphic Story Bookshop. Looking to localize the best comics in the world, Patten corresponded with Japanese publishers, namely Akita Shoten, and became an early pioneer importing Japanese manga. He began writing about anime and manga in 1979. From 1991 to 2002, Patten worked at Streamline Pictures under CARL MACEK. In March 2005, he suffered a stroke and retired from fandom. His collection of almost 900 boxes containing around 220,000 comics, paperbacks, records, tapes, anime, manga, and convention memorabilia dating back to the 1930s, was donated to the J. Lloyd Eaton Collection, at the University of California, Riverside. He has been honored many times for his service to the otaku community, including the Sampo Award in 1971, the Inkpot Award in 1980, and a Life Achievement Award at the 64th World Science Fiction Convention in 2006.

FRED PATTEN'S *WATCHING ANIME, READING MANGA*

ANIME ESSENTIALS BY GILLES POITRAS

Pechapai (ペチャパイ): See MUNYUU.

Pico (ぴこ): Little-boy characters drawn to look smooth, glossy, and feminine, often with overemphasized nipples on their flat chest in a way similar to LOLICON. Pico is derived from the 2006 OVA *Boku no Pico*, and it is an outgrowth of that series more than a genre unto itself. *Pico* is mostly consumed by men who are low-key, closeted fans of this pedophilic material.

Pink (ピンク): Slang for "pornographic." In Japan "blue movies" are pink (*pink eiga*).

Poitras, Gilles Lee: Born in 1951 in Quebec, Canada. A long-term proselytizer of ANIME, and one of the forefathers of American OTAKU. He is the author of *The Anime Companion* and *Anime Essentials* and has written magazine columns for the likes of *Otaku USA* and *Newtype USA*. He also sits on the senior board of *Mechademia*, an annual scholarly anthology covering otaku culture. He has been a speaker at over twenty fan and industry conventions, introduced anime at the Smithsonian, and lectured on anime at the animation studio Pixar.

***Pokémon* (ポケモン):** One of Japan's most successful character franchises, created by Tajiri Satoshi as role-playing video games for NINTENDO's Game Boy system in 1996. The word "Pokémon" is a contraction of "pocket monsters," and the objective of the game is to capture and collect all the Pokémon and train the strongest team possible. There are five hundred or so fictional monsters in the series, and the franchise spans video and card games, ANIME, MANGA, and various other product lines. The most recognized Pokémon is the cuddly yellow mascot, Pikachu, an electric mouselike creature.

The story in the TV anime follows a young boy named Satoshi (or Ash Ketchum in the English version) as he and his friends quest to become Pokémon Masters and thwart the diabolical Team Rocket. Apart from the TV series, there has been a movie every year since 1999, with the eleventh movie, *Giratina and the Sky Warrior*, released in 2009. When the *First Movie* opened in 1999, attendance at schools around the US dropped in what would be deemed the "Pokeflu." That year, the series made the cover of *Time* magazine. The film was number one at the box office and made $10.1 million in a single day, growing to $85 million in total US sales. There have been two Pikachu balloons in the Macy's Thanksgiving Day Parade; a Boeing 747 decorated with Pokémon; and theme parks in Nagoya, Aichi Prefecture, and Taipei.

Pokémon is the second most successful video game–based media franchise, behind only the *Mario* series, which Nintendo also owns.

Pokémon was the first worldwide mainstream breakout success story for Japanese animation and was a turning point for the globalization of anime and manga. In 1999, the *Pokémon* game was selling in seventy countries, the anime was broadcast in sixty-one countries and two territories, the movies had been shown in forty-four countries, and the card games had been translated into eight languages. In 2003, the franchise was valued at $15 billion worldwide.

Pokémon opened the door for the COOL JAPAN movement but has also been criticized as promoting materialism. In 1999, Nintendo was unsuccessfully sued on the grounds that the *Pokémon Trading Card Game* caused two nine-year-old boys to become addicted to gambling.

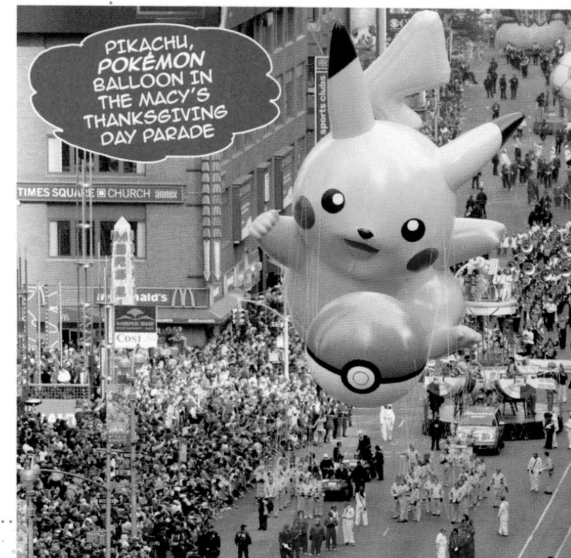

PIKACHU, POKÉMON BALLOON IN THE MACY'S THANKSGIVING DAY PARADE

PHOTO: JEFF CHRISTENSEN / AP

p

***Pokémon* Doujinshi Incident (ポケモン同人誌事件):** At the height of the POKÉMON Boom in 1999, NINTENDO sued the creator of a DOUJINSHI that featured *Pokémon* and human characters in unwholesome ways. It was a reminder that the ANMOKU NO RYOKAI—or silent agreement between companies and fans to let doujinshi be—is a tenuous balance, and amateur creators have to be very careful not to go too far in flouting intellectual property rights.

***Pokémon* Shokku (ポケモンショック):** POKÉMON Panic. On December 16, 1997, over six hundred children were hospitalized for epileptic seizures within thirty minutes of watching *Pokémon* season one, episode thirty-eight, "Computer Soldier Porygon," on TV Tokyo and its affiliates. The suspected cause was a series of flashing blue and red backgrounds showing the character Pikachu shocking the villainous Team Rocket. The media jumped on the case and reports could be found on every major TV channel throughout the day. Over the course of the next few days, some 12,000 more cases of photosensitive-onset "disorientation" and nausea were reported. While *Pokémon* recovered to become a lasting franchise, all ANIME now carries the preface warning screen that anime should be watched in a well-lit room and viewers should sit a respectable distance away.

Pon (ぽん): A cute name suffix used for IDORU and fan favorites. For example, Kusanagi Tsuyoshi from boy band SMAP is called "Tsuyo-pon."

Ponchi-e (ポンチ絵): *Punch* pictures. Satirical cartoons printed in the British magazine *Japan Punch*, created and published in Yokohama in 1862 by Charles Wirgman (1832–91), a British correspondent for the *Illustrated London News* from 1861 to 1887. The conflict among the Tokugawa Bakufu Government, revolutionaries, and foreign powers gave Wirgman much to write on. *Japan Punch* continued for 2,500 pages, and found popularity among foreigners in Yokohama and Japanese. "Ponchi-e" became a term for Western manga, which were seen as more meaningful than the "fanciful pictures" (manga) associated with artists such as Hokusai. Wirgman's works contained word and thought balloons, which influenced Japanese artists such as Kawanabe Kyosai and the later development of postwar manga.

Pong (ポン): A computer tennis game. Designed by electrical engineer Allan Alcorn and released in 1972 by ATARI. It was the first successful, well-known video game to hit arcades and home consoles, and it started the gaming boom.

Pororoca (ポロロッカ): Or *Pororoca gyakuryuu genshou*, the "Pororoca reverse current phenomenon." Introduced in the MANGA *Sayonara Zetsubou Sensei* (2006) to suggest that renewed interest in older ANIME, manga, and other media, stems from people getting hooked on them through MEDIA MIX tie-ins—for example anime themed PACHINKO machines—and then tracing it back to the original source.

Pre-scoring (プレスコ): Prerecording. A dubbing method in animation where the audio track is recorded beforehand and the images are drawn to match. Many animation companies, including DISNEY, use this method, which improves the harmony between voice and picture. See also AFUREKO.

***Princess Maker* (プリンセスメーカー):** Or *Purime*. *Princess Maker* was an early brainchild of GAINAX and is often considered one of the best GYARUGE of all time. In 1991, Gainax released the first installment of the game in which you raise your virtual daughter with the intention of marrying her. The game was a hit and produced several sequels and spinoffs. In *Princess Maker 5*, released in 2007, the player could choose to be either father or mother and simply raise the daughter in an ideal Japanese setting.

PRINCESS MAKER 5 FROM GAINAX

Private production: See JISHU SEISAKU.

Production committee system (製作委員会システム): A system of producing ANIME with a fund of investment dollars, rather than simply a single studio's money. Many companies contribute funds to lower the risk of investment, and then get a proportionate percentage of the return. The production committee system is a remnant of the days when TEZUKA OSAMU was struggling to put together enough money to make his works. Indeed, the system means small studios can put out work, but it also means that the profits are divided up among the contributing sponsor companies. If the work is too high risk or expensive, costs are cut and the actual creators of the anime might not make much money. Those animators disadvantaged by the system often call it "*Osamu no noroi*," referencing the "curse" Tezuka left behind. Another problem with the system is that there is a preference for potentially profitable, mainstream, and safe works, which weeds out experimentation.

Production I.G: A Japanese production studio (also known simply as I.G) that's involved in the design and development of ANIME (TV, OVA, and film) and videogames. The initials I and G are those of the company founders Ishikawa Mitsuhisa and Goto Takayuki. The company began as a subsidiary of Tatsunoko Productions to produce the anime *Zillion* in 1987. The staff got along and formed a company of their own, I.G Tatsunoko Limited, which KYOTO ANIMATION supported. It worked on both the 1987 and 1993 *Patlabor* movies by OSHII MAMORU, and in 1993 became Production I.G. It continued to work with Oshii and in 1995 released its most famous title, *GHOST IN THE SHELL*. It broke with Tatsunoko in 1998 to form Production I.G, Inc. In 2000 it merged with the production company ING.

Production I.G is at the fore of digital animation and is reknowned for its amazing digital compositing and digital effects. It has produced some of the world's most-watched anime, including all of the *Ghost in the Shell* TV series and movies, the *xxx-Holic* series, the films *Evangelion: Death and Rebirth* and *The End of Evangelion*, and the OVA *FLCL*. In 1995 *Ghost in the Shell* marked the first time computer-generated visuals were overlaid onto a hand-drawn background. With *Blood: The Last Vampire* in 2000, I.G seamlessly mixed hand-drawn and computer animation. In 2007, the studio commemorated its twentieth anniversary with *Shinreigari/Ghost Hound*, which it co-created with SHIROW MASAMUNE. In 2008, it again collaborated with Shirow on *Real Drive*, put out another anime, *Library War*, and animated Oshii's film *Sky Crawlers*. I.G also created the animated sequence in Quentin Tarantino's *Kill Bill: Vol. 1.* in 2003 and the micro-series *IGPX Immortal Grand Prix* for the Cartoon Network (Toonami) in 2003. As far as games go, it is responsible for the classic *Xenogears* and a host of others, including *Grandia III, Namco × Capcom, Star Ocean: First Departure*, and *Valkyrie Profile 2*.

In 2007 Production I.G merged with the publisher Mag Garden.

Puchi (プチ): From the French word "petite," this means cute, little, or super-deformed (see SD).

Puramo (プラモ): Or Plamo. Plastic models kits. Collectible FIGURES and models that are assembled or snapped together.

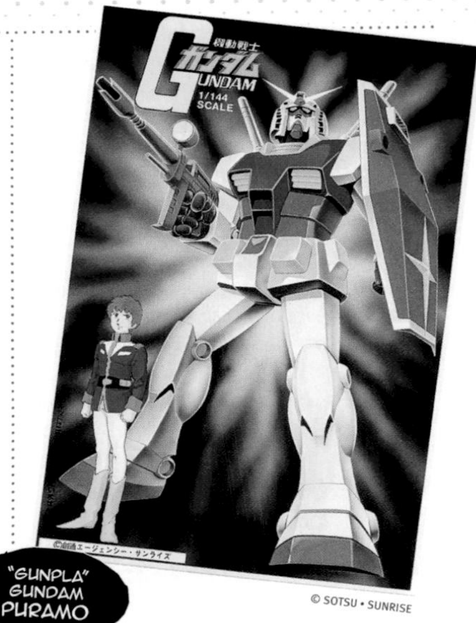

"GUNPLA" GUNDAM PURAMO

In 1958, the Marusan toy company released a plastic submarine, the first *puramo* in Japan. War machine replicas continued to be the main trend for puramo until the hit British marionette show *Thunderbirds* established the character market in 1965. This was followed by super car and train toys. The big boom in puramo came after BANDAI's flagship ANIME *Mobile Suit Gundam* was aired in 1979. Bandai's 1/144 scale robot models were a smash hit with fans of the series, hobbyists, and collectors, and now comprise the "Gunpla" (GUNDAM plastic model) subset of puramo. While many character models have followed, Gunpla comprise 90 percent of the plastic character model market in Japan.

There are many events and competitions devoted to constructing puramo, including the Bandai Action Kits Universal Cup, and *Dengeki Gunpura Ou Ketteisen* (Electric Assault Gunpla King Qualifier).

Purikura (プリクラ): Print Club. Photo booths that produce bright, colorful sticker photos that can be personalized with text and various graphics. They are especially popular among Japanese girls, who often collect thousands of stamp-sized sticker pictures taken with friends.

Print Club machines appeared in 1995, when Sasaki Miho of the arcade-game developer Atlus suggested the idea to her bosses. Atlus then teamed with Sega to develop sticker pictures to target women. The first machine was called Print Club, shortened and Japanized as Purikura, a trademark of Atlus but nonetheless now used as a generic name for these machines. Sega and Atlus first tried to promote the machine for business card photos and placed them in the department store Tokyu Hands. But it wasn't until megahit boy band SMAP showed Purikura on their television show SMAPxSMAP that the phenomenon took off. In 1996, Atlus shipped 20,000 Print Club machines to arcades across Japan. There were soon numerous different Purikura venues offering changing stalls, editing services, makeup, and special backgrounds. Many restrict male presence to keep the perverts away. Most Japanese have at least one Purikura picture on a cell phone, folder, or wallet. In 2004, Purikura was a $200 million business.

PURIKURA STICKER PICTURE

PV: Promotional Video. Roughly equivalent to music video, trailer, or teaser for an upcoming ANISONG or a new product.

QR Code: Quick Response Code. A type of square barcode created by Denso Wave in 1994 and popular in Japan. They were first used for tracking parts in vehicle manufacturing. One popular contemporary application is "mobile tagging," where QR Codes are displayed on signboards and fliers, especially at COMBINI and in magazines, and read by code-readers built into the cameras on Japanese mobile phones. As QR Codes can store URLs, they are ideal for advertising, as viewers can quickly access websites on their mobile phones to get information or discount coupons.

READ THIS QR CODE TO VISIT ME ONLINE!

R

Raa (ラー)**:** In the late 1990s, attaching the suffix "raa" to a word became a popular slang term meaning to be in love with something. For example, Chanel-raa (Chanel lover) or Amu-raa (Amuro Namie lover). The most famous example is mayo-raa, or mayonnaise lover. This came about on the *SataSuma* TV program in 1998 when Katori Shingo of the boy-band SMAP made a habit of cross-dressing and drinking mayonnaise straight from the tube, what he called the "*mayo chu chu*." Those who mimicked him, or simply liked mayonnaise too much, were called "mayo-raa." Doll-raa (DOLL lover) and yao-raa (YAOI lover) are examples of this word in contemporary use.

Race Queen (レースクイーン)**:** Promotional motor racing model. They're usually sexy young girls in their late teens or early twenties, and dress in swimwear, miniskirts, or hot pants, adorned with a company's logo. Technically their job is to simply hold an umbrella over a driver while he is parked, but it doesn't hurt if they attract the attention of wandering cameras. They started appearing in the 1960s. See AYAKAWA YUNMAO INTERVIEW ON PAGE 54.

Real time (リアルタイム)**:** Commonly used phrase among Japanese to indicate they watched an ANIME on TV at the time it was first aired. For example, "I watched *Evangelion* in real time." This is distinct from someone who watched it on reruns, VHS, DVD, or online. Real-time viewing tends to make the series more important to a fan.

REDISU COMIKKU SWEET

Redisu comikku (レディースコミック): Ladies' comics; often shortened to *redicomi*. These are explicitly pornographic MANGA for female readers depicting women having sex with various obscure male characters. They are typically written by women for women, for example Ogawa Yayoi's *Tramps Like Us* or Hazuki Kanae's *Voices of Love*. Despite their female readership, their content often features rape and torture. The fact that a significant number of women choose to read this pornography is intriguing and far removed from the traditional image of demure Japanese women. Ladies' comics are known to have write-in sections where readers explain their own sordid escapades to everyone's embarrassment and delight.

Reiyaa (レイヤー): The shortened form of "cosplayer," used among devoted fans of cosplay as a term of endearment for fellow enthusiasts.

Renai simulation game (恋愛シミュレーションゲーム): Dating simulator game. See GYARUGE.

Rensai (連載): Serialized MANGA. Expansive and episodic story manga with weekly or monthly installments, such as those that are typically featured in manga magazines. They have lots of cliffhangers and are highly addictive reading.

Rental comics: See KASHIHON.

Rental showcase (レンタルショーケース): A glass box located in a specialty store and rented by collectors to sell their own goods on consignment. These are found in spots like AKIBA and NAKANO BROADWAY, and cost around $20 a month to rent. The boxes are a chance for users to show off their collections, and sell excess stuff. Many contain rare merchandise, but they are often disorganized. Prospective buyers don't know what a box might hold, and part of the fun is window shopping at these living OTAKU museums.

Riajyuu (リア充): Someone satisfied with life. Japanese online denizens, including HIMOTE and KATO TOMOHIRO, have said they despise such people.

Riba (リバ): Short for "reversible" in Japanese. Used to indicate characters in YAOI DOUJINSHI or BL MANGA that can change between dominant (SEME) or submissive (UKE). That is, the submissive can suddenly switch on the dominant in the sexual encounter. This flexibility is one of the yaoi genre's most unusual features. The opposite word is *koutei*, or "set" roles in the narrative.

Rin (りん): A cute name suffix used for idoru and fan favorites. For example, GRAVIA IDORU Ogura Yuko becomes "Yukorin."

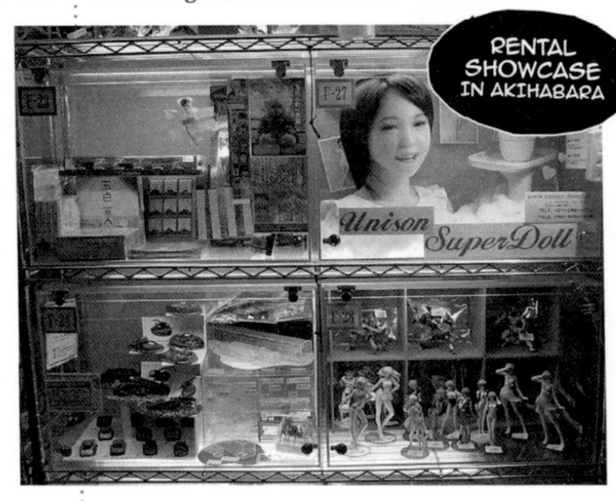

RENTAL SHOWCASE IN AKIHABARA

Robot (ロボット): A machine that performs human work, often humanoid in appearance and equipped with sensors and artificial intelligence. The word first appeared in 1921 in a play by Czech writer Karel Capek, *R.U.R.* (*Rossum's Universal Robots*). Robots, androids (artificial humans) and cyborgs (technologically enhanced humans) are a staple of science fiction. However, in the West their image is almost universally bad. Robots are often shown as being cold, unfeeling, dangerous, or suspicious.

Japan, on the other hand, has little if any negative bias against robots. In its rapid and intense modernization, Japan largely escaped the nightmare of the Industrial Revolution, leaving robots as a source of hope or entertainment in the postwar period. Robots are a staple of Japanese SF, MANGA, ANIME, and pop culture, and anime icons such as TEZUKA OSAMU's *TETSUWAN ATOMU*, and "real-robot" series such as *Mobile Suit Gundam*, greatly influenced the development of real-life robots, including Honda's Asimo, Sony's Aibo, Murata Seisakusho's Murata Boy, Kokoro's ultra-real Actroid, and Sakakibara Kikai's mobile suit–like Land Walker 01.

In 2008, half of the functioning 1 million robots worldwide were located in Asia. It's interesting that most robot research in Japan and other parts of Asia focuses on creating bipedal humanoid robots, whereas in the West the direction is toward more machine-like functional robots.

In 2008 SEGA released the E.M.A. (Eternal, Maiden, Actualization) robot that includes a "love mode" and greets you with a kiss, and in 2009 Japan's National Institute of Advanced Industrial Science and Technology unveiled the HRP-4c, a walking and talking female humanoid robot, designed to mimic a fashion model.

THE HRP-4C FASHION ROBOT

JAPAN'S NATIONAL INSTITUTE OF ADVANCED INDUSTRIAL SCIENCE AND TECHNOLOGY (AIST)

***Robotech*:** See MACEK, CARL.

Rough (ラフ): An incomplete, or conceptual, sketch.

RPG: Role-playing game, especially one in which players adopt AVATAR characters to narrate through fantasy realms (*Dungeons & Dragons*), but also including board games (*Hero Quest*) and video games (*Dragon Quest* and *Final Fantasy*).

Ryousei (両性): Both sexes. Androgynous.

Sakakibara Incident (酒鬼薔薇事件): "Sakakibara" is the alias of a juvenile murderer from Kobe whose name cannot be released; he is often called "Shonen A." In March 1997, at age fourteen, he murdered a ten-year-old girl, and then in May of the same year murdered and beheaded an eleven-year-old boy, leaving the mutilated head in front of his school gate with a note stuffed in the mouth. The note said in part that the murderer intended to punish the world for "years of great bitterness." The incident was said to resemble the Zodiac Killings in the US in the 1960s. When Sakakibara was captured, the press called him a HIKIKOMORI who could only verify his existence by hurting others; and when ero-MANGA, ANIME, and pornography were found in his room, parallels were made to other the infamous "otaku" criminals MIYAZAKI TSUTOMU and AUM SHINRIKYO.

Sakuga kantoku (作画監督): Illustration director. The person who checks the frames of an animation to make sure they match and meet quality standards. They check the GENGA, the key frames that govern the continuity, and when necessary fix them to maintain the integrity of the whole animation. The look and feel of an ANIME changes drastically depending on the sakuga kantoku. The smallest unit of their work is an entire episode, as the scenes within have to be consistent. Changing the sakuga kantoku often explains the inconsistency of style between episodes.

Sarariman (サラリーマン): Salary man; a salaried male worker. Typically a white-collar paper jockey in a suit. Slaves to the corporate hierarchy, they constantly work overtime—so much so that some die of overwork, a phenomenon known as *karoshi*. Many are hard drinkers, and it is surprisingly common to see *sararimen* passed out drunk on trains in the evening. They don't get much respect in the media and are the often the brunt of jokes, especially in MANGA. Sararimen who work

hard by day and GEEK OUT at night are called "*otariman*," and Yoshitani's manga *Boku, Otariman* (*I am, Otariman*) about one such guy, had sold over 500,000 copies as of 2007. The term "sarariman" became famous in the West in WILLIAM GIBSON's 1984 novel *Neuromancer.*

Satsueikai (撮影会): Photography event where an organizer or agency rents some sort of space and sells tickets to take photos of IDORU. Unlike most idoru events, where buying a DVD or photo album allows a minute of free photography, at a satsueikai customers pay a time-based fee to take as many photos as they want. This is usually between $50 to $100 an hour, depending on the popularity of the idoru, and includes the use of studios and professional lighting.

SATSUEIKAI PHOTO OF GRAVIA IDORU SHINOZAKI AI

Scanlations: Unlicensed MANGA translations done by fans and disseminated illegally online. The originals are scanned in and the Japanese text is replaced digitally.

Schodt, Frederik L.: Born in 1950 in Washington, DC. An author who has written widely on Japanese history, technology, and pop culture but is best known for his enormous contributions to MANGA studies. Either alone or with partners, Schodt has worked on translating some of the greatest manga of all time, including TEZUKA OSAMU's *Phoenix* and *Astro Boy*, Ikeda Riyoko's *The Rose of Versailles,* and SHIROW MASAMUNE's *Ghost in the Shell.* His books *Manga! Manga! The World of Japanese Comics* in 1983 and *Dreamland Japan: Writings on Modern Manga* in 1996, were the first, and are arguably still the best, to introduce foreign readers to the depth and complexity of manga. He has since written dozens upon dozens of articles on manga and Japanese popular culture and regularly appears at fan conventions. In recognition of his contributions to the global spread of manga popularity, Schodt received the Special Category of the *Asahi Shimbun*'s prestigious Osamu Tezuka Culture Award in 2000. That same year, his translation of Kiyama Yoshitaka's *The Four Immigrants Manga* (1931) was selected as a finalist for the Pen West USA translation award. He has also written *The Astro Boy Essays: Osamu Tezuka, Mighty Atom, and the Manga/Anime Revolution* (2007).

SCHODT'S CLASSIC

SD: Super deformed. Also called *derforme*. The miniaturization of characters or exaggeration in a drawn image. Their large heads make them look like awkward, cute, babies. See PUCHI.

SEGA: Video and arcade game developer based in Tokyo. The company was founded in 1940 as Standard Games by Martin Bromely, Irving Bromberg, and James Humpert in Hawaii to provide coin-operated games to American servicemen. It moved to Tokyo in 1951 and officially registered as Service Games of Japan in 1952. The company merged with Rosen Enterprises Inc. in 1965 and became Sega Enterprises (from SErvice GAmes).

In 1983, Sega released its first game console, the SG-1000; the first 3D arcade video game, *SubRoc-3D*; and the first LaserDisc arcade game, *Astron Belt*. In 1984, the Japanese conglomerate CSK bought the company and renamed it Sega Enterprises Ltd. The technically superior Sega Master System was released in 1986 but lost out to the NINTENDO Entertainment System (NES) due to ineffective marketing. Sega fought back by developing the Sega Mega Drive (or Sega Genesis) in 1989, and got a new mascot character in *Sonic the Hedgehog* in 1991. The combination was a hip image that won out against Nintendo in America for a time. *Sonic the Hedgehog 2* sold 6 million copies.

Sega's ingenuity in game arcades continued, and in 1993 it revolutionized arcade gaming with the 3D game *Virtua Fighter*, which has since been put on display at the Smithsonian. It followed up with *Daytona USA*, the most profitable arcade game in history. Its console successes, however, were still up and down, and when the Sega Saturn was released in 1995, it failed despite great software titles such as *Sakura Taisen, Panzer Dragoon, House of the Dead*, and *Grandia*. Sega continued its console projects with the Dreamcast in 1999, which was cheaper and technically superior to both the Nintendo 64 and Sony PlayStation. The ambitious project was the first console that offered online gaming, and it ushered in the hits *Phantasy Star Online*, the first console-based MMORPG; *Jet Set Radio*, the first cel-shaded game; and the cult classic *Seaman*, which involved communicating via headset with a salty fish-man. Unfortunately, Sega failed in Japan again by not putting out enough games at the Dreamcast's launch, and it was ignored by gamers waiting for Sony's Playstation2 (PS2). In the States, Dreamcast fared slightly better, selling 500,000 consoles in a week, then the most successful launch in history, but it ultimately lost out to the PS2.

In 2002, Sega left the console market to become a third-party game software publisher—one not attached to any particular system. This ultimately also failed, and it was bought up by Sammy, which cut back on the console game development for more profitable arcade games and cabinets. Sega Sammy Holdings is now one of the biggest game manufacturing companies in the world. The company rallied with strong sales of PACHINKO games, arcade game franchises, and tie-ups with international developers.

Sega Joypolis (ジョイポリス): An amusement park run by Sega. Founded in 1996 and located in Odaiba, Tokyo. It's three stories high and has 9,600 square meters of floor space. There are two other locations, Umeda, Osaka, and Okayama City, Okayama, but Odaiba is the seat of the empire. The company partnered with Namco Nanja Town in 2001 to form a game center amusement park coalition. At the peak of Sega's popularity, Sega also had several SegaWorld theme park–arcades located around the world, although most have since closed.

Seichi junrei (聖地巡礼): Pilgrimage. For OTAKU, sojourns to locations seen in ANIME and MANGA. As settings and backgrounds became realistic enough for fans to identify the actual places used as inspiration, otaku started making pilgrimages to these "holy" sites. The most well-known examples are the walk through Nishinomiya in Hyogo Prefecture from *The Melancholy of Suzumiya Haruhi*, and the journey to Saitama Prefecture, from *Lucky Star*—which culminated in otaku MATSURI as fans converged on Washinomiya Shrine in 2007 and 2008 to pray to the anime gods. Other popular seichi junrei destinations include Tokyo's Azabu area (*Sailor Moon*); Sendai, Miyagi Prefecture (*Jojo's Bizarre Adventure*); Tokyo's Kokubunji and Fuchu areas (*School Days*); and various other settings from *Full Metal Panic*, *Neon Genesis Evangelion*, *R.O.D*, *Kodomo no Jikan*, and *Mimi wo Sumaseba*. Seichi junrei can also mean visiting the major otaku areas of AKIHABARA, OTOME ROAD, NAKANO BROADWAY, OSU, in Nagoya, and Osaka's NIPPONBASHI.

Seifuku (制服): A uniform. The stylized sailor-suits and military uniforms adopted by Japan from Europe during the Meiji period (1868–1912) are still models for school dress codes today. Boys wore the first seifuku in Japan in 1879, and girls began wearing them in 1910. Sailor-style uniforms became the standard girls' school uniform by 1930. By the 1950s, girls in seifuku had begun to be seen in pornography and other media. In 1985 writer Mori Nobuyuki published his *Tokyo High School Girl Uniform Fieldbook*, which combined ethnographic anthropology and fetishism. The media fixation with girls'

FANS OF THE ANIME *LUCKY STAR* AT WASHINOMIYA SHRINE FOR *SEICHI JUNREI*

JSG*S HAVE THE BEST UNIFORMS!
*JAPANESE SCHOOLGIRL

seifuku has accelerated since media coverage of ENJOKOSAI in the 1990s, and the sexy schoolgirl character is now standard in ANIME and MANGA. See also KOGAL.

Seinen manga (青年漫画): Manga for youth or young adults. They typically have harder content and more adult themes about growing up and taking on life's challenges.

Seiyuu (声優): Voice actor or actress. Many seiyuu gain enough credibility in the ANIME industry to green-light projects. The First Annual Seiyuu Awards was held in 2007 in Tokyo as part of the attempt to glamorize and mainstream anime and its production. Seiyuu such as HAYASHIBARA MEGUMI, Hirano Aya, and Mitsuishi Kotono have also had successful singing and acting careers.

Sekai-kei anime (世界系アニメ): World-style ANIME. Stories in which the protagonist's world equals the entire world. Personal emotions and relationships determine the fate of the world; there is no difference between wanting to die and wanting the world to end. Because this outlook is so selfish and immature, these stories tend to feature young antiheroes. These include anime such as *Evangelion*, *Voices of a Distant Star*, *The Melancholy of Suzumiya Haruhi*, and *She, the Ultimate Weapon*.

Seme (攻め): The dominant member in gay COUPLINGS, such as those in BL or YAOI. Common types include narcissistic seme (*oresama* seme), cruel seme (KICHIKU seme), exhausted seme (*tsukushi* seme), younger seme (*toshi shita* seme), non-gay seme (NONKE seme), and loser seme (HETARE seme). A character that's a seme in all couplings and DOUJINSHI works is called *soseme*, or general seme. The term usually relates to fictional relationships and shouldn't be confused with "*tachi*," the actual term for the dominant partner in a gay relationship.

Semi-homo (セミホモ): A put-down for OTAKU in the 1980s and 1990s. Derived from the observation that otaku are constantly with other guys and without female companionship, so must be "kind of gay." Also applied to the gender-bending content of some ANIME, MANGA and video games.

Senga (線画): Line art; graphic. Typically black on white.

Sentai (戦隊): Teams of superheroes that usually wear brightly colored suits and masks or helmets, and battle it out with enemy monsters (KAIJU). They often pilot MECHA and use martial arts. The red costumed figure usually leads, but this pattern was challenged by the white (and female) leader in *Ninja Sentai Kakuranger* (1994–95). The shows typically carry a message of good conquering evil, and are noted for

S

their wild monster designs, stylish poses, and speeches. Representatives include the *Super Sentai* series (from 1975). Many superhero shows were inspired or written by ISHINOMORI SHOTARO, who created the first Japanese superhero team in the MANGA *Cyborg 009* in 1964, and the TV show *Himitsu Sentai Goranger* in 1975.

Sentai are hugely popular among OTAKU of the generation that grew up with these hero archetypes. They have always been popular in other parts of Asia, which has taken to making its own. Sentai really hit the US with the phenomenal *Mighty Morphin Power Rangers* from 1993 to 1995, which was adapted from *Kyouryuu Sentai Zyuranger* from the *Super Sentai* series.

S

Sento bishojo (戦闘美少女): Fighting girls. Applies to any female warrior or soldier in ANIME or MANGA character who can kick butt. Examples abound, but the most noted is the international smash hit *Sailor Moon* (manga 1992–97, anime 1992–97).

TAKEUCHI NAOKO'S FAMOUS SENTO BISHOJO *SAILOR MOON*

Seoul International Cartoon and Animation Festival (SICAF): An annual trade show for animation held in Seoul, South Korea, since 1995. In 2003, the South Korean president addressed the event, saying he hoped the country would become a global leader in animation. In 2008, 1,307 movies from sixty-three countries competed for exhibition space.

Serialized manga: See RENSAI.

7-Zark-7: The iconic ROBOT narrator in *Battle of the Planets*—the United States adaption of *Science Ninja Team Gatchaman*. He was added to explain things to viewers, filling in missing information and making up for jumps in the edited work. Among the many heavy-handed edits in localizing *Science Ninja Team Gatchaman*, fans particularly found 7-Zark-7 insulting because it was not in the original series and bore a striking resemblance to R2D2 from *Star Wars*.

Sex doll: See DUTCH WIFE.

SF: Abbreviation of science fiction, or Sci-Fi. See also CYBERPUNK.

Shadow animation: See KAGE ANIMESHON.

Shashoku (写植): Photo typesetting. Special fonts and script seen in MANGA; these are handwritten not by the MANGAKA but by an assistant or editor during typesetting.

Shibuya (渋谷): One of the twenty-three wards of Tokyo. Shibuya is known as one of the fashion centers of Japan, particularly for young people, and has a major night life and club scene. Both of these factors come to bear on the most famous local culture: that of the colorful and brash Shibuya gals, who cluster around the 109 BUILDING (see GYARU). Shibuya generally refers to the business district surrounding Shibuya Station, which is famous for having the busiest pedestrian crosswalk in the world, nicknamed

SHIBUYA

"Scramble Crossing." There is also a popular meeting spot near the station at a memorial to a famous dog called Hachiko, who loyally waited years for his deceased master to return from work.

Taku Hachiro, who was among the first successful OTAKU TARENTO in the media, describes himself as a "Shibuya-kei" otaku.

Shinjinrui (新人類): New-breed humans. Refers to Japanese born after 1960 who disdain conformist lifestyles, and often criticized as lazy, selfish outcasts. The word is rarely used these days

Shinkai Makoto: Born 1973 in Nagano Prefecture. An ANIME film director and producer. While working as a graphic designer at the video game company Falcom, he started to produce his own anime on his Macintosh computer. He quit his job in 2001 and in just seven months put together a quality twenty-five-minute OVA entitled *Voices of a Distant Star*. He and his financée did the voices, and his friend Tenmon provided the soundtrack. The work was so popular that he has since put out *The Place Promised in Our Early Days* (2004), *5 Centimeters per Second* (2007), and opening movies for adult games from Minori.

Shin Seiki Evangelion **(新世紀エヴァンゲリオン):** *Neon Genesis Evangelion*, often shortened to *Evangelion* or *Eva*. A MECHA-ANIME written and directed by ANNO HIDEAKI. It was produced by GAINAX and aired on TV Tokyo from 1995 to 1996. It is still the most influential anime series since the 1990s. It became an international sensation when dubbed into English by ADV Films. Character designer Sadamoto Yoshiyuki began the MANGA in 1994; in 2009 it was up to eleven volumes and still running.

The story is set fifteen years after a global cataclysm called "The Second Impact" wiped out half the world's population in the year 2000. It's revealed that a shadowy organization called Seele had sent its research arm, Gehirn, to Antarctica to experiment on an unearthed alien, or "Angel," called Adam—which went berserk, causing the destruction. Seele predicts sixteen more Angels will appear. The aliens are invincible because they possess AT (Anti-Terror) force fields, but Gehirn uses the remnants of Adam to make genetic and engineering breakthroughs to help fight the Angels. The result of the experiments are the Evangelion robots. The rub is that only those born after The Second Impact can pilot the machines—meaning all the pilots are fourteen years old.

The main protagonist is a boy named Shinji who's been summoned by his estranged father to pilot one of the Evangelions (Unit 01) for a paramilitary organization called Nerv.

SPOILER ALERT!! STOP READING NOW IF YOU DON'T WANT TO KNOW WHAT HAPPENS!

At Nerv, he joins the other pilots, Ayanami Rei (Unit 00) and Asuka Langley Soryu (Unit 02) and is taken

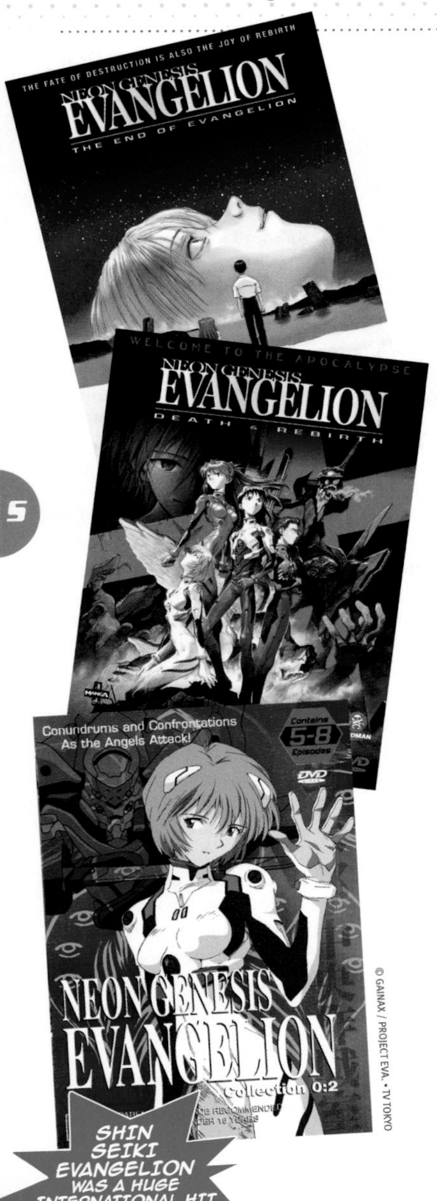

SHIN SEIKI EVANGELION WAS A HUGE INTERNATIONAL HIT FOR GAINAX

under the wing of Major Katsuragi Misato, with whom he shares an apartment. All the characters are emotionally scarred, disturbed people, but somehow they pull it together to fight the Angels.

Anno was suffering from depression before he made the series, and *Evangelion* is full of human suffering and deep psychoanalytic questions. The twist in the tale that separates *Evangelion* from every fighting robot series since *Gundam* is that the robots are in fact biomechanical machines encasing living Angels that in turn contain the souls of the children's dead mothers. Because of this only the correct child can mentally synchronize and control each machine.

The story was incredibly ambitious and convoluted, and the studio famously ran out of money during the final episodes. In an attempt to stretch the budget, the end of the series was mostly just line art, sketches, and flashbacks illustrating Shinji's mind as he struggles to come to terms with the events in his life.

In the final episode Shinji suddenly wakes up from his internal conflict, surrounded by the entire cast of *Evangelion*, who applaud him. This ending was controversial, and Gainax was threatened by fans who wanted a different ending.

In an attempt to tie up some of the loose ends, Gainax released two movies in 1997 that retold the story. The first, *Death and Rebirth*, summarized the story from episodes one to twenty-four and added a new version of the story from episode twenty-five. *The End of Evangelion* retold the story from episodes twenty-five and twenty-six. This film was even more apocalyptic and shocking than the original series. Fans had said they wanted Asuka to fight more often, so Anno really stuck it to them by placing the emotionally devastated girl in a fight with nine mass-produced Evangelions. The animation is brilliant and the action blistering, but eventually she is torn to pieces and eaten. Shinji witnesses this and flips out, losing the last remnants of his sanity and all will to fight. At this point in the story things get really strange, as Ayanami merges with the remnants of a creature called Lilith that has been kept in Nerv's basement and grows into a supreme being the size of the planet, absorbing all humanity into her. She places the future of all humans in Shinji's hands. He eventually realizes that without pain there can be no joy and decides to live as an individual rather than as part of the mass human consciousness. The giant Ayanami crumbles, and in the last scene Asuka and Shinji rematerialize. Shinji tries to strangle Asuka but can't, and he collapses on top of her crying. Asuka utters the words "*kimochi-warui*" ("that's disgusting") and the movie ends.

SPOILER ALERT!! STOP READING NOW IF YOU DON'T WANT TO KNOW WHAT HAPPENS!

It was not the last of the Evangelion franchise, however, as Anno has been reworking the story ever since, including the *Rebuild of Evangelion* series of four movies that will retell the story. The first, *Evangelion: 1.0 You Are (Not) Alone*, was released in 2007. The second, *Evangelion: 2.0 You Can (Not) Advance*, came out in summer 2009, with the other two set to follow. There is also a live-action film version rumoured in the works. It will be produced by ADV Films, Gainax, and Weta Workshop Ltd., but the release date has not been pinned down and is due anytime between 2010 and 2015.

Shirow Masamune (士郎正宗): Born in 1961 in Kobe, Hyogo Prefecture. A MANGAKA internationally renowned for his MANGA *GHOST IN THE SHELL*, which has since been turned into several ANIME movies and anime TV series, and several video games. Shirow is also popular for creating erotic, humorous, and technological art. He's a reclusive genius who never explains himself or the meanings behind his often-frightening CYBERPUNK images of the future. While studying oil painting at Osaka University of Arts, he developed an interest in manga. His first work, *Black Magic*, was published in the manga fanzine *Atlas*, where it caught the eye of the Seishinsha publishing company president Aoki Harumichi, who offered to publish his next work. The result was *Appleseed*. The story was a sensation, and it won the 1986 Seiun Award for Best Manga. After that he published *Dominion*, *Ghost in the Shell*, and *Shinreigari*.

Shitagi dorobo (下着泥棒): Panty thief. Thieves who steal female underwear. It's not unheard of in Japan for one thief to collect as many as 4,000 pieces of lingerie before being captured. Most don't sell their prizes to BURUSERA stores; they treasure their booty, as it were.

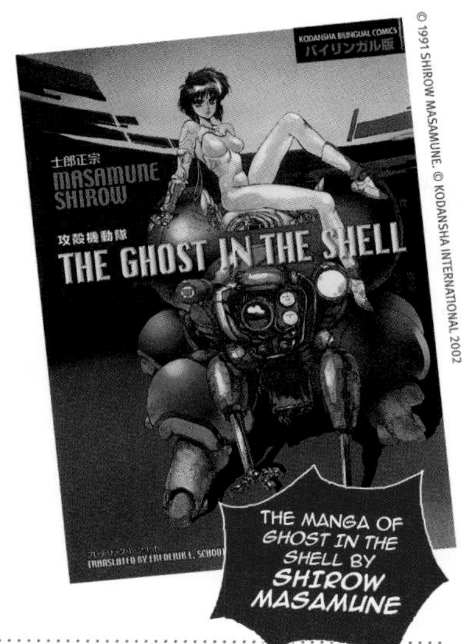

THE MANGA OF GHOST IN THE SHELL BY SHIROW MASAMUNE

Shitamachi (下町): Lower city or downtown. The concept of high and low city is common in fiction in Japan, including ANIME and video games such as *Battle Angel* and *Final Fantasy VII*.

Shitsuji café (執事カフェ): Butler café. Cafés in which staff dress up as butlers. These are the FUJOSHI answer to MAID CAFÉS. Found mostly on OTOME ROAD in Ikebukuro, Tokyo. They feature good-looking men who speak in extremely polite Japanese and wait hand and foot on their "lady" (*ojosama*) customers. There is at least one example in Shibuya of a café with Western men playing the part of butlers. For service, customers merely have to ring a bell that is provided. Butler cafés tend to be expensive and classy, but they are so popular that they are booked solid for months. If guests are so inclined, they can even ask a butler to say, "Your horse is waiting outside, madam," when it's time to go. This is distinct from the DANSO CAFÉ, where women cross-dress as beautiful boys to emulate fantasies drawn from YAOI. Danso cafés are mostly populated by fujoshi, while butler cafés serve a broader demographic.

I'M A SHOJO CHARACTER TOO!

Shobunkan Saiban (松文館裁判): The Shobunkan Trial. A trial stemming from arrests made in 2002 that finally ended in a conviction in 2007. The case involved the company president, an editor, and a MANGAKA at Shobunkan, a publishing house specializing in adult magazines and MANGA. They were accused of obscenity violations in the SEINEN MANGA *Misshitsu* (*Closed Room*) when a letter complaining about it arrived on the desk of an influential politician. Police were dispatched and arrested the three. The highly publicized trial was the first time obscenity in manga was contested, and it was a landmark failure for free speech in Japan. See also WAISETSU and the DOUJINSHI ISSUE.

Shojo (少女): Young girl. The term also refers to anything for or about school-age girls, for example SHOJO MANGA. The term is interesting because it's relatively new. Before Japan modernized at the turn of the 20th century, all children were called *shonen*, meaning simply "few years" or "child." With the advent of the word "shojo," the word "shonen" came to mean "boy." The shojo category was invented along with all-girl schools and ideas of femininity and is tied to ideas of innocence and purity. Shojo characters also dominate popular media such as ANIME and MANGA.

Shojo-ai (少女愛): Girl love. Love of girls between the ages of seven and twenty, be it a physical desire or platonic feeling. This is roughly analogous to LOLICON in Japan, but shojo-ai is usually directed to a real rather than fictional person, so is closer to the English word "pedophilia." Among fans outside of Japan, shojo-ai is sometimes used to describe ANIME, MANGA and video games where beautiful girls fall in love. It's even sometimes called GL, or "Girl's Love," like the manga genre BL, or "BOY'S LOVE." However, this usage is not common in Japan, which favors the term "YURI" for the lesbian genre. "Shojo-ai" was used interchangeably with "lolicon" in the 1980s.

Shojo manga (少女漫画・少女マンガ): Girls' MANGA. Manga targeting girls between the ages of seven and twenty. They're romantic comics that focus on relationships between sets of girls and boys who struggle with feelings for each other and eventually fall in love.

SHOJO magazines grew out of the girls' sections in magazines for boys at the turn of the 20th century; the first publication specifically for girls was *Shojo Kai* in 1903, and the most famous was *Shojo no Tomo* in 1908. Comics appeared around 1910, and sophisticated works such as Matsumoto Katsuji's *Kurukuru Kurumi-chan* (1938) in the 1930s. Ironically, it was a man, TEZUKA OSAMU, who popularized shojo manga after the war with his intense drama *Princess Knight* (1954–68). For a time after this most of the writers were men, including Chiba Tetsuya, ISHINOMORI SHOTARO, and MATSUMOTO LEIJI. In the mid-1960s, however, female artist Nishitani Yoshiko began to create stories about contemporary Japanese teenagers in love. This marked the beginning of shojo manga as distinct from SHONEN MANGA, which more often focused on action. The genre changed again in the 1970s with the MAGNIFICENT 49ERS (Takemiya Keiko, Hagio Moto, and Oshima Yumiko), a group of young female manga artists who focused on SHONEN AI stories and earned shojo manga critical acclaim. At the same time, Ikeda Riyoko's *The Rose of Versailles* and Yamamoto Sumika's *Aim for the Ace!* were smash hits. As a result, most shojo manga artists are now female, as is the readership. About 30 percent of the manga market is devoted to shojo titles.

王子さまの〜〜〜
おでまし〜〜〜い!
Here comes the prinncccee!

PRINCESS KNIGHT, AN EARLY SHOJO MANGA BY TEZUKA OSAMU

Shojo manga have a very distinctive feminine look and feel. They are often highly decorative and feature much finer lines than the lines of shonen manga. They typically have flowery or ornate patterns, full-page close-ups, and characters that are crossing or breaking out of the panels on a page. Shojo manga have unattributed words written in the blank spaces of the page that might be narration, the thoughts of the character, or the commentary of the mangaka. Large eyes that brim with emotion were originally a specialty of shojo manga but later became standard across genres for boys and girls. Shojo characters can seem very androgynous, causing critics to call this a form of narcissistic self-love in which girls explore themselves through the characters.

Representative examples include Ikeda Riyoko's *The Rose of Versailles* (1972–73), Watase Yuu's *Fushigi Yuugi* (1992) and Kamio Yoko's *Hana Yori Dango* (1992–2008), which in 2006 was the highest grossing shojo manga in Japanese history. In the United States, the most influential might be Takeuchi Naoko's *Sailor Moon* (1992–97). When this manga made it to the United States from *Mixxzine* in 1997, it offered girls in the US something they had never had before: interesting comics with appealing feminine aesthetics. The most popular shojo manga in the United States in 2006 was Takaya Natsuki's *Fruits Basket* (1999–2006). Shojo manga are now so popular in the United States that Harlequin has started releasing manga-styled romance comics.

Shoko-tan (しょこたん): Nakagawa Shoko. Born in 1985 in Tokyo. A model and TV talent (TARENTO) known for her OTAKU tastes. She debuted in 2001 after winning a *Popolo* magazine new face award, and in 2002 she was chosen as Miss Shonen Magazine. In 2004 she started an official blog, where she compulsively posts on the minutiae of her life. In April 2005 she posted 600 times, and on January 28, 2006, she posted seventy times in one day.

SHOKO-TAN SEE INTERVIEW P. 214

She was a regular on the *Osama no Bunch* TV show in 2005, where she often explained ANIME and MANGA to the other panelists. She soon came out as an okatu and has since become the photogenic symbol and charismatic spokesperson for all the geeks in Japan. In February 2008, the *Mainichi Shimbun* newspaper reported her blog had been accessed 1 billion times. By 2008, the "New Queen of Blogs" (apparently there was an old one) had projects as a photo IDORU, TV talent, SEIYUU, and ANISONG singer. After singing the theme for hit GAINAX anime *Gurren Lagann*, she made her first national tour of Japan and performed at the Nokia Theater in Los Angeles for ANIME EXPO 2008, her first visit overseas. Over 4,000 fans showed up, and she was soon featured in numerous magazines, including *Wired*. She released the albums *Big☆Bang!!!* (2008) and *Magic Time* (2009). She has an encyclopedic knowledge of Bruce Lee movies, and has manga (such as *Shocotan Quest*) serialized in a literary journal and glamor magazine.

Shokugan (食玩): Short for *shokuhin-gangu*. Toys that traditionally came packaged with food and candy to promote sales—kind of like cereal extras in North America. Early versions such as *gangu gashi*, literally "toys with candy," appeared in Japan as early as 1922.

Under the pioneering efforts of KAIYODO, high-quality shokugan exploded in popularity in 1999 with the release of Furuta's "Choco Egg," which had a toy figure inside. Estimates place the value of this industry at some $500 million annually, and rare shokugan become collector's items. Pop artist MURAKAMI TAKASHI famously promoted his work by making shokugan versions of his art works.

Shokushu-kei (触手系): Tentacle style; as in "tentacle sex." The weirdest and most emblematic genre of ERO-GURO ANIME—or HENTAI as it is known outside Japan—where monsters, demons, or aliens with multiple tentacle appendages molest or rape beautiful women. This bizarre kind of imagery is not new in Japan, as can be seen in Hokusai's *The Dream of the Fisherman's Wife* (1820), which depicts a woman with her kimono open being ravaged by two giant octopuses. Artist Teraoka Masami remade the image in 2001 with *Sarah and Octopus/Seventh Heaven*, and fellow artist Aida Makoto parodied it in 1993 with *Kyodai Fuji Taiin vs. King Gidora*.

The first modern shokushu-kei anime was *Cream Lemon: Part 3* in 1984. But the *Urotsuki-doji* series, released in 1986 by Maeda Toshio, is considered the genre's most seminal work. At the time, it was illegal to show genitals rubbing together in animated images, as was the depiction of pubic hair and reproductive organs. This resulted in the development of unique erotic imagery in Japan, including tentacle sex, because if the attacker was a monster, unusual sexual practices were possible. Maeda was also responsible for *LA Blue Girl* (1989), another well-known title in this genre.

Shonen A (少年A): See SAKAKIBARA INCIDENT.

Shonen-ai (少年愛): Stories featuring homosexual male romances between impossibly beautiful and sensitive men. This term is often used to describe YAOI—except in Japan where it has much longer ties to classic literature.

***Shonen Jump* (週刊少年ジャンプ):** *Shukan Shonen Jump*. Also known as *Weekly Shonen Jump* or *Weekly Jump*. It's one of the longest-running weekly MANGA magazines in Japan and has a circulation

5

of over 3 million. It targets young males, featuring manga with lots of action and adventure and young, male protagonists with special powers or abilities. So many popular manga, such as *Naruto* and *Dragon Ball*, have been born from these hallowed pages that they comprise a category known as "*Jump-kei*." The magazine was launched in 1968 by Shueisha to compete with the successful *Shonen Magazine* and *Shonen Sunday* manga. At its most popular, in the mid-1990s, *Weekly Jump* had a regular circulation of over 6 million. *Weekly Jump* manga titles, and even the anthologies, have been translated and redistributed in many countries. When *Shonen Jump* was released in the United States by VIZ in 2002, 300 pages of manga sold for $5 and the circulation quickly grew to around 250,000.

Shonen manga (少年漫画): Boys' MANGA. Typically encompasses stories about action, sports, adventure, fighting, collecting, and so on. There is also a significant crossover with SHOJO MANGA these days in style and content. Stories are characterized by bawdy humor, action, and sexuality, and feature narratives about becoming a stronger man.

Shotacon (ショタコン): Male version of LOLICON. Indicates a love of young boys or a woman with that tendency. Indicators of this status include hairless legs, shorts, caps, and *randoseru* (school bags based on military ruck sacks). It's mostly popular with FUJOSHI. The name is an abbreviation of "Shotaro complex," indicating Shotaro, the little-boy protagonist of *Tetsujin 28-go* (1963).

Shuchusen (集中線): Impact lines. In MANGA and ANIME, concentration or focus lines that draw and keep the viewer's focus, often to deliver a powerful effect or message.

Sister café (シスターカフェ): Not little sisters, but sister nuns. These are cafés that look like churches where waitresses dress as nuns in short skirts. The fetishism of nuns is nothing new, as the word in Japanese, *ama*, happens to be a homonym of the Japanese word for bitch.

Smith, Toren: Born in 1960 in Alberta, Canada. An important figure in the history of MANGA in North America. In 1981, he moved to California. He was introduced to manga in 1982, and advised Horibuchi Seiji in the founding of VIZ. Frustrated with the company's slow pace licensing outside the Shogakukan library, Smith sold his possessions and moved to Japan in 1986 to found his own company, Studio Proteus (est. 1988). His first year in Japan, Smith was invited to DAICON V in Osaka and also visited General Products (which would become GAINAX). At the convention, Smith met OKADA TOSHIO and TEZUKA OSAMU, among others, and received the rights to localize SHIROW MASAMUNE's *Appleseed*, which received the Seiun Award for best manga. Smith was soon able to arrange more licenses. After seeing an article in which Smith severely criticized the localization of *NAUSICAÄ OF THE VALLEY OF THE WIND*,

MIYAZAKI HAYAO handpicked Studio Proteus to adapt the *Nausicaä* manga for Viz. After a brief stint in the US to publish his licensed manga with Eclipse Comics, Smith returned to Japan, this time hosted by Okada. He lived and worked out of a walk-in closet in Gainax House, a semi-hygienic flop for animators. One of the characters in *Gunbuster* (1988) is named after Smith, who also contributed voice-overs. Also in 1988, Studio Proteus entered an exclusive co-publishing deal with Dark Horse Comics. Aside from producing duties, Smith co-translated thirty-four manga series, totaling nearly 80,000 pages. This includes *GHOST IN THE SHELL* and the script for the ANIME, both enduring classics. He also co-wrote the first three American *Dirty Pair* comics. Appalled by the "quantity over quality" trend in localization, Smith sold most of his rights to Dark Horse in 2004 and retired from the world of manga.

Soramimi (空耳): Air ears. Listening to a song or spoken words and mistakenly hearing what is said. The phenomenon really took off on the TV show *Tamori Club* in 1982. The most popular part of the show was the soramimi hour, in which lyrics in songs by overseas artists were replaced with similar-sounding Japanese to hilarious effect. Soramimi has also become a popular form of comedy on the video-sharing site NICO NICO DOUGA, where users write alternative lyrics to unintelligible domestic and foreign songs and share them with others. Some soramimi become cult classics. For example, a video of the hit song "Moskau" by the German band Dschinghis Khan was put online in 2005 with a completely different set of lyrics. The 2CHANNEL mascot cats do Cossack dances, and characters from *The Rose of Versailles, Gundam*, and *Laputa* also make appearances.

SOS: Save Our Sailors. The largest and most successful ANIME-revival campaign in history, launched in 1996 when *Sailor Moon* was taken off the air before the entire series had been shown. Distributor DiC brought over only sixty-five of the 200 episodes and none of the movies based on Takeuchi Naoko's 1992–97 MANGA. The show was edited for kids and aired in poor time slots in Canada and the United States. The SOS campaign was launched to get everything else brought over to the English-speaking world with as little editing as possible. Within fourteen months, SOS had over 78,000 supporters and a huge petition going. The group retired in 2004 after reaching its goal of getting the entire *Sailor Moon* franchise brought over to the US—except the final *Sailor Stars* story arc.

Soshuhen (総集編): Highlights; summary. A recap and review episode near the middle of a broadcast ANIME series—somewhere between episodes twelve and fourteen—to introduce the main characters and events and to explain important narrative points to new viewers. The anime business, infamously and habitually strapped for funds, often also uses these edit-and-recycle episodes as rest periods for overworked staff and a break in the budget.

Sotsugyoushitahito (卒業した人): Graduated person. If someone grows out of being an OTAKU or decides that they can no longer be part of a fandom, they are said to have "graduated" (see DATSU-OTA). Similarly, this extends to MAIDS who "graduate" from their fantasy and COSPLAY work. M's Melody café in Nagoya was the first café to hold a graduation ceremony for staff on February 15, 2003.

Sound drop (サウンドドロップ): A type of Gashapon toy developed by BANDAI (see GACHAPON). These popular keychain buttons make sounds—especially sound effects and lines from ANIME—when pressed. Forerunners include Sound Gears, Watanabe Pro Neta Voice, and so on. Bandai revolutionized the market in 2006 by releasing about 2 million units, and by June 2008 there were more than 20 million on the market. Popular examples include "*Ikimasu!*" from *Gundam*, "*Kamehameha!*" from *Dragon Ball Z*, and the phrase "*Okaerinasamase, goshujinsama*" (Welcome home, Master), as heard in MAID CAFÉS.

***Space Battleship Yamato*:** See *UCHU SENKAN YAMATO*.

Speech or thought balloon: See FUKIDASHI.

Speed lines: See DOUSEN.

S

Stamp rally (スタンプラリー): Buying products or attending events to fill in a stamp card, which can then be traded for the privilege of buying a limited product or attending a special event.

Stop-motion animation: See KOMATORI.

Storyboard: See EKONTE.

Story manga (ストーリーマンガ): Narrative-driven comics, graphic novels.

Street idoru (路上アイドル): Amateur singers, dancers, and models who use the street as their space to practice and perform before fans. This happens regularly in parks and in front of train stations in Tokyo, but outdoor shopping arcades are particularly likely spots for IDORU encounters. AKIHABARA became the ideal place to make a name in the mid-2000s, and many street idoru would show up to perform on the weekend. Popular idoru often had scores of fans doing OTAGEI dances at the impromptu shows. Unfortunately, the fun ended when new regulations for public display were imposed after Sawamoto Asuka, a self-proclaimed "sexy idoru," was arrested in 2008 for flashing her panties in public and inciting mass chaos on the streets of Akiba.

Studio 4°C (スタジオ4°C): A renowned Japanese production company and early adapter of digital techniques. It specializes in high-impact ANIME with progressive hybrid imagery. Founded in 1986 by director Morimoto Koji, producer Tanaka Eiko, and animator Sato Yoshiharu. Morimoto worked on OTOMO KATSUHIRO's "The Order to Stop Construction" segment of the anthology film *Neo-Tokyo*, and later as animation director on Otomo's landmark feature *AKIRA*. He did the concert scene in *Macross Plus* as well as the manic short film *Noiseman Sound Insect*. Tanaka Eiko worked as line producer on MIYAZAKI HAYAO's *My Neighbor Totoro*, and *Kiki's Delivery Service*. Studio 4°C also did the animation for Otomo's *Memories* in 1996, and in 2003 collaborated with Warner Bros. to put out *The Animatrix*. In 2004, it made award-winning avant-garde works such as *Mind Game* and *Tekkon Kinkurito*, the latter nominated at the Berlin Film Festival. While most of its portfolio is theatrical, it has also made TV series such as *Tweeny Witches*, music video clips for popular artists including Utada Hikaru, visuals for games such as *Street Fighter IV*, and commercials for the likes of Nike. The studio is located in Kichijoji, near the Ghibli Museum.

STREET IDORU DOING THEIR THING IN AKIBA

MINDGAME FROM STUDIO 4°C

Studio Ghibli (スタジオ・ジブリ)**:** A Japanese animation film studio beloved the world over for its wholesome family entertainment. This hit machine holds most of the records for yearly box office sales in Japan. The name "Ghibli" is Italian slang from WWII meaning "hot blowing wind," a force the studio hoped to bring to the Japanese ANIME industry. The founders are MIYAZAKI HAYAO, Takahata Isao, and Suzuki Toshio, who came together to produce the animated film *NAUSICAÄ OF THE VALLEY OF THE WIND*. Released in 1984, *Nausicaä* was a monsters and BISHOJO extravaganza destined for glory. Spurred by the film's success, the core members of the production founded Ghibli in 1985. Miyazaki continued to turn out massive costly and popular productions, including *Laputa: Castle in the Sky* (1986), *My Neighbor Totoro* (1988), and *Kiki's Delivery Service* (1989), all of which took the Animage Anime Grand Prix award.

Other important works by Ghibli include Takahata's soul-crushing war-orphan drama *Grave of the Fireflies* (1988), and his nostalgic *Only Yesterday* (1991). Others are Miyazaki's *Porco Rosso* (1992), Takahata's *Pom Poko* (1994), and Kondo Yoshifumi's *Whisper of the Heart* (1995). Ghibli did some animation work for Anno Hideaki's *NEON GENESIS EVANGELION* in 1995, the same year that Miyazaki directed his darkest work, "On Your Mark," a music video for the musical duo Chage & Aska that follows two policemen as they rescue an angel from a cult massacre and subsequent government experimentation.

Most of Ghibli's works are distributed in Japan by the major studio Toho, and in 1996 Ghibli's parent company Tokuma provided the Walt Disney Company with international home video distribution rights to its catalog. This was a major turning point for Ghibli, as demonstrated by the success of Miyazaki's next work, *Princess Mononoke*, in 1997. The work not only became the most successful film in Japanese history at the box offices—15 million tickets sold—but it was also widely distributed in the United States and won the studio and director legions of fans. In 2003, Miyazaki's *Spirited Away* (2001) became the first anime to win an Academy Award for Best Animated Feature. Ghibli then worked with Production I.G to co-produce OSHII MAMORU's *Innocence: Ghost in the*

Shell 2 in 2004. That year, Miyazaki put out another film, *Howl's Moving Castle*. His son, Goro, directed *Tales from Earthsea* in 2006, and Miyazaki put out *Ponyo on the Cliff by the Sea* in 2008.

Ghibli has a museum and playground in KICHIJOJI outside Tokyo, a forest retreat in suburban Saitama Prefecture, and a two-year professional school to train incoming Ghibli animators located in Aichi Prefecture.

Suginami Animation Museum (杉並アニメーションミュージアム): Japan's first museum devoted to ANIME rather than a single artist or creator. Opened in 2005 in Suginami Ward of Tokyo, where some seventy of Japan's 230 anime studios are located—the second most of any ward after Nerima.

Sukebe (スケベ): Someone who thinks too much about sex. The term originated in the Edo period (1600–1868).

Sukumizu (スクミズ): Abbreviation of "school *mizugi*"; a girl's swimming suit for school. From grade school to high school, the designs are set and everyone wears the same uniform. They tend to be navy blue and very plain and were first adopted by schools in the early 1960s. Female characters often wear them in MANGA and ANIME, and they are are part of the fetishized SEIFUKU wardrobe.

Suré (スレ): Pronounced "sue-ray," it's an abbreviation of the Japanese pronounciation of "thread" (su-re-do), as in the discussion threads on a BBS. For example YAOI-sure.

Sweets (lol) (スイーツ(笑)): A derogatory term used among OTAKU and FUJOSHI, especially in online discussions, to ridicule others who follow mainstream fashion and culture magazines and then presume they are cool or sexy. It first appeared on 2CHANNEL in late 2007 when some groups began to euphemistically describe arrogant people as fancy "sweets," because they were all show and no substance. Most commonly used to describe young women who attempt to be stylish.

Symbolic speech: See MANPU.

ONIICHAN!
I'M A LITTLE
COLD . . .

5

RANMA ½ BY TAKAHASHI RUMIKO

Tachiyomi (立ち読み): Standing and reading. The practice of standing in front of magazine and book racks in convenience and bookstores and reading for hours on end. It is a great way to save money. Many Japanese can be found killing time this way. In an effort to increase sales, weekly MANGA anthologies have started closing products with bindings removed at the counter, and TANKOBON manga are often shrink-wrapped.

Takahashi Rumiko (高橋留美子): Born in 1957 in Niigata Prefecture. The best-selling female MANGAKA in Japan. Her hits include *Urusei Yatsura*, *Maison Ikkoku*, *Ranma ½*, *Inu-Yasha*, and countless others. She was dominating TV as soon as her works were first broadcast, with the end of *Urusei Yatsura* providing the promotion hook for her next series, *Maison Ikkoku*. Because Takahashi had the foresight to keep the rights to her creations, she became a millionaire many times over soon after *Urusei Yatsura*; she routinely makes the list of the richest Japanese with an annual income of over $3 million. She has a knack for the poignant portrayal of relationships, making the awkwardness of young boys and girls ring true, even for the most jaded readers, in stories of immature love that unfold over the course of long, sprawling story arcs. She is known for her focus on and bending of gender roles. Takahashi was one of the first female artists to break down the barriers and write for a male audience (see SHONEN MANGA). She did this by tying her female sensibilities to action adventure, sexy girls, and bodily (often bawdy) humor.

tarento • 中川翔子

NAKAGAWA SHOKO

NAKAGAWA SHOKO, OR "SHOKO-TAN" as she is usually called, appears regularly on Japanese TV as a *tarento* and is loud and proud about being an
OTAKU. Her blog is one of the most widely read blogs in the world.

PG: What kind of stuff do you do in your free time?

NS: Watch ANIME, draw, read MANGA, play on the Internet, and sing anime songs . . . here just isn't enough time in the day! So when I get back from work I do them all at once. Like, while I'm watching anime, I play games, use the computer, and draw.

PG: What got you so intensely interested in all this?

NS: Ever since I was young I liked to draw, and my parents bought me manga and stuff. I wanted to be a *MANGAKA*. In grade school I liked anime, games, and manga, but just in a normal way, like any child. Then when I got into middle school, people suddenly started calling me an otaku. It's been that way ever since. I still like the things I did as a kid.

PG: What's your favorite work?

NS: I like *Final Fantasy VII*. It had a huge impact on me when it came out. Suddenly, games were so real. There was this boss character, Sephiroth-sama, and I loved him so much! I recorded the movies he appeared in and spent all my allowance on Sephiroth merchandise. It was intense, and his existence was a big part of my life. As for anime, well, there are so many I like! But *Sailor Moon* is the best. It was playing on TV when I was a little girl, and it was what got me into drawing. It's like, how should I say, perfect, you know? It has every single kind of cute, all packed into one work, or that's what I thought. Ever since I was a kid, not a day has gone by that I haven't thought about *Sailor Moon*.

PG: Are you an otaku?

NS: I think someone like me is still "soft," so maybe I'm not qualified to be an otaku. "Otaku" can be really widely applied. An anime otaku and an IDORU otaku are different after all, and there are people who like figures, and others with no interest in them at all. It's hard to use "otaku" to summarize and group people together, right? I think it basically means someone going all out for a hobby. I'm really happy when people say that about me, but I need to work hard to be more of an otaku. Back in school, I was really sad when people called me otaku, because they were saying it as an insult. Now, it's the opposite, I can enjoy life as otaku. Like, I finally understand, everyone is an otaku.

PG: How did you go from otaku to tarento?

NS: Being holed up in my room watching anime, playing games, and reading manga all the time, I was the last person anyone would think would become famous. Singing in front of people seemed impossible. I got into it because I wanted to become a SENTAI hero. I was a total groupie of the Pink Ranger from *Power Rangers*. I wanted to be just like her, so I really dieted and stuff. I collected swimsuit pinups, GRAVIA idoru pictures, and thought "that's what I want to do." When I first made it as an

doru I hid my real hobbies. But then I thought, "Why not?" and asked my management to make a blog where I could be more open about my hobbies. I wanted to keep a diary, to talk about anime and stuff, but I didn't think anyone would read it. However, the more I talked about those things, the more people started to read it. That was about 2003 or 2004.

PG: What do you like best about your life now?

NS: When I go straight home from work and am in my own room. All the shelves are filled with manga. I even threw out my bed to make room for manga! I have my computer, my cats are there, all my figures are displayed, and there's even a special wardrobe for COSPLAY. The rare *Sailor Moon* goods I bought on auction are there. I'm surrounded by all the things I love. My room is really a disaster, but it's all stuff that's important to me and I'm in bliss.

PG: How often are you online?

NS: When I'm home my computer is always on, and I update my blog from my cell phone throughout the day. On busy days, I post maybe twenty times.

PG: The words you use in your blog, where are they from?

NS: *Giza*, which means "very," was a mistake when I was trying to type *giga* on my blog. I thought it was kind of cute and kept using it because I thought no one would see it. It became kind of like a habit, so I still use it. There are lots of words that I use only on my blog. When you're writing words rather than speaking them, it kind of seems natural that it would be different. I keep up with 2channel words, but I don't write anything there.

PG: You went to Anime Expo 2008 and performed live. What was it like?

NS: When I first heard I was going to perform in the United States, I was like, "No way, it's impossible! I can't!" Really, I'm the quiet and reserved type. I never ever raised my hand in school. But when I got to LA everyone was wandering around in cosplay and having a great time. I really felt that otaku are no different anywhere so I relaxed. The concert was scary, but I'd taken a bunch of costumes with me and went out there and sang anime songs. People really got into it! When it came time for the last song I asked, "Do you know the anime *Gurren Lagann*?" And even though it hadn't yet aired in the United States everyone knew it and screamed! Seriously otaku are amazing. It was giza! I want to try and write my blog in English to keep up the energy I felt at the concert, but I suck at English.

PG: What are your plans for the future?

NS: My dream is to be the Queen of Anime Songs and have a concert in Hong Kong where they love anime so much. And I'd like to sing at Anime Expo again! I've been doing some work as a SEIYUU, as well, so hopefully there will be a chance to do more. I also want to draw my own manga, get that made into an anime, and play the main role. That'd be a dream come true.

TALK LIKE SHOKO-TAN

Giza very
Giganto very very
Gigantic very very very
Bikku ban big bang level
Galactica galactic level
King royal level
Rai rai greeting
Tutturuu excited
Bocchiboon shock
Horuusu emotional response
Mepo good morning

Tan (たん): A cute name suffix used for IDORU and fan favorites. For example SHOKO-TAN.

Tanbi (耽美): Aesthetics. Used among FUJOSHI to discuss beautiful boy characters.

Tankobon (単行本): A compact, usually paperback book, with color dust jacket and thicker-than-normal paper. These are usually released as collections of stories of a popular MANGA after it has run in the pages of a manga magazine.

Tape traders: People who made and sold bootleg VHS tapes of ANIME series that they had translated and subtitled. This was a pre-Internet form of piracy, but most companies looked the other way as long as these sellers didn't distribute licensed series or properties already on the market. The tape traders sold the tapes for around $15 each at SF conventions and did a lot to help spread anime fandom in the late 1980s and early 1990s.

Tarento (タレント): Talent. A catchall term meaning anyone who is famous or lucky enough to become a celebrity in the Japanese media. These people function as a rotating talent pool for variety shows and late-night TV. Ironically, tarento are not usually especially talented at anything but are beautiful, funny, crazy, or stupid, and play along with the skits they are given. Foreign celebrities are typically called *serebu*.

Tashiro Matsuri (田代祭): The Tashiro Festival. A 2CHANNEL movement that began in December 2001 with the aim of getting entertainer Tashiro Masashi voted in as *Time* magazine's Person of the Year. Tashiro was, at the time, in trouble for taking pictures of women's underwear and peeping at a man in the bath. 2channel folk cast tons of online votes so he could become a "HENTAI legend." They even created a computer script for voting automatically. As a result, Tashiro was at one point in the lead with twice the votes of Osama Bin Laden. American mediators realized it was a fraud and called the vote off, instead electing former New York Mayor Rudy Giuliani. This international prank resulted in the formation of the Matsuri thread on 2channel in 2002. While they were no longer allowed to vote for *Time*, they attempted to get Tashiro voted into Asian Heroes 2002, Hat Grand Prix 2003, and the Yahoo! Japan artist search rankings. There still exists a hardcore minority that votes for him to this day.

Tasogare (黄昏): Twilight. This term also describes a time and space when all things are equally true and false, right and wrong, good and bad. A lot of ANIME, MANGA, and OTAKU culture falls into this twilight zone.

Tatsunoko Productions: See YOSHIDA TATSUO.

Tecchan (鉄ちゃん): Nickname for train otaku (*tetsudo otaku*). These guys are true "train spotters" and their obsession covers everything from train parts, interior styles, and sounds, to collecting goods, memorizing schedules, and photographing retiring trains. The female version is *tekko*.

Techie: A term used to describe fanatics or specialists of computers, electronics and other technologies. They often build and maintain their own machines, meaning that they know all the specs. Because

MAYBE I SHOULD CHANGE MY NAME TO MOÉ-TAN

T

of their passion for IT and stereotyped social inability, techies are often compared to the early radio, computer, and ROBOT OTAKU of AKIBA, who still gather there to browse the newest advances.

Telop: (テロップ): Television opaque projector. In Japan, this is used to mean text superimposed on the screen. Most of the time these are subtitles, but they can also be scrolling messages or credits. In 1997 some ANIME viewers complained of averse physical effects from watching anime (see POKÉMON SHOKKU), prompting a telop message at the beginning of episodes warning viewers to maintain a safe distance from the TV and to keep the room bright when watching anime.

Terebi game (テレビゲーム): TV game; video games. While most video games are now Japanese, gaming technology was actually developed by a group of computer boffins at Massachusetts Institute of Technology (MIT) in the US, who made the first video game, *Spacewar!*, in the 1960s. In 1971 Nolan Bushnell and Ted Dabne created the first commercial video game, *Computer Space*, and went on to found the first video game company, ATARI. Their game *PONG* opened up mass arcade and home console gaming in 1972. But it was Japanese games like Taito's *Space Invaders* in 1978, Namco's *Galaxian* and *Pac-Man* in 1979 and 1980, and NINTENDO's *Donkey Kong* and *Mario Bros.* in 1981, that really sparked the video game boom.

Japan still rules the roost in console and arcade games, but competitive e-Sports for the computer and on the Internet are dominated by its neighbor, South Korea. At Tokyo Game Show 2008, the feeling was Japan was going to lose out unless something was done. In 2006, the global video game market was $31.6 billion, and analysts estimate it will increase to $48.9 billion by 2011.

Terekura (テレクラ): Telephone clubs. Places where people record personal ads on a voice mail system and then wait for contact. Despite the pretense of being a fun way to meet friends and singles, such services are usually used for phone sex, prostitution, and most notably, in the mid-1990s, by KOGALS who used them to arrange meetings with older men for ENJOKOSAI. Similar to DENGON DIAL (answering services).

TETSUDO CAFÉS APPEAL TO TETSUDO OTAKU

Tetsudo Hakubutsukan (鉄道博物館): The Train Museum. Founded in AKIHABARA in 1936 and relocated to Omiya, Saitama Prefecture, in 2007. The new 41,600-square-meter modern facility cost $112 million to construct. It boasts Japan's largest train diorama, a miniature train ride, Japan's first steam locomotive, and thirty-five other engines, including a snowplow model. There are also outdoor facilities and a restaurant serving only train station boxed lunches (*ekiben*). An estimated 50,000 people showed up to pay the $10 entrance fee during opening week. It is now a popular date spot. Soon after, a train station pub opened in Akihabara complete with uniformed conductors who welcome customers aboard and a TV playing only scenery shot from a train window. See also TETSUDO OTAKU and TETSUDOL.

Tetsudol (鉄ドル): A cute female IDORU who likes trains. The archetypes are Kimura Yuko and Toyoka Masumi. Toyoka lent her voice to the wildly popular 2007 ANIME *Tekko no Tabi* (*Train Girl's Journey*), which helped legitimize and mainstream train OTAKU. These girls are also called tetsudol TARENTO because they appear on TV and at promotion events dedicated to trains.

Tetsudo otaku (鉄道オタク): Train otaku; an extremely devoted fan of trains. In 2005, the Nomura Research Institute suggested there are 140,000 tetsudo otaku in Japan. That number is likely to have gone up drastically following the opening of the new TETSUDO HAKUBUTSUKAN in 2007 and the train boom that followed with ANIME such as *Tekko no Tabi* aimed at train fans. Also in 2007 *Kamen Rider Den-o* became a hit with female train fans because it had beautiful boys and a time travelling train. There are numerous subcategories, including *noritetsu* (likes to ride trains), *rosen kenkyu* (likes to memorize what trains on what lines do what things in what conditions), *toritetsu* (likes to take pictures of trains), *mokeitetsu* (likes to build train models and dioramas), *ototetsu* (likes to analyze train sounds), *ekibentetsu* (likes the special box lunches sold at train stations), *jikokuhyoutetsu* (likes to analyze the train time schedules), *ekitetsu* (likes to memorize information on train stations), and *soshikitetsu* (likes to memorialize retired trains and lines). Tetsudo otaku are also called *tetsuota*, *denshamania*, TECCHAN or *tekko*

***Tetsuwan Atomu* (鉄腕アトム):** A MANGA and ANIME by TEZUKA OSAMU, known as *Mighty Atom* or *Astro Boy* around the world. Aired in 1963, the series was the first successful TV anime in Japan, and the first to adopt serialized thirty minute episodes. The story revolves around Atom, a little robot boy with an atomic heart, who was created by Doctor Tenma to replace his son Tobio, who died in a car accident. Atom is abandoned by Tenma because he cannot physically grow or emotionally express himself in the same ways Tenma's son did. Atom is rescued by the kindly Dr. Ochanomizu, who helps him learn. Atom, the robot that is more human than humans, teaches a universal lesson about love and respect; he guides 21st-century society toward a brighter tomorrow. The work touches on issues of atomic energy, militarism, racism (as seen in the treatment of robots), and industrialization in a post-Hiroshima world. The series set the tone for cute, violent, symbolic, and subtly cerebral anime to come.

TETSUWAN ATOMU BY OZAMU TEZUKA

The very same year it aired in Japan, producer Fred Ladd poured money into adding cels to the US adaption, *Astro Boy*, which was sponsored by NBC and received national syndication. This was the beginning of the First Wave of international anime fans. It was also the beginning of pressure groups complaining to broadcasters about adult themes and violence, which denied American audiences the last episode of *Tetsuwan Atomu* and resulted in restrictions on imports to come. Imagi Animation is putting out a CG anime of *Atomu* for Hollywood release in 2009.

In Takadanobaba, where Tezuka Productions has its studios, the train station has adopted the *Tetsuwan Atomu* theme song as the boarding chime. There is also a mural in front of the station, and in Hanno-shi in Saitama Prefecture there's a statue dedicated to the little robot.

Tezuka Osamu (手塚治虫): Born in 1928 in Toyonaka, Osaka. A pioneering MANGAKA and the father of Japanese ANIME as we know it. At the end of WWII, at age sixteen, he worked in a munitions factory. He went on to study medicine at Osaka University, and received his doctorate before turning to MANGA full time.

He debuted as a mangaka at age seventeen in 1946 with *Diary of Ma-chan*, a newspaper comic strip about a little boy who wants to learn the ABCs from the GIs occupying his country. Tezuka became famous with the AKAHON MANGA *Shin Takarajima* in 1947, an update of Robert Louis Stevenson's *Treasure Island*. He went on to pen such classics as *Metropolis* (1949), *JYANGURU TAITEI* (1950–54), *TETSUWAN ATOMU* (1952–68), the first SHOJO MANGA *Ribon no Kishi* (1953–56), *Dororo to Hyakumaru* (1967–68), and *Hi no Tori* (1956–89), a massive epic often called his lifework. In the 1970s Tezuka

TEZUKA OSAMU
"THE GOD OF MANGA"

produced some of his more adult works, including the raunchy *Cleopatra: Queen of Sex* (1970), the panty-fest *Marvelous Melmo* (1970–72), and *Yakeppachi no Maria* (1970) about a lovedoll that comes to life. He also created the cutesy *Mitsume ga Tooru* (1974–78) and *Yuniko* (1976–79). Tezuka finished out his career with more mature and sophisticated works, including *Black Jack* (1973–83), *Buddha* (1974–84), *Tell Adolf* (1983–85), and *Neo Faust* (1988).

During the US occupation of Japan, he spent time with US soldiers, who took him to animated picture shows and shared their cartoons with him. Tezuka actually wanted to be a filmmaker, but settled on the emerging manga scene, which he innovated with his cinematic style and stories. He borrowed heavily from Walt Disney and Max Fleischer and was enthralled with *Bambi*, which he claimed to have seen a hundred times and later licensed to adapt as a manga. He memorized the work, praising the visual realism but rejecting the unrealistic characters and interactions. Tezuka innovated manga with ideas such as speed lines, temporal shots, sweat, and exclamation marks. He then brought all this to the table in 1963 with *Tetsuwan Atomu*, the first full-fledged TV broadcast anime in Japan. From the beginning, his works were cinematic in style and theme and highly narrative. At the 1964 World's Fair, Tezuka met Disney, who praised his work. Tezuka continued to experiment with anime techniques, creating a variety of themes—such as technological utopia, robots, human resilience—that define the Golden Age of Anime. Tezuka became so prolific and popular that even Stanley Kubrick was a fan; Kubrick wanted Tezuka to do the designs for his *2001: A Space Odyssey*, but the "God of Manga" was too busy contributing to his own 150,000-page, 700-work corpus.

The Tezuka Osamu Memorial Museum is located in Takarazuka, Hyogo Prefecture, where the legendary mangaka spent much of his youth.

TEZUKA'S RAUNCHY *YAKEPPACHI NO MARIA*

3DCG: Three Dimensional Computer Graphic animation. Animation made up of three-dimensional objects generated on computers. Computer graphics developed rapidly in the 1990s, and it became possible to create complex images that are indistinguishable from actual motion pictures. 3DCG animation is now used to create backgrounds and special effects in film.

Tobirae (扉絵): A title page, usually a highly detailed, colorful illustration.

Toei Animation (東映アニメーション): A major animation studio. Founded in 1948 as Japan Animated Films, but changed its name to Toei Douga when bought by Toei in 1956. In 1998 *douga*, an older word for animation, was officially replaced, and the company became Toei Animation. Toei is a shareholder in the Japanese ANIME satellite network, ANIMAX, along with other noted anime studios and production enterprises such as Sunrise.

This was Japan's first large-scale animation studio, and it remains one of the biggest and most successful. Its original goal was to become the "Disney of the East," and its animators insisted they were not making anime, but art. Toei Douga introduced the division of labor system to involve hundreds of people on a single project (see SAKUGA KANTOKU). In 1958, it made the first color animated film in Japan, *HAKUJADEN*, which inspired MIYAZAKI HAYAO to go into anime. The 1959 work *The Adventures of Little Samurai* was the first anime shown to the emperor. Former animators include NAGAI GO, Miyazaki, and Takahata Isao. In 1964, Miyazaki was the chief secretary and Takahata the vice chairman of Toei Douga's labor union, where they formed the lasting partnership that led to them founding STUDIO GHIBLI. Toei Douga laid the

groundwork for many future anime by training animators, importing ideas, and refining ideals. For example, Takahata made his directorial debut with *Little Norse Prince Valiant* (1968), a benchmark classic featuring abstract interior shots, a purple-haired, mysterious heroine, otherworldly beings, and animal sidekicks. Miyazaki was chief animator, concept artist, and scene designer.

In the 1960s, Toei Douga animated ISHINOMORI SHOTARO's *Cyborg 009* (1968) and Mizuki Shigeru's *Ge Ge Ge no Kitaro* (1968–69), and it was at the cutting edge of the magical girl genre with Yokoyama Mitsuteru's *Sally, the Witch* (1966–68) and *Akko-chan's Secret* (1969–99). In the 1970s, it brought out the works of Nagai Go, including *Devilman* (1972–73), *Mazinger Z* (1972–74), and *Cutie Honey* (1973–74). It also put out MATSUMOTO LEIJI's *Captain Harlock* (1978–79) and *Galaxy Express 999* (1978–81) and animated his *Yamato* films from 1977 to 1983. It still managed to squeeze in classics including *Majokko Megu-chan* (1974–75) and *Candy Candy* (1976–79).

In the 1980s, Toei Douga also provided animation work for American animation, including *Teenage Mutant Ninja Turtles*, *My Little Pony*, *Transformers*, and *G.I. Joe*. In Japan, it brought to the screen *Fist of the North Star* (1984–88), one of the most beloved martial arts-action series of all time. They also put Toriyama Akira on the map with *Dr. Slump* (1981–86) and *Dragon Ball* (1986–97), the latter a ten year-long franchise considered the pinnacle of the *shonen* style.

In the 1990s, Toei struck gold again with Takeuchi Naoko's *Sailor Moon* (1992–96), which shaped a generation of young women in Japan. It has since continued to be a hit machine, with series such as *Slam Dunk* (1993–96), *Yu-Gi-Oh!* (1998), *Digimon* (1999–2007), *One Piece* (from 1999), and *Pretty Cure* (from 2004).

Other arms of Toei Company Ltd. were critical to the development of TOKUSATSU, KAIJU, and SENTAI. The Toei Animation Gallery is in Nerima Ward, where most of Japan's 230 anime studios are located.

***Tokimeki Memorial* (ときめきメモリアル):** A popular PC dating simulator released by Konami in 1994. In 2006 it was voted the twenty-third best game of all time, and is a classic dating simulator, or GYARUGE.

Tokusatsu (特撮): Special effects. Japanese live-action films and television shows using special effects such as miniature models and sets, elaborate costumes and pyrotechnics. These are usually SF, disaster or horror films. Classic examples are KAIJU monster movies, like *Godzilla*; hero stories such as *Ultraman*; SENTAI task force shows, such as *Power Rangers*; and MECHA dramas, like *Giant Robo*. Tokusatsu emerged with *Godzilla* in 1954 and kaiju ruled until 1957, when hero stories emerged with *Super Giant*. In 1966 the genres merged with a hero fighting giant kaiju in *Ultraman*. That same year, *Maguma Taishi* became the first color

TOKUSATSU: ULTRAMAN MEBIUS VS KAIJU

tokusatsu series to air in Japan, based on TEZUKA OSAMU's manga. The transforming hero genre took off after ISHINOMORI SHOTARO's *Kamen Rider* in 1971.

Tokusatsu series are extremely popular among OTAKU, who watched them as kids and studied the techniques as young adults. For example, *Ultra Seven*, who used capsule monsters not unlike *POKÉMON*, has become an icon for many since appearing in 1967. At SF conventions around Japan in the 1980s, young creators, including Daicon Film (see GAINAX), made parody tokusatsu films. Marionette tokusatsu *X Bomber* (1980–81, by NAGAI GO), or *Star Fleet*, as it was known in England, inspired the album *Star Fleet Project* by Brian May of Queen.

Tokyo Game Show (東京ゲームショウ): Or TGS, was founded in 1996 and has grown to be the world's largest event for electronic entertainment. The expo is on par with E3 in Los Angeles and the Leipzig Games Convention. TGS is a four-day event; two days for business and two days for the general public. It was originally held twice a year at Tokyo BIG SIGHT, but in 2002 the schedule changed to once a year in fall at MAKUHARI MESSE in Chiba prefecture. In 2008 209 exhibitors manned 1,768 booths, the highest numbers ever. TGS occupied eight halls (dwarfing C3xHobby, the other notable event hosted by Makuhari Messe), a whopping 54,000 square meters, and some 180,000 people visited. TGS also included tie-ins to the Japan International Contents Festival, the world's largest and longest season of comprehensive content events. A full 879 titles were displayed, up from 702 in 2007 because of what organizers described as a boom in sequels for popular franchises on console, hand-held, and mobile platforms, and a growing market for games targetting women and seniors.

Tokyo International Anime Fair (TAF) (東京国際アニメフェア): Japan's largest trade fair for ANIME. The event is held over fours days in spring at the massive Tokyo BIG SIGHT convention center. Industry and press are allowed on weekdays, and the general public pays around $10 for a

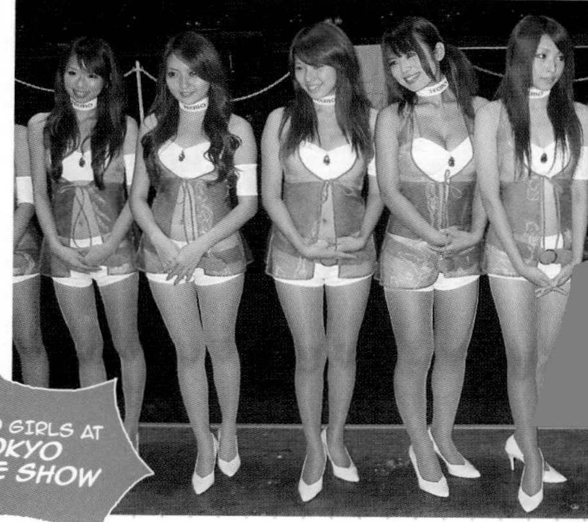
TECMO GIRLS AT TOKYO GAME SHOW

weekend ticket. During the business days, symposia on the potential of the anime market are held. It was founded in 2002 as New Century Tokyo International Anime Fair 21 (the 21 was a reference to the 21st century) and was presided over by Tokyo Mayor Ishihara Shintaro, who has made brash remarks suggesting Japanese artists should make something "more uniquely Japanese" to aid the nation's image.

The event includes the Tokyo Anime Awards, Japan's first major domestic awards for anime. TIAF is supported by government agencies including the Ministry of Economy, the Tokyo Metropolitan Government, and its Association of Japanese Animation. Although the event has a short history, the political clout gives it credibility in the industry.

Tokyopop: An American publishing company specializing in Japanese media. It was originally called Mixx Entertainment and was responsible for running *Sailor Moon* almost unedited in its *Mixxzine* MANGA magazine in 1997. It changed its name to Tokyopop in 2002 and began releasing manga that was not FLOPPED and kept the original Japanese text for the sound effects words. The CEO, Stuart Levy, called this "100% Authentic Manga," and it hit big. It was also cheaper than manga previously released in the US because staff were not needed to retouch the manga that had been mirrored to read left to right. Tokyopop started releasing manga by Shueisha; and the strength of the content, the affordability, and the increased speed of production, were all part of the driving force behind the manga revolution in the US.

TOKYOPOP MANGA

MANGA FROM TOKYOPOP

Tome-e (止め・止め絵): A static image or still shot in a motion picture or ANIME. In particular these are stop-motion pictures that depict a certain moment of movement. Another term for this is "drawn picture" (*kakie*). It was started by Dezaki Osamu in *Ashita no Joe* (1970) as a method to emphasize and express movement in an anime with a small number of pictures. It's commonly used to give a strong impression to a certain scene and is still used in digital animation.

Tomino Yoshiyuki (富野由悠季): Born in 1941 in Odawara, Kanagawa Prefecture. Influential ANIME director best known for his work on the seminal *GUNDAM* franchise. Tomino began his career in 1963 with TEZUKA OSAMU'S MUSHI PRODUCTIONS, scripting the storyboards and screenplay for *TETSUWAN ATOMU*. Later, with Studio Sunrise, Tomino revolutionized the transforming-super-giant-robot genre with the realism and wartime themes of 1979's *Mobile Suit Gundam*. He famously stated that anime is not kids' stuff, justifying his broadening of themes and appeal to the older crowd with *Gundam*, (see ANIME SHIN SEIKI SENGEN), but later revoked this claim. This capriciousness is now referred to as "pulling a Tomino." Tomino apologized openly after AUM SHINRIKYO attacked in 1995, claiming it was his work's apocalyptic vision that inspired adults to fantasize in a way that was unhealthy too long past childhood.

Toonami: Cartoon Tsunami. The name of a programming block on the Cartoon Network TV channel launched March 17, 1997. In theory it was dedicated to active and exciting titles in general, but it actually became a major source of ANIME for Americans. It originally only had *Thundercats*, *Voltron*, *The Real Adventures of Jonny Quest*, and *Super Adventures*, but in 1998 it started airing *Sailor Moon*, *Dragon Ball Z*, and *Robotech* reruns. Cartoon Network posted its highest ratings ever, and Toonami became the premier destination for anime series such as *Gundam Wing*, *Blue Submarine No. 6*, *Tenchi Muyo*, *Outlaw Star*, *The Big O*, *Martian Successor Nadesico,* and countless others. This free source of anime opened the eyes of many Americans to the width and depth of anime. Toonami even spawned Reactor, an online subscription-based anime channel in 2001. Unfortunately the party ended when Toonami was cancelled on September 20, 2008.

Topcraft: A Japanese animation studio founded in 1972 in Koenji, Tokyo, by former Toei Douga staff. The president, Hara Toru, worked on 1968's *Little Norse Prince*, a foundational work in the development of a unique Japanese ANIME style. It was also the directorial debut of STUDIO GHIBLI's Takahata Isao and features the design work of a young MIYAZAKI HAYAO. Topcraft's staff included Kubo Tsuguyuki of *Speed Racer* fame and Yamada Katsuhisa, who was known for *Gatchaman*. Yamada later worked for MADHOUSE. Topcraft collaborated with Toei on a few episodes of *MAZINGER Z* before becoming a favorite subcontractor of Rankin/Bass, an American animation firm known for its stop-motion animation and seasonal specials. Topcraft's first work for Rankin/Bass was *Kid Power* (1972–73), an adaptation of the comic strip *Wee Pals*—noted for its racially diverse cast. Even as TEZUKA OSAMU's MUSHI PRODUCTIONS and Toei Douga stopped working on overseas productions, Topcraft worked with Rankin/Bass to put out *20,000 Leagues Under the Sea* (1972), *Willie Mays and the Hey-Say Kid* (1972), and *The Hobbit* (1977). The 1980s saw Topcraft working on some of the most beloved and visually stimulating animation in US history: *The Last Unicorn* (1982), *Flight of Dragons* (1982), and *Return of the King* (1980). The studio was especially known for its background art. Takahata and

TOKYOPOP, TOMINO, TOONAMI, AND TOPCRAFT! WOW! THIS IS AN IMPORTANT PAGE!!

TORANOANA IN AKIHABARA

Miyazaki hired Topcraft to work on *NAUSICAÄ OF THE VALLEY OF THE WIND* in 1984, and brought on core members when they founded Studio Ghibli in 1985. Because Miyazaki adopted the pay by commission system for his animators, the same system that had caused many to leave Toei before, Hara did not join and left what remained of Topcraft. Others went on to join newly founded Pacific Animation Corporation (PAC), which worked with Rankin/Bass on the sprawling TV epic *ThunderCats* (1985–90). PAC was sold to DISNEY in 1989.

Toranoana (虎の穴): A major retailer of DOUJINSHI and MANGA. It started selling doujinshi in a small backstreet shop in AKIHABARA in 1994, and changed the landscape of Chuo-dori street in the 1990s when it prominently displayed giant banners of OTAKU style art on its new store. Toranoana was named after the pit used to train wrestlers in *Tiger Mask* (manga 1968–71, ANIME 1969–71). The company now holds a 75 percent share of the year-round doujinshi consignment sales market and reports $2.7 million a month in online sales and $30 million in annual sales.

Toukou (透過光): The depiction of light in animation, including shiny eyes, stars, lightning, sunlight, and neon signs. Also called "*T-kou*." In analog animation, this was accomplished by exposing light on the film while shooting the painted cells, but it is done digitally these days.

Trekkie: An intensely devoted *Star Trek* fan. Started to appear in 1966 and are known to COSPLAY, collect goods, and write amateur works. "Trekkie" is often used as the functional English translation of "otaku," though the uniqueness of both movements should not be downplayed.

Tsubo (ツボ): Pressure point; "the spot." Used among many OTAKU to label the thing that makes them get all MOÉ.

Tsukkomi (つっこみ): The intelligent, calm, serious character in traditional Japanese pair standup comedy (see MANZAI).

Tsukuba-kei (ツクバ系): As distinct from AKIBA-KEI, some people in AKIHABARA now identify theselves as "Tsukuba-kei," or Tsukuba-style. Tsukuba City in Ibaraki Prefecture is home to a massive research university and suburban housing for middle-class executives and their families. The daily commute to Tokyo has been cut down dramatically, from an hour and a half to forty-five minutes by the new Tsukuba Express Line, which terminates in Akihabara. This massive transport project brings wealthy, family-orientated Japanese into the OTAKU heartland, prompting projects to raise the image of Akiba. Use of the term "Tsukuba-kei" is an attempt to be separated from the riffraff of Akiba. The Tsukuba Express Line even used it in a campaign ad that read, "Let's Get Going With Tsukuba-kei."

Tsundere (ツンデレ): Word combining the onomatopoeia *tsun tsun* (which suggests turning your head away in disgust) with *dere dere* (to turn all lovey dovey). As the literal translation implies, this means characters who're particularly moody. It's important to note that tsundere is not a character type per se but rather a developmental process wherein an icy character shows their warm side over the course of time. Relationships between rivals, and deeply important relationships (soul mates, best friends) in ANIME and MANGA often follow this pattern. The term "tsundere" was first made popular in the hit GYARUGE *Kimi ga Nozomu Eien*. There are now tsundere events at Akihabara maid cafés where the waitresses go out of their way to be mean to customers but finally melt down when he or she is about to leave.

TSUN!
I DIDN'T ASK YOU TO READ THIS BOOK!

SEIYUU Kugimiya Rie is the "Queen of Tsundere," playing characters such as Shana (*Shakugan no Shana*), Nagi (*Hayate no Gotoku!*), Louise (*Zero no Tsukaima*) and Aisaka Taiga (*Toradora!*).

Tsuu (通): An authority, expert, or connoisseur. Someone extremely well versed in a certain area of hobby or leisure. The interest has to be broad in order to be a tsuu. Examples are, *nihon* tsuu (Japan expert), *eiga* tsuu (movie buff), or GUNDAM tsuu (Gundam authority). At times it approaches OTAKU-type knowledge, but the term "tsuu" has been around much longer and doesn't have the negative connotations.

Twin-tail (ツインテール): A type of hairstyle, usually seen on young girls and involving two pony tails. Calling this "twin-tail" is not common practice in Japan, but it is a common-use phrase among OTAKU. This gap might be explained by the *Ultraman* KAIJU Twin Tail (appearing in the 1971–72 series *Return of Ultraman*), which sports a giant forked inverted tail. This popular kaiju might have inspired the otaku name for two ponytails. This is a preferred style for female characters among otaku, and many with twintail are TSUNDERE.

Uchu Senkan Yamato **(宇宙戦艦ヤマト):** A TV ANIME by MATSUMOTO LEIJI known as *Star Blazers* or *Space Cruiser Yamato* around the world, although *Space Battleship Yamato* is a more correct translation.

The story is set in the year 2199, when an alien race known as the Gamilas shell the Earth with radioactive bombs, erradicating life on the surface. The outgunned Earth forces are helpless to stop them; humanity is shut up in shelters deep underground, and the radiation is slowly seeping down. A message is found by humans on Mars, in which Queen Starsha of the planet Iscandar conveys that she has a device called Cosmo Cleaner D that can cleanse the Earth. She provides blueprints for a space battleship to come to her planet and retrieve it. Japan's sunken WWII flagship, the *Yamato*, is raised and rebuilt into a space battleship renamed *Argo*, the hope of humanity. The story follows the 114 brave souls aboard the ship as they make a desperate journey through the Gamilian line to save the Earth.

This is Matsumoto's masterpiece, and it changed the way anime was perceived in Japan and abroad. *Yamato*'s epic story featured sweeping narrative plots and compelling character development. The romantic vision of heroes, villains, and battle in space was true space opera, and it captured the hearts and minds of a generation of adults. At the time, *Animage*, Japan's first adult-oriented OTAKU magazine, carried facts, figures, and details on *Yamato*.

When *Yamato* came to the United States in 1977 as *Star Blazers*, it was extremely accurate to the original plotlines and dialogues and only had minor changes—including the censorship of the sinking of the *Yamato* by Americans in WWII; rewriting scenes of the crew getting drunk on saké at critical moments; and toning down references to the *Yamato*'s gallant suicide mission. These relatively minor changes were in stark contrast to the heavy edits of *Science Ninja Team Gatchaman* before and *Macross* after, making *Yamato* an even more important series in developing a hardcore, purist anime fan base around the world. *Space Battleship Yamato* was the first anime to make it to theaters in the US in 1977 and 1978, over a decade before *AKIRA* (1988).

UFO Catcher (UFOキャッチャー): The name of an arcade game from SEGA and now used as a generic term for any crane-style game where a claw is controlled and used to collect toys or goods, usually stuffed animals or characters from popular ANIME. The ability to win items to sell at second-hand stores or to give to the ladies can make skilled players prosper both economically and socially.

UFO CATCHER 7 FROM SEGA

SEGA

Uke (受け): The submissive member in a COUPLING in BL or YAOI (not to be confused with *neko*, the actual term for a gay male submissive). These characters are typically extremely feminine and are the leads of these romance stories—not surprising given the predominantly female readership. The most common types are seductive uke (*sasoi uke*), old man uke (*oyaji uke*), cool uke (*kuuru uke*), narcissist uke (*oresama uke*), buff uke (*kinniku uke*), laudable uke (*kenage uke*), impish uke (*shoakuma uke*), queen uke (*joousama uke*), and princess uke (*hime uke*). A character that is imagined as an uke in all couplings and DOUJINSHI works is called *souke*, or general uke. See also SEME.

United Archives (複合アーカイブ): Code name for a planned "OTAKU museum" associated with Meiji University and currated by MORIKAWA KAICHIRO of the School of Global Japanese Studies. The main exhibition will contain six four-ton trucks of goods from the *Otaku: Persona = Space = City* exhibit in Venice from 2004, and a new section on the history of otaku culture. The archive will catalog and preserve 1.5 million DOUJINSHI from the COMIKET warehouse and some 200,000 MANGA titles formerly housed at the private Gendai Manga Bijutsukan in Waseda. It will open sometime after 2010, prefaced in 2009 by the Yonezawa Yoshiro Memorial Museum, housing the massive collection of the man who chaired Comiket for twenty-six years before his death in 2006. Aside from the art, museum, and archive space, there will be an ANIME theater and a hall to host doujinshi events.

Vector toward damé: See DAMÉ SHIKOU.

Veoh: Veoh Video Network; a massive video-sharing community site particularly known for its strong ANIME content. Another popular site is Crunchyroll.

VHS (ビデオ): Video Home System. A tape recording technology developed in 1976 by Victor (JVC) in Japan to record and play back visual material. This caused a revolution in the home video market because television shows, movies, and ANIME, could now be recorded, watched repeatedly, and shared. This was a crucial turning point in the evolution of OTAKU, as it made collection and study of anime possible. The convenience and cost efficiency of VHS, along with the fact that the format was adopted by the porn industry, meant that by the late 1980s VHS had won out against the less prevalent and more complicated Sony BETAMAX and MCA LaserDisc (see LD).

Video market (ビデオマーケット): A place to buy old VHS and Betamax tapes.

Virtual idoru (バーチャルアイドル): An IDORU that exists only in the digital realm, as in they don't really exist at all. Distinct from ANIME or game characters, these digital idoru are created as independent media entities. The first was Hori Pro's computer-generated Date Kyoko (codename DK-96, or Digital Kid 1996) in 1996. Visual Science Laboratory, one of Japan's top computer graphics software houses, was brought on board to bring a walking, talking virtual girl to life. The studio made early use of "full motion capture," a technique now widely used in video game and film production, to give her realistic movements. Her first CD single was "Love Communication" with the spookily real Date walking the streets of Tokyo and New York City. As a NETA, this was a wild success, but it all ended in 1997 when fans got tired of not being able to see her perform live.

DK96: THE FIRST VIRTUAL IDORU

V

In the early 2000s Japan had something of a virtual idoru renaissance, including Fuji TV's involvement in the Virtual Idoru Project that turned out the trio Yukari, Aya, and Miharu. Then came Terai Yuki, a hit bigger than Date, at least among a certain fan base. She put out photo albums and videos like any other idoru, and was joined by Fei Fei and CG idoru unit Super Honey Bee.

3D idoru in general have failed to maintain their popularity with fans the way more pliable 2D characters do, and they tend to fade away fairly quickly. Recently 2D virtual idoru such as the cartoony VOLCALOID Hatsune Miku have become global sensations among OTAKU, and many more are bound to follow. See also IDOLM@STER.

Visual-kei (ビジュアル系): A rock music genre. Members of visual-kei bands are generally beautiful, brooding boys who wear flashy gothic- and punk-inspired outfits, cross-dress as Lolitas, have big hair, and moan and groan and growl into the microphone. The emphasis is on the visual presentation and style more than the music. Visual-kei boomed in the 1990s, especially among young female fans, who emulated the androgynous members in dress and followed along with their dance moves en masse. After the trend died down, visual-kei bands toured Asia looking for new markets, finding unexpected support in Europe. Pink Jisatsu (Spain), Tokio Hotel (Germany), and Anorexia Nervosa (France) are just a few examples of international visual-kei copies. Visual-kei invaded the United States along with ANIME in the 2000s. The popularity of anime with theme songs performed by visual-kei bands, and the beauty of their appearance and performances at anime events around the world, won these bands legions of new fans. These ambiguous studs have, along with IDORU singers, become synonymous with J-POP in the global imagination. Visual-kei is sometimes colloquially called "vizzy" by female fans outside Japan. In 2006, Dir en Grey's "Saku" took the grand prix on MTV's *Headbangers Ball* program, beating out Iron Maiden and the Deftones. In 2007, the band was introduced on the Grammy Awards website as one to keep an eye on. That same year, X Japan performed the theme song for *Saw 4*. These charismatic bands then rode the COOL JAPAN wave back into stardom in their country. The reemergence of visual-kei in Japan is described as "neo visual-kei," but if anything the only thing that has changed is that the costumes are a bit tamer.

VISUAL KEI BAND VISTLIP, KNOWN FOR THEIR SONG "PUBLIC GAME" ON THE PSP GAME YUUSHA 30 SOUNDTRACK

VIZ: One of the first major American distributors of Japanese MANGA, established in the San Francisco area in 1987 as a branch of Shogakukan. The president was Horibuchi Seiji, in part responsible for the early custom of FLOPPING manga pages to read left to right for US readers. See also SMITH, TOREN.

Vocaloid (ボーカロイド)**:** A voice synthesizer software developed by Yamaha to allow users to produce singing from their computers by simply typing in lyrics and choosing the melody. "Vocaloid" also refers to the characters created by third party developers to embody the voices included in the software. There is something about the imperfect tone and pronunciation that approaches a cute, innocent "non-ability" idoru singer, and the software became a smash hit with computer-savvy Japanese OTAKU, who could now be creative and produce their own virtual idoru. The most popular vocaloid is Hatsune Miku, a green-haired idoru with pigtails and a leek baton, created by Crypton Future Media. She fueled a popular music revolution on NICO NICO DOUGA that spilled over into DOUJINSHI, COSPLAY, and FIGURES. Miku's famous baton first appeared in fan movies on the video-sharing site.

In 2006 the Finnish band Loituma's a capella version of the folk song "Levan Polka" was matched by a Russian fan to a twenty-six-second looped video of a *Bleach* ANIME character (Inoue Orihime) dancing with a leek. The idiocy of the dance, the funny music, and the mystery of the leek fueled copycat projects. Japanese fans then synched "Levan Polka" to Hatsune Miku, and she has waved her leek baton ever since.

Volks Inc.: A Kyoto hobby maker founded in 1972. It was big in GARAGE KITS in the 1980s, but is now most famous for its Super Dollfie series of ball-jointed, resin dolls, which it has been producing since 1999. These 25- to 65- centimeter-tall dolls cost between $300 and $1,500, but they are more affordable than imported French porcelain dolls. They are articulated, customizable, and posable, making them perfect for photography. At first Super Dollfies were especially popular with female GOTH-LOLI and VISUAL-KEI fans. However, in 2000 Araki Gentaro, who pioneered figure sculpting in the 1990s, started designing dolls for Volks, which greatly contributed to their popularity among men as well as women. Many retailers in AKIHABARA now cater to doll-OTAKU, who like to create their ultimate fantasy doll from a vast array of parts, such as wigs, different-colored eyes, and body shapes.

In winter 2008, about 15,000 people gathering at Tokyo BIG SIGHT for Dolls Party 20, the tenth anniversary of Super Dollfie; organizers estimate 20 percent were male. Some users carry these dolls around with them constantly, treating them like children or friends, and will pose them for photographs in various situations. Stores in the United States dealing in ball-joint dolls jumped from 25 to 150 from 2007 to 2008. Dolls Parties for Super Dollfies can now be found overseas. See also DOLL and DOLPA.

VOCALOID HATSUNE MIKU CHARACTER FIGURE BY GOOD SMILE COMPANY (SEE P. 90)

Waisetsu (猥褻・わいせつ): Obscenity, especially in media and art. An artist can be arrested for this in Japan. The obscenity laws states that anything that would inspire shame in a "normal person" can be considered waisetsu, but practical application is limited to the explicit portrayal of genitals, sexual penetration, and pubic hair. Obscenity is prohibited by the Criminal Code, Fixed Tariff Law, Entertainment Facilities Law, Broadcast Law, Prison Law, Law Regulating Business Affecting Public Morals, Child Welfare Law, and thirty-nine local ordinances. However, any amount of lasciviousness is allowed (incest, rape, bestiality) as long as commercial works pixellate the genitals (see MOSAIC). Amateur or artistic works are generally safe if they are not strictly for profit or pornographic purposes. This seems a very awkward legal position, as a lot of HENTAI and DOUJINSHI is criminal from a Western point of view.

Japan's obscenity laws originated with Article 175 of the Criminal Code in 1907 and Article 21 of the Customs Tariffs Law in 1910, intended to purge behavior and customs that made Japan seem hedonistic to outsiders. In 1918 the government officially drew the line at the depiction of genitalia and pubic hair, the public exposure of which had drawn great criticism in the 1800s. In 1991, Japan ruled that the vagina and pubic hair can be shown in an artistic way (see HAIR NUDE), but ANIME, MANGA, and doujinshi are not included (see SHOBUNKAN SAIBAN).

Waisetsu Doujinshi Jiken (わいせつ同人誌事件): The Obscene DOUJINSHI Incident. In 1990, the fallout from the MIYAZAKI TSUTOMU INCIDENT had much of Japan rallying against dangerous MANGA, with the *Asahi Shimbun* newspaper leading the media charge. As a result, the Seinen Comic mark was adopted in January 1991 to mark adult manga and all manga were required to blur out genitals. Further, the inspections of manga expanded to doujinshi, which were found to have obscene (WAISETSU) content and no mosaics. In February, five people were arrested, including the manager and two staffers at Shosen Book Mart, the manager of Comic Takaoka, and the manager of Manga no Mori Shinjuku. Two more joined them in prison in March, along with sixty-seven taken into custody for questioning. The media lapped it up, and the image of doujinshi got ever worse. A TBS announcer covering Comiket proclaimed, “There are 100,000 Miyazaki Tsutomus here.” In March, after being informed that there were obscene materials at Comiket, the Chiba Police went to question organizers. Makuhari Messe thus refused to host Comiket in August 1991. The organizers convinced the Harumi Tokyo International Exhibition Center to host the event by agreeing to screen all the content, impose MOSAICS, and censor obscene works before authorities got involved. The right to free speech would once again come into question in the Shobunkan Trial of 2002 (see SHOBUNKAN SAIBAN).

Wapanese: A put-down for a non-Japanese who attempts to be Japanese by appropriating Japanese culture as experienced through ANIME, MANGA and video games. This is most often used among international fans to discourage foreign OTAKU behavior. Another way to say this is *weeaboo*, originally a fictional game from webcomic *Perry Bible Fellowship* where anyone who said “weeaboo” got spanked with a paddle. This was adopted as a 4CHANNEL meme when use of the insult Wapanese was no longer allowed.

Watanabe Shinichiro (渡辺信一郎): Born in 1965 in Kyoto. One of the best-loved ANIME directors in the United States, known for *Cowboy Bebop, The Animatrix*, and *Samurai Champloo*. He wanted to make film but changed his mind after thinking how long it would take to break into the business. At age nineteen, he saw MIYAZAKI HAYAO’s *Nausicaä* and OSHII MAMORU’s *Beautiful Dreamer* and decided to go into anime. He got started at Sunrise studio in the late 1980s and worked on a variety of small TV series and OVA until making his debut in 1994 co-directing *Macross Plus*. Watanabe is keen on music and makes it a focal point of his works. His first project was marked by the music of KANNO YOKO, the insurmountable composer who brought in the Israeli Philharmonic Orchestra for the project. When Watanabe was given free reign to make a story with spaceships, he came up with *Cowboy Bebop* in 1998. It mixed multiple genres, such as Westerns, detective noir, and Hong Kong martial arts films. He used American cityscapes and outstanding jazz music, again by Kanno, in a story about drifters in space. The series was all about flow, deliberately following the intermingling lives of the characters along the twisting jazz-like riffs toward the climax. It was shown on late-night TV in Japan, but it made a huge impact in the United States. When the film, *Knockin’ on Heaven’s Door*, came out in 2001, US fans swarmed the theaters. In 2003, Watanabe directed his first anime in English, the short films “Kid’s Story” and “A Detective Story” from *The Animatrix*. He then mixed samurai and gangsters in the anime *Samurai Champloo* in 2004, with hip-hop music by Tsutchie, fat jon, and the Nujabes. His short film “Baby Blue” was included in the *Genius Party* compilation in 2007. He has also directed the music for *Michiko to Hacchin* (2008) and *Mind Game* (2004), the latter a big hit in art circles.

Web-anime (ウェブアニメ): ANIME created for or shown on the web. They can be more niche and free in topic, form, and expression. Closely related to *doujin* movements, international fandom, and exchange.

Web-comic or Web-manga (ウェブ漫画): Digitized MANGA created for or shown on the web. They can be more niche and free in topic, form, and expression. Closely related to *doujin* movements, international fandom, and exchange. See MCCLOUD, SCOTT.

W

WEB-COMIC BY SCOTT McCLOUD

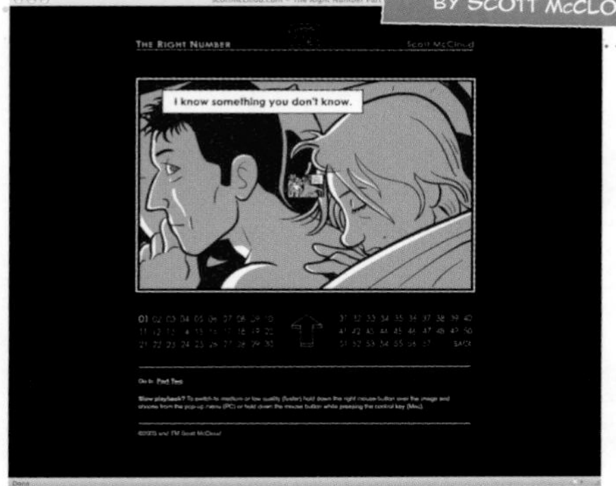

White Day: (ホワイトデー): March 14. A day on which men who received chocolate from women on Valentine's Day (February 14) give a small return gift. The chocolate given to men in February is called either *giri choco*, when it is given out of mere obligation, or *honmei choco* when it is given out of love. Similarly, on White Day men will give either small candies or expensive jewelry, depending on their feelings or status. Japan's National Confectionery Industry Association founded White Day in 1978 as a way to drum up sales. Koreans have added an interesting twist to all this with Black Day on April 14, a holiday where single people who did not receive gifts on Valentine's Day, and did not return them on White Day, can get together and eat black noodles (*jjajang-myeon*) to commiserate.

Wonder Festival (ワンフェス): Or WonFes. A twice annual, massive event in Tokyo to display and sell amateur and professional GARAGE KITS, FIGURES, toys, and models. Started in 1984 as an event run by General Products, which went on to become GAINAX but was taken over by KAIYODO in 1992. This is the biggest convention for modelers and hobby enthusiasts in a country renowned for them, and many companies use the time to unveil new products and sell rare stock. These models are extremely detail-oriented, and many of these sculptures appear in very small quantities. The winter 2008 Wonder Festival was cancelled due to an escalator malfunction in the summer, in which hundreds of OTAKU got dumped into a sweaty, angry pile. The event was moved to MAKUHARI MESSE in summer 2009.

Working characters: Mascots doing a job such as PR spokesperson rather than acting as commercial characters in and of themselves. A term coined by Matt Alt and Hiroko Yoda in their book *Hello, Please: Very Helpful Super Kawaii Characters from Japan* (2007). This includes YURU-KYARA.

World Cosplay Summit (世界コスプレサミット): Or WCS. An international gathering and tournament for COSPLAYers held annually since 2003 in Nagoya, Aichi Prefecture. In the first year, only three teams participated—Italy, Germany, and France. But in 2008, the World Cosplay Championships pitted teams from thirteen countries in judged three-minute stage performances. Over 12,000 spectators attended, many cosplaying themselves.

THREE VERY CUTE COSPLAYERS AT THE *WORLD COSPLAY SUMMIT*

X JAPAN: One of the earliest examples of Japanese VISUAL-KEI rock music. Founded in 1982, they made their debut in 1989 and signed with Sony. In 1992, they left Japan and signed with Atlantic Records in the US. Around that time band member Yoshiki read Clamp's apocalyptic MANGA *X* and wrote the rock ballad "Forever Love" as a tribute to the many soulmates who die in the story. This was used as the theme song for Rintaro's theatrical ANIME *X* in 1996. The following year, X JAPAN broke up and all the members started solo careers, with the understanding they would come back together in 2000. On May 2, 1998, backup vocalist and guitarist Hide was found dead. The mass media said it was suicide, though investigators later decided it was an accident. Fans were in such a state of despair over this Kurt Cobain–like episode that seven people committed suicide. The members of X Japan publicly denounced this, saying Hide wouldn't have wanted it. Around 50,000 people gathered to bid him farewell. Former Prime Minister Koizumi Junichiro, a fan of X JAPAN, used "Forever Love" in a campaign advertisement in 2001. After numerous quarrels, X JAPAN reunited in 2007.

X JAPAN

Y

Yabai (ヤバい): Terrible; crap; sick; amazing; awesome; cool.

Yaba-puri (ヤバプリ): *Yabai* PURIKURA (sticker photos). A subgenre of sticker photos in which people, especially young women, try to look as strange and outrageous as they can. See also ERO-PURI, ONNA NO KO SHASHIN, and GYARU-MOJI.

Yakuza (ヤクザ): A mobster. Used outside of Japan to refer to the Japanese mafia or organized crime in general, but not so in Japan, where such groups are known unromantically as *boryokudan*, or gangs. The name "yakuza" is derived from a losing hand at the card game *Hanafuda* totaling a score of 20 made up of 8 (*ya*), 9 (*ku*), and 3 (*za*). Yakuza have been around since at least the Edo period (1600–1868) and are often seen as outlaw heroes in Japan, like cowboys or gangsters in American fiction. The practice of covering the body with tattoos has traditionally been associated with yakuza, meaning tattoos are still taboo in Japan.

Yamamba (ヤマンバ): Mountain witch. A type of GYARU (gal). Roughly analogous to GANGURO, but their hair is white, in stark contrast to their tanned skin.

Yandere (ヤンデレ): "*Yan*" means mental or emotional illness, and "*dere*" means to show affection. The term is used to describe a character whose good will toward their partner crosses the bounds of sanity and often comes to express itself in violent or brutal ways. The character type can be traced all the way back to

Four Murasame in the *Mobile Suit Z Gundam* ANIME (1985), although the first conscious use of the term was in the GYARUGE *Giniro* (2000) and *School Days* (2005). Basically, these are mentally unstable, and potentially physically hostile, characters who can't control their massive emotional reserves.

Yandere characters have been criticized because of the increasing violence in anime such as *School Days* (2007) (see NICE BOAT) and *When They Cry* (*Higurashi no naku koroni*) (2006). There is an extreme variant called "*yangire*," derived from *Magical Girl Lyrical Nanoha StrikerS* (2007), wherein the character is yan, or mentally ill, but does not show any signs of dere, or affection. He or she simply snaps, or gire. Also check out *Kamen Rider Kiba*.

Yankii (ヤンキー): Bad adolescent. A word used after WWII to describe Japanese youth who in fashion and hairstyle mimicked American youth. Though the origins are obscure, the word seems to have emerged in the late 1970s in Osaka around the America Mura neighborhood, known for imported and second-hand clothing. Disenfranchised youth wore loud aloha shirts and baggy pants and strutted around the area. It spread around Japan in rural and suburban areas in the early 1980s and became well known after Kamon Tatsuo's popular song, "Yankii Oniichan no Uta" in 1983. It became synonymous with *furyo* (no good) and *tsuppari*, the Tokyo-area word for "bad boy" at the time. There was overlap between yankii and BOSOZOKU, or biker gangs, as can be seen in the magazine *Champ Road* (from 1987), the so-called "yankii bible" that covered bikes and cars. Yankii characters have appeared in *Kamikaze Girls* (film, 2004), *Yasuko and Kenji* (manga, 2005–2006), and *Gokusen Gokusen* (TV drama, 2007).

Yaoi (ヤオイ): An acronym for no climax (*YAma nashi*), no punchline (*Ochi nashi*), and no meaning (*Imi nashi*). This is a genre of MANGA featuring male-male homosexual romance and pornography for heterosexual female readers. Like SHOJO MANGA, the focus is human relationships, but in yaoi women are as a rule absent, leaving only the juicy man meat. Most often yaoi take characters from mainstream commercial media and couple them in romance in alternative worlds, settings, and stories. The story is irrelevant, thus the term "yaoi." Lots of intense sex means the acronym is sometimes reinterpreted as, "Stop! My ass hurts!" (YAmete! Oshiri ga Itai). It's also referred to as "801" by fans, because those numbers sound like "yaoi" in Japanese (8 = *ya*, 0 = *oh*, 1 = *ee*).

Mori Mari wrote Japan's first male-male romance novels in 1961, setting the stage for the MAGNIFICENT 49ERS to experiment with homosexual themes in SHOJO MANGA—especially Takemiya Keiko's *Ringo no Tsumi* in 1968. Influential works followed, including Takemiya's *Natsu e no Tobira* in 1975 and Moto Hagio's *The November Gymnasium* in 1972, which became *The Heart of Thomas* in 1974. When asked why she focused on homosexual men rather than women, Moto said it was because she felt two men was an "equal, pure union."

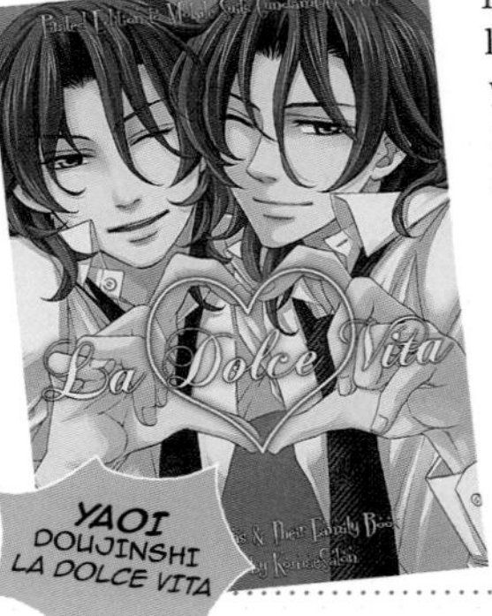

YAOI DOUJINSHI LA DOLCE VITA

Whereas two women was too close to the female readers and "gooey like *natto* (fermented soy beans)." Takemiya opened the floodgates with the series *Kaze to Ki no Uta*, which ran for seventeen volumes between 1976 and 1984 and inspired the first yaoi ANIME in 1987. This was also the first manga to show two young boys in bed—and they weren't sleeping. Yaoi spread when specialty magazine *June* was founded in 1979, 50 percent manga with "lesbian" ads for YURI friendship to boot, followed by the more literary *Allan* (1980–84) and *Gecko* (1984–2006).

Amateurs experimenting with this theme were the core of the DOUJINSHI movement. In the 1980s, women ruled doujinshi and conventions, and homosexual male romance using *Six God Combination Godmars* and *CAPTAIN TSUBASA* characters was their favorite topic. After amateur MANGAKA Sakata Yasuko's *Loveri* in 1980 was characterized as lacking narrative and focusing only on men, young ANIPARO writers begin calling their works "yaoi" in self-depreciation. This is still used to describe the genre and the amateur doujinshi, while commercial products with original characters are typically called BL (boys' love). In 1995, *June* had a circulation of 180,000, and yaoi claimed 3.8 percent of the manga market. According to the Fuji TV documentary *FUJOSHI NO SAKI NI ARU MONO* (Beyond Fujoshi) released November 22, 2007, FUJOSHI account for a $129.5 million market. Yaoi is growing in popularity overseas as well, with events like Yaoi-con in America and the Pop Travel Japan's "Fujoshi Paradise" tours to Tokyo. In 2007, *L'Etoile Solitare* became the first yaoi title written for an English-speaking, overseas audience.

Yaoi-chan (やおいちゃん・801ちゃん): A put-down for fans of YAOI or female OTAKU in general.

Yashigani (ヤシガニ): Slang for a poorly animated work. For details, see ANIME BUBBLE.

Yohaku (余白): The blank space or margin of a MANGA page layout.

Yokoyama Mitsuteru (横山光輝): Born in 1934 in Kobe, Hyogo Prefecture. Died in 2004. A MANGAKA best known for *Tetsujin 28-go* (*Gigantor*), one of Japan's most popular giant robot MANGA, and *Mahotsukai Sarii* (*Sally, the Witch*), at the fore of the magical girl genre. He also wrote the sixty-volume sprawling epic *Sangokushi* (*Romance of the Three Kingdoms*), which was made into an ANIME in 1991. He was inspired by American culture, and in turn the anime versions of his work did much to popularize Japanese pop-culture abroad.

YONGSAN IN SEOUL, SOUTH KOREA

Yongsan (용산): An area of Seoul, South Korea, that resembles the old AKIHABARA Electric Town. There are twenty or so buildings with about 5,000 stores, mostly dealing in PCs and electronics but also with plenty of software, games, videos, CDs, "pirated" DVDs, and electronic parts. There are also cinemas and a group pro-gaming tournament venue. Near the train station is a large building that resembles the Radio Kaikan in Akihabara. There are some shops selling OTAKU-oriented goods, with more to be found in the Dongdaemun-sijang area, but import regulations on media and merchandise from Japan mean it must keep a low profile. In Myeongdong, another area of Seoul, that's similar to Tokyo's SHIBUYA or HARAJUKU, there was a MAID CAFÉ called AmuAmu, but it has since closed

Yoshida Tatsuo (吉田竜夫): Born in 1932 in Kyoto. A self-taught MANGA artist and co-founder of Tatsunoko Productions with his brothers Kenji and Toyoharu (a.k.a. Kuri Ippei). The studio's name is a double-entendre meaning "Tatsu's child" and "sea dragon," which inspired the studio's emblematic seahorse logo. In 1967 Yoshida released the ANIME *Mach Go Go Go*, a modest hit in Japan that would become a worldwide blockbuster as *Speed Racer*. He is also responsible for the classic *Kagaku Ninjatai Gatchaman* (*Battle of the Planets*) in 1972, which was a huge success in Japan and abroad. Yoshida also created *Shinzo Ningen Casshan* (1973), *Time Bokan* (1974), and *Yattaman* (1977), all of which have recently received critical acclaim or been remade into new films or anime series. Although most active in the 1970s, Tatsunoko is still respected for unique MECHA and character designs.

GATCHAMAN CREATED BY YOSHIDA TATSUO

Yoshimoto (吉本): The largest agency for comedians, MANZAI, and humorous TARENTO in Japan. They are for comedians what JOHNNY'S is for boy bands.

Yuri (百合): Lily. Used by editors at the gay magazine *Barazoku* in 1971 to describe lesbians as opposed to gays, who were referred to as *bara* (rose). The term "yuri" was adopted by YAOI magazine *June* and used for its personal ads section. The word was used in "Roman Porno" (the predecessor of PINK *eiga)* in a string of hit movies in the 1980s, beginning with *Seifuku Yurizoku* in 1982 and followed by *Sailor Fuku Yurizoku*, *OL Yurizoku 19 sai*, and *Onna Kyoshi Yurizoku*. The mass media picked it up and yuri became a common word for "lesbian." For this reason, in Japan "yuri" is often considered to be little more than a buzzword from the 1980s. On the contrary, however, since the series *Maria-sama ga Miteru* began in 1998 the word is now a genre unto itself in the world of ANIME and MANGA. In this context, "yuri" means a relationship between two submissive characters. Given the history, this is typically understood to be female characters—sometimes implied or explicitly lesbian and often erotic. FUJOSHI fans also use "yuri" to mean two UKE-type passive males in a YAOI coupling.

Yuru-kyara (ユルキャラ): A term invented by commentator Miura Jun to describe regional mascots. An example would be Sento-kun, Nara's deer/Buddha boy.

Yutori (ゆとり): Dumbass. 2CHANNEL slang derived from *yutori kyouiku*, or the "slow education" system adopted by the Japanese government in the 1990s to ease pressure on students. Students who were educated since are said to be a little slow themselves. Now, anytime anyone says something stupid on 2channel they run the risk of being called "yutori." See also DQN.

y

ONIICHAN. I CAN'T DECIDE... WHICH IS BETTER FOR YOU? RIGHT OR LEFT?
Z

Zettai ryoiki (絶対領域): The absolute barrier. Fans on 2CHANNEL adopted this word to mean the stretch of exposed flesh above knee-high stockings and below the mini-skirt. Because the rest of the body is covered, the eyes are drawn to this bare flesh, which looks especially tempting and erotic because it appears carelessly uncovered. Female fans have answered this male definition by claiming the "true" zettai ryoiki is the exposed space between a glove and a suit jacket sleeve on males. The term may be a reference to the "absolute terror field" from ANNO HIDEAKI's *NEON GENESIS EVANGELION*. See also CHAKUERO.

Zokusei (属性): Attribute. First used to describe the traits, class, abilities, and so on of characters in table-top and video game RPGs. In the late 1990s, zokusei became conflated with MOÉ to describe the attributes of the characters deemed moé and the type of fans who like these characters.

OTAKU ESSENTIALS

To really understand otaku you have to go further than this book. You need to watch anime, read manga, and play games. The following list is a good start.

Essential anime

Adieu Galaxy Express 999
Akira
Bleach
Bubblegum Crisis
Code Geass: Lelouch of the Rebellion R2
Cowboy Bebop
Death Note
Ebichu Minds the House
Elfen Lied
Excel Saga
Fist of the North Star
FLCL
Fullmetal Alchemist
Ghost in the Shell
Little Norse Prince Valiant
Lupin III: The Castle of Cagliostro
Magical Princess Minky Momo
Martian Successor Nadesico
Mazinger Z
Megazone 23
Mobile Suit Gundam
Nadia: The Secret of Blue Water
Nausicaä of the Valley of the Wind
Neon Genesis Evangelion
Ninja Scroll
Oh My Goddess!
Otaku no Video
Paranoia Agent
Revolutionary Girl Utena
Rozen Maiden
Samurai X: Trust & Betrayal
Serial Experiments Lain
Sexy Commando Side Story: That's Amazing!! Masaru-san
Sgt. Frog
Space Battleship Yamato
Spirited Away
Super Dimension Fortress Macross
The Girl Who Leapt Through Time
The Grave of the Fireflies
Trigun
Urusei Yatsura

Moé Anime (for those moé fans out there)

Azumanga Daioh
Cardcaptor Sakura
Club to Death Angel, Dokoro-chan
Ichigo Marshmallow
Idolmaster: Xenoglossia
Lucky Star
Panyo Panyo Di Gi Charat
Popotan
Magical Lyrical Girl Nanoha
Magical Nurse Witch Komugi-chan
Moetan
My-HiME
Red-Eyed Shana
She, the Ultimate Weapon
Strike Witches
The Melancholy of Haruhi Suzumiya

Manga you can't miss

Akira
Berserk
Cyborg 009
Dragon Ball
JoJo's Bizarre Adventure
La Blue Girl
Lone Wolf and Cub
Maison Ikkoku
Monster
Phoenix
Sailor Moon
Slam Dunk
The Rose of Versailles
The Song of the Wind and Trees
Tomorrow's Joe

Videogames including gyaruge

Air
Chrono Trigger
Final Fantasy III
Final Fantasy VII
Gladius II
Golden Eye 007
Grand Theft Auto
Gunstar Heroes
Ico
Legend of Zelda: A Link to the Past
Legend of Zelda: Ocarina of Time
Metal Gear Solid 3
Princess Maker
Pokémon

ONIICHAN, HAVE YOU SEEN ALL THESE?

Street Fighter II
Super Mario Bros. 3
Super Mario 64
Tokimeki Memorial

Tokusatsu

Ambassador Magma
Choujin Sentai Jetman
Destroy All Monsters
Gamera: Guardian of the Universe
Gamera 2: Attack of Legion
Gamera 3: Awakening of Irys
Ghidorah, the Three-Headed Monster
Godzilla (1954 and 1985)
Godzilla, Mothra and King Ghidorah: Giant Monsters All-Out Attack
Godzilla vs. Biollante
Johnny Sokko and His Giant Flying Robot
Kamen Rider Black
Kyouryuu Sentai, Zyuuranger (*Mighty Morphin Power Rangers*)
Negadon: The Monster from Mars
Space Sheriff Gavan
Ultra Seven
War of the Gargantuas

SELECTED BIBLIOGRAPHY

Books

Allison, Anne. *Permitted and Prohibited Desires*. Berkeley, CA: University of California Press, 2000.

—. *Millennial Monsters*. Berkeley, CA: University of California Press, 2006.

Alt, Matt, and Hiroko Yoda. *Hello, Please! Very Helpful Super Kawaii Characters from Japan*. San Francisco, CA: Chronicle Books, 2007.

Aoyagi, Hiroshi. *Islands of Eight Million Smiles: Idol Performance and Symbolic Production in Contemporary Japan*. Cambridge, MA: Harvard University Asia Center, 2005.

Azuma, Hiroki. *Mojo genron efu kai: Posutomodan otaku sekushuariti* [F-kai network meeting: Postmodern otaku sexuality] Tokyo: Seidosha, 2003.

—. *Dobutsuka-suru Postmodern: Otaku kara mita nihon shakai* [Animalizing Postmodern: Japanese society as seen from otaku] Tokyo: Kodansha, 2001.

Clements, Jonathan, and Helen McCarthy. *The Anime Encyclopedia: A Guide to Japanese Animation Since 1917*, Revised and Expanded Edition. Berkeley, CA: Stone Bridge Press, 2006.

Comic Market Preparation Committee. "What is the Comic Market?" Official Comic Market Site. http://www.comiket.co.jp/ (accessed June 2, 2008).

Fujimoto, Yukari. *Watashi no ibasho wa doko ni aru no?* [Where do I belong?] Tokyo: Gakuyo Shobo, 1998.

Gill, Tom. "Transformational Magic: Some Japanese super-heroes and monsters," in *The Worlds of Japanese Popular Culture*, ed. Dolores Martinez. Cambridge, England: Cambridge University Press, 1998: 33-55.

Horibuchi, Seiji. *Moeru Amerika: Beikokujin wa ikani shite manga wo yomu youni natta ka* [Budding America: Have Americans finally come to read manga?] Tokyo: Nikkei BP, 2006.

Ishii, Shinji. *Manga ronso!* [Manga Debate!] Tokyo: JICC Shuppan Kyoku, 1979.

Ishiko, Jun. *Nihon manga shi* [The History of Japanese Comics] Tokyo: Kyoyo Bunko, 1988.

Ito, Go. *Tezuka izu deddo: Hirakareta manga hyougen e* [Tezuka is Dead: Toward Open manga expression] Tokyo: NTT Shuppan, 2005.

Iwabuchi, Koichi. *Recentering Globalization: Popular Culture and Japanese Transnationalism*. Durham, NC: Duke University Press, 2002.

Jenkins, Henry. *Fans, Bloggers, and Gamers: Media Consumers in a Digital Age*. New York: New York University Press, 2006.

Kato, Hidetoshi. *Handbook of Japanese Popular Culture*. Santa Barbara, CA: Greenwood Publishing Group, 1989.

Kelts, Roland. *Japanamerica: How Japanese Pop Culture Has Invaded the U.S.* New York: Palgrave Macmillan, 2007.

Kinsella, Sharon. "Cuties in Japan," in *Women, Media and Consumption in Japan,* eds. Lise Skov and Brian Moeran. Honolulu, HI: University of Hawaii Press, 1995: 220-254.

—. *Adult Manga: Culture and Power in Contemporary Japanese Society.* Oxon, England: Routledge, 2000.

Kitabayashi, Ken. *Otaku shijo no kenkyu* [Otaku Market Research] Tokyo: Nomura Research Institute, 2005.

Lent, John A. *Animation in Asia and the Pacific*. Bloomington, IN: Indiana University Press, 2001.

Leonard, Sean. "Progress against the law: Anime and fandom, with the key to the globalization of culture," *International Journal of Cultural Studies* 8. 2005: 281-305.

Levi, Antonia. *Samurai from Outer Space: Understanding Japanese Animation*. Chicago, IL: Open Court, 1998.
Machiyama, Tomohiro. *Otaku no hon* [The Book of Otaku] Tokyo: Bessatsu Takarajima, 1989.
Macias, Patrick. *Otaku in USA: Ai to gokai no yunyushi* [Otaku in USA: Love and Misunderstanding! The History of Adopted Anime in America] Tokyo: Ota Shuppan, 2006.
— and Tomohiro Machiyama. *Cruising the Anime City: An Otaku Guide to Neo Tokyo* Berkeley, CA: Stone Bridge Press, 2004.
McCloud, Scott. *Understanding Comics: The Invisible Art*. New York: Harper Collins Publishers, 1994.
Miyasako, Chizuru. *Cho shoujo e* [Toward the Hyper-girl] Tokyo: Shueisha, 1989.
Morikawa, Kaichiro. *Shuto no tanjo: Moeru toshi Akihabara* [Learning from Akihabara: The Birth of a Personapolis] Tokyo: Gentosha, 2003.
Murakami, Takashi. *Little Boy: The Arts of Japan's Exploding Subculture*. New Haven, CT: Yale University Press, 2005.
Nagatani, Kunio. *Nippon mangaka meikan* [A Directory of Japanese Manga Artists] Toyko: Data House, 1994.
—. Nippon meisaku manga meikan [A Directory of Great Japanese Manga] Tokyo: Data House, 1995.
—. Nippon manga zasshi meikan [A Directory of Japanese Manga Magazines] Tokyo: Data House, 1995.
Napier, Susan J. *Anime from Akira to Howl's Moving Castle*. New York: Palgrave Macmillan, 2005.
—. *From Impressionism to Anime: Japan as Fantasy and Fan Cult in the Mind of the West*. New York: Palgrave Macmillan, 2007.
Natsume, Fusanosuke. *Natsume Fusanosuke no mangagaku* [Natsume Fusanosuke Mangalogy] Tokyo: Daiwa Shobo, 1985.
Okada, Toshio. *Otakugaku nyumon* [Introduction to Otakuology] Tokyo: Ota Shuppan, 1996.
—. *Otaku wa sudeni shindeiru* [Otaku are already dead] Tokyo: Shinchosha, 2008.
Otsuka, Eiji. *Shojominzokugaku* [Ethnography of little girls] Tokyo: Kobunsha, 1997.
—. *Shojotachi no kawaii tenno* [The emperor of little girls] Tokyo: Kadokawa, 2003.
—. *"Otaku" no seishinshi senkyukyakuhachiju nendai ron* ["Otaku" intellectual history in the 1980s] Tokyo: Kodansha, 2004.
Patten, Fred. *Watching Anime, Reading Manga: 25 Years of Essays and Reviews* Berkeley, CA: Stone Bridge Press, 2004.
Pink, Daniel H. "Japan, Ink," *Wired* 15.11 (November 2007): 216-222.
Poitras, Gilles. *The Anime Companion*. Berkeley, CA: Stone Bridge Press, 1999.
—. *Anime Essentials*. Berkeley, CA: Stone Bridge Press, 2000.
—. *The Anime Companion 2*. Berkeley, CA: Stone Bridge Press, 2005.
Saito, Tamaki. *Sento bishojo no seishin bunseki* [Analysis of the spirit of fighting girls] Tokyo: Ota Shuppan, 2000.
Schodt, Frederik L. *Manga Manga! The World of Japanese Comics*. Tokyo: Kodansha International, 1983.
—. *Dreamland Japan: Writings on Modern Manga*. Berkeley, CA: Stone Bridge Press, 1996.
Shimizu, Isao, "Red Comic Books: The Origins of Modern Japanese Manga," in *Illustrating Asia: Comics, Humor Magazines, and Picture Books*, ed. John A. Lent Honolulu, HI: University of Hawaii Press, 2001: 137-150.
Silverberg, Miriam, *Erotic Grotesque Nonsense: The Mass Culture of Japan in Modern Times*. Berkeley, CA: University of California Press, 2006.
Takatsuki, Yasushi, *Nankyoku ichigo densetsu: Dacchi waifu kara rabu dooru made* [The Legend of South Pole No. 1: From Dutch Wives to Love Dolls] Tokyo: Basilico, 2008.
Taylor, Emily, "Dating-Simulation Games: Leisure and Gaming of Japanese Youth Culture," *Southeast Review of Asian Studies* 29 (2007): 192–208.
Thompson, Jason, "How Manga Conquered America," *Wired* 15.11 (November 2007): 223-233.
Yanagihara Hideya, *Akiba ga chikyu wo*

nomikomu hi [The Day Akihabara Swallows the World] Tokyo: Kadokawa, 2007.
Yomota, Inuhiko, *Kawaiiron* [Cute Theory] Tokyo: Chikuma Shobo, 2006.
Yonezawa, Yoshihiro, *Sengo shojo manga shi* [A History of Postwar Shojo Manga] Funabashi, Chiba Prefecture: Shinposha, 1980.

Websites

Akiba Blog
http://www.akibablog.net
Anime News Network
http://www.animenewsnetwork.com
Anime Research
http://www.AnimeResearch.com
Danny Choo
http://www.dannychoo.com
Gilles Poitras
http://www.koyagi.com
Heisei Democracy
http://heiseidemocracy.com
Kotaku
http://kotaku.com
Matt Alt
http://altjapan.typepad.com
2channel
http://www.2ch.net
Otaku2
http://www.otaku2.com
Otasuke
http://www.ota-suke.jp
Patrick Macias
http://patrickmacias.blogs.com
Sankaku Complex
http://www.sankakucomplex.com
Sci-fi Japan
http://www.scifijapan.com
Wired
http://www.wired.com

Magazines

Animage (Japan). 1978–.
Animedia (Japan). 1981–.
Anime Insider (US). 2001–.
The Comics Journal (US). 1977–.
Comptiq (Japan). 1983–.
Famitsuu (Japan). 1986–.
Hobby Japan (Japan). 1969–.
Otaku USA (US). 2007–.
Newtype (Japan). 1985–.
Protoculture Addicts (Canada) 1987–.

IMAGE CREDITS

All illustrations of Moé-pon character by Akashiro Miyu
Pages 15, 23, 55, 87, 107, 108, 135, 151, 175, 215, Asaki Katsuhide (www.asakiphoto.com)
Pages 42, 66, 110, 137, 139, 148, collection of Patrick W. Galbraith
Pages 51, 53, 210, Adrian Lozano
Page 10, AYA/Ojou no Yokushitsu
Page 12, courtesy Office 48. Page 18, Kodansha Rights Division. Page 20, Kodansha Photo Library. Page 21, courtesy Gainax. Page 25, courtesy Shogakukan Productions. Page 26, courtesy Anime Expo. Page 27, courtesy Tatsunoko Production. Page 28, courtesy Anime Festival Asia. Page 31, courtesy Vap Video. Page 32, courtesy Saito-Production.
Page 35 bottom, courtesy Josh Barnett.
Pages 37, 70–72, 75, 77, 83, 113, courtesy Kaiyodo
Page 39, courtesy Orient Industry. Page 40, Courtesy Jump Comics/Shueisha. Page 43, courtesy Danny Choo. Page 49, courtesy Japan Media Arts Festival. Pages 50, 52, Hayashi Shoji. Page 57 bottom, Panther Science Fiction.
Page 58 bottom, used with permission of Okada

Toshio. Page 60, courtesy K Dash Stage. Page 61, top courtesy Niwano Noriko. Page 61 bottom, courtesy Fuji TV/Pony Canyon. Page 62 bottom, courtesy Digital Hollywood University. Pages 63–65, Kohji Shiiki.
Page 68, courtesy Blast Books, Inc.
Page 81, courtesy Gainax. Page 84, courtesy GDH/FUNimation/Takashi Okazaki. Page 88, courtesy Anno Haruna. Pages 90, 91 top, courtesy Good Smile Company. Page 91 bottom, courtesy Index Communications. Page 92, courtesy *Young Magazine*/Kodansha.
Page 94, courtesy Choubunsha. Page 95, courtesy Toei Animation. Page 98 right, courtesy Dynamic Planning. Page 99, Anime 18/Central Park media. Page 101, Visipix.
Page 103, courtesy Sunrise. Page 104 left, courtesy Toho Advertising. Page 104 right, courtesy International Manga Award.
Page 111, courtesy Tezuka Productions.
Page 113 top, courtesy Kaikai Kiki. Page 117, courtesy Wani Books. Page 118, courtesy Only-One. Pages 119, 120, courtesy Sunrise. Page 121, courtesy Anikao Shizuka. Page 123, Kodansha Rights Division.
Page 127 top, courtesy Takara Tomy. Page 127 bottom, courtesy Kodansha. Page 130 top, Kato Pleasure Group. Page 130, courtesy Lucca Comics and Games SRL.
Page 132, courtesy *Otaku USA* magazine. Page 141, courtesy Jump Comics/Shueisha. Page 142, courtesy Manboo. Page 143, courtesy Manga Koshien. Page 144, Kodansha Photo library. Page 145, courtesy Toei Animation. Page 146, courtesy Dynamic Planning. Page 149, Courtesy of Shueisha Bunko. Pages 152, 153, Kodansha Photo library. Page 154, courtesy Mode Gakuen Cocoon Tower. Page 158, courtesy Kaikai Kiki.
Page 159, Kodansha International. Page 160, courtesy K Dash Stage. Page 161, courtesy of Amane Ramu. Page 162, Nice Boat. Pages 163, 164, courtesy Nintendo.
Page 166, courtesy Tengu Canning. Page 170 top, courtesy Madman. Page 170 bottom, courtesy Production I.G. Page 178, courtesy Gainax. Page 179, Okada Toshio. Page 180, courtesy Kodansha. Page 183, Fumino Osada.
Page 184, courtesy Sankyo. Page 186 top, courtesy Frederik W. Patten. Page 186 bottom, courtesy Gilles Lee Poitras. Page 187, AP Photo. Page 189, courtesy Gainax. Page 190, courtesy Sunrise.
Page 192, courtesy Ayakawa Yunmao. Page 193, courtesy Kasakurashuppansha. Page 194, courtesy Japan's National Institute of Advanced Industrial Science and Technology (AIST)
Page 195, courtesy Chukei Publishing. Page 196 left, courtesy of Danny Choo. Page 196 right, Kodansha International. Page 197, courtesy Sega. Page 198, courtesy Washinomiya Chamber of Commerce. Page 200, courtesy Kodansha. Page 202, courtesy Madman Entertainment. Page 203, Kodansha International. Page 205, courtesy Tezuka Productions. Kodansha International. Page 206, courtesy Watanabe Entertainment. Page 208, courtesy Shueisha. Page 211, courtesy Madman Entertainment.
Page 213, courtesy Shogakukan. Page 218, courtesy Little TGV. Page 219, courtesy of Tezuka Productions. Page 220, Kodansha Photo Library. Page 221, courtesy of Tezuka Productions. Page 222, courtesy Toei Animation. Page 223, courtesy Tsuburaya Productions. Page 224, courtesy Tokyopop.
Page 228, courtesy Tohokushinsha Film Corporation. Page 229, courtesy Sega.
Page 230, courtesy Hori Productions. Page 231, courtesy Marvelous Entertainment. Page 232, courtesy Good Smile Company.
Page 235 top, courtesy Scott McCloud (www.scottmccloud.com). Page 235 bottom, Hayashi Shoji.
Page 236, courtesy Hideo Kanno/Ongakusenkasha
Page 238, Komae Salon/Matsumoto Azusa. Page 240, courtesy Tatsunoko Production.
All other images by Kodansha International.

THANKS TO . . .

Keiko, my wife, for her support and bearing with me through it all. You're my best friend and the only flesh-and-blood girl I'll ever love.

My mother, for teaching me the joys of reading and study. I owe all that I am to you. Except the otaku bit. That's not your fault.

Andrew Lee for being a great editor. I owe you immensely for giving this otaku some perspective. Without your patience, guidance, and tireless effort this book would never have been possible. In the end, I think you even turned a little otaku for the cause.

Asaki Katsuhide for his fantastic interview portraits, and Akashiro Miyu for bringing Moé-pon to life.

Akiyama Masumi for her wonderful design, and my apologies that you had to do it several times over on my account.

Otake Tomomi for her editorial assistance, and for introducing me to Oono Norihiro—as hardcore an otaku as ever there was, and a saint for his many sleepless nights fact checking.

In addition I would also like to thank Frederik L. Schodt, who pioneered the inquiry into Japanese pop culture and remains an inspiration. Matt Alt and Hiroko Yoda, Danny Choo, Brian Ashcraft, Patrick Macias, and Philomena Keet, for their input and insight. Okazaki "Bob" Takashi and Tezuka Makoto for their generous help in acquiring images. Morita Yuko for helping us find Ms. Akashiro. And to everyone who agreed to be interviewed despite busy schedules and random alien attacks.

Also special thanks must go to David Slater, a scholar and a gentleman. Steve Trautlein, for giving me a chance. And Adrian, Steffen and Eva, my circle, my comrades.

But most of all thanks to the many otaku out there, who have the curiosity to research, the conviction to stick to it, and the heart to share. You are the revolution.

Patrick W. Galbraith
Tokyo 2009

（英文版）外国人のためのヲタク・エンサイクロペディア
The Otaku Encyclopedia

2009年 6月　第1刷発行
2009年 12月　第3刷発行

著　者　パトリック・ウィリアム・ガルバレス
発行者　廣田 浩二
発行所　講談社インターナショナル株式会社
〒112-8652 東京都文京区音羽 1-17-14
電話　03-3944-6493（編集部）
03-3944-6492（マーケティング部・業務部）
ホームページ　www.kodansha-intl.com
印刷・製本所　大日本印刷株式会社

Printed in Japan
ISBN 978-4-7700-3101-3

ONIICHAN, WHAT SHOULD I WEAR TODAY?
(SEE KISEKAE NINGYO P. 122)
Moé